AI is more profound than... electricity or fire.
—Google CEO, Sundar Pichai

All of us—not only scientists, industrialists, and generals—should ask ourselves what we can do now to improve the chances of reaping the benefits of future AI and avoiding the risks.
—Stephen Hawking

Most people don't understand just how quickly machine intelligence is advancing, it's much faster than almost anyone realized, even within Silicon Valley.
—Elon Musk

Also by Charles Simon

Computer Aided Design of Printed Circuits: The Guide for Evaluating, Purchasing, and Using Computer Aided Design Systems

Computer Aided Design and Design Automation Book Section in Clark's *Handbook of Printed Circuit Manufacturing*

Quickstart Circumnavigation Guide

Software/Hardware, Charles Simon

Printed Circuit CAD Graphics

The BRAIN Simulator: Tutorial Software for Neural Circuit Design

EEG System (Brainwave Monitoring)

Cynthia Voice-activated Intercom

Synthetic Intelligence

3-D ComputerScape

3-D MiniCAD for Windows

Continuum: Software for Enterprise CAD

Committee Boat Suite

Flying Media: Museum Interactive System

3-D Mouse

Passport to Discovery: Museum Interactive System

WILL
COMPUTERS
REVOLT?

PREPARING FOR THE FUTURE OF
ARTIFICIAL INTELLIGENCE

CHARLES J. SIMON

Future AI
Annapolis, MD

http://willcomputersrevolt.com

Published, October 30, 2018, in the United States by Future AI,
3 Church Circle #238, Annapolis, MD 21401, info@futureAl.guru

ISBN-13 (eBook): 978-1-7326872-3-3
ISBN-13 (Paper): 978-1-7326872-1-9
ISBN-13 (Hardcover): 978-1-7326872-2-6
Library of Congress Control Number: 2018909542
Printing Version: 9/14/18
First Edition

Book Sales, worldwide:
Amazon, other retail outlets, and distributed through Ingram.

Section Header I & III: Images by Tatiana Shepeleve, Shutterstock, Section II by metamorworks, Shutterstock

Publisher's Cataloging-in-Publication Data
Names: Simon, Charles J., author.
Title: Will computers revolt? Preparing for the future of artificial intelligence / Charles J Simon.
Description: Includes bibliographical references and index. | Annapolis, MD: Future AI, 2018.
Identifiers: ISBN 978-1-7326872-2-6 (Hardcover) | 978-1-7326872-1-9 (pbk.) | 978-1-7326872-3-3 (ebook) | LCCN 2018909542
Subjects: LCSH: Artificial intelligence. | Human-computer interaction. | Computers and civilization. | Machine theory. | Robotics. | Singularities (Artificial intelligence) | Conscious automata. | BISAC: COMPUTERS / Intelligence (AI) & Semantics | TECHNOLOGY & ENGINEERING / Robotics
Classification: LCC Q335 .S56 2018 | DDC 006.3--dc23

To my wife, Cathy, for never failing in her encouragement.
Also to our son, Steve, for his continuing support on all my adventures.

Table of Contents

Preface

I originally wrote this book in the 1980s as a companion to software I wrote, *The Brain Simulator*, which simulated an array of 1,200 neurons on a PC. Many of the ideas in this book were mere speculations at the time but are facts now. In a nutshell, the software was released but the book wasn't.

In 2003, I updated the text as a companion to the software I wrote called *Synthetic Intelligence* (SI) which included larger functional modules. Instead of individual brain cells, the SI software allowed the creation of arbitrarily complex modules such as video edge detection, various speech-process modules, etc. and was used in AI (Artificial Intelligence) classes. A unique capability of the system was that various modules (and multiple instances of the modules) could run simultaneously on different networked computers. Once again, the software gained traction while the book wasn't completed.

This time, I decided to finish the book first.

I have had a variety of professional experiences which have contributed to my ability to write this book. Primary among them were several years writing software for neurological test equipment. In writing most of the software for one of the first paperless EEG (brainwave monitoring) systems, I became familiar with brains and the kinds of normal characteristics and malfunctions they exhibit. My subsequent work on software for NCV/EMG/EP (Nerve Conduction Velocity/Electromyography/Evoked Potential—all of which measure signals in neurons) helped me gain insight into the capabilities and limitations of the biological neuron as a computational device.

Along the way, I earned degrees in Electrical Engineering and Computer Science, founded companies, and managed software projects. I worked in the semiconductor industry and participated in the development of an early microprocessor, giving me insight into the capabilities and limitations of integrated circuits, how these have evolved over past decades, and what the future will hold.

I've always been interested in intelligence and the possibilities of mimicking human intelligent behavior in computers. At the first company I founded which did automated printed circuit design, we wrote algorithms which attempted to fit patterns to the problem of routing circuit boards. In this way, the software mimicked the way we observed human designers solving the same problem.

These experiences combined to create the model of intelligence detailed in Section II of this book. Based on this model of intelligence, we can make reasonable predictions of what the behavior, capabilities, and limitations of future thinking machines will be.

The question remains as to how much computer horsepower will be required to implement a system along the lines I will describe in this book. This is an open question, primarily because we can't predict how software efficiency will be able to short-cut the need for brute-force computing. If we need machines which equal (or exceed) the computational power of the human brain, these are still decades away. If, as I contend, we'll be able to devise algorithms which are orders of magnitude more efficient than the human brain (which evolved to make use of the neuron as its building block), this is a project which, if started today, will be complete in five to ten years. That's five years to develop the system/software and five years to train it and create any custom hardware which will make it fast enough to be useful.

I believe that for each of us, intelligence and insight are based on our experiences. Because I have had a unique set of experiences, this book contains some unique ideas and a singular point of view on intelligence and our ability to replicate it in machines.

As a future of thinking machines will be sooner than most people think, **the time to start getting prepared is *NOW!***

Foreword

This book is about the creation of super-intelligent thinking machines. The first section presents the overall case that intelligent thinking machines are not only possible but inevitable.

Then I present a model of capabilities that a system needs in order to appear intelligent, and the behaviors we can expect from a system built following that model. The details of the explanation are a bit more technical but I have endeavored to include examples which will make the process clear.

The final section extrapolates the behaviors that result from a system created along the lines of the model of Section II so we can reach conclusions about what such machines will be like and what we might do to coexist with them. It isn't critical to the thesis of this book that the model be correct in every detail. In fact, any goal-oriented learning system which interacts with our physical environment is likely to exhibit similar behavior.

What is the point of this book?

- To show that computers more intelligent than humans are possible.
- To explain why such computers are inevitable.
- To argue that machine intelligence will be created sooner than most people think.
- To demonstrate that, subsequently, vastly more powerful intelligences will be created only a few decades later.
- To conclude that such "genius" machines will lead to options and opportunities for how humans will coexist with (and prepare for) them.

As you continue through this book, you'll see a block diagram of intelligence in terms of capabilities which you can observe for yourself. The conclusion is that a reasonably sized software project can implement everything which we know about human intelligence—a fact which I'll reinforce later. Underlying this book is my contention that human intelligence is not as complex as it appears. Rather, it is built of a few fundamental capabilities, operating on an immense scale within your brain.

Over the next chapters, I intend to prove it to you. Not only that, but I make some predictions on how future intelligent machines will behave—how they will be similar to human intelligence and how they will necessarily be different. Based on these predictions, we will be able to consider how such computers and people will coexist.

AI today

Recent developments in AI (Artificial Intelligence) have been astonishing. In 1997, IBM's Deep Blue supercomputer system beat the World Chess Champion Garry Kasparov. In 2014, IBM's Watson beat champions at the TV game, *Jeopardy!* In 2015, Alphabet/Google's AlphaGo program began beating world-class players at the ancient Chinese game of Go. What's more astounding is that the October 2017 version, AlphaGo Zero, was not programmed to play Go. It was programmed to *learn* to play. And over a period of just three days of learning, playing against itself, it was able to achieve such a level of play that it could consistently beat the 2015 version.

Other fields of AI research, including speech recognition, computer vision, robotics, self-driving cars, data mining, neural networks, and deep learning, have had equally impressive successes. But are such systems intelligent? The general consensus is that they are not (although this is a matter of how we define "intelligent"). When applied to a problem outside their specific field of "expertise", most systems fail miserably. Many people use the evidence that AI has not achieved the holy grail of true general intelligence over the past 70 years as proof that either (a) true intelligence in machines is impossible or (b) true intelligence in machines is still a long way off. I disagree with both contentions.

Because of the generally limited scope of AI applications, the AI community has adopted the term AGI (Artificial General Intelligence, also called "strong AI" or "full AI"). This represents the idea of a true "thinking" machine and might represent an agglomeration of many AI technologies of more limited domain or entirely new technologies.

Why not yet? AI to AGI

Why hasn't AI already morphed into AGI? There are three primary reasons:

1. Computers have not been powerful enough to solve the problems.
2. The problems to be solved in creating intelligent systems turned out to be a lot more difficult than they initially appeared.
3. We do not yet know fully how human intelligence works.

In the next few chapters, I'll show why these roadblocks will be going away soon. I'll also expand on these and a host of other issues which have confronted the AI community.

Bringing it all together

In summary, AI has lots of bits of intelligence, but none has any underlying "understanding". I contend that AI programs have (mostly) been developed to solve specific problems. They have no contact with the "real world". Then, after they are running, we wonder why they don't have any real-world understanding. AGI will necessarily emerge in the context of robotics, as robots are the only technology based on real-world interaction.

Consider the self-driving car, which is just a big, autonomous, mobile robot. Currently being created as narrow AI, abstract concepts like "obstacle", "destination", and "pedestrian" will eventually need real-world meanings—meanings which would be impossible within the controlled verbal-only environment of Watson, for example.

Once this real-world understanding emerges in various robotic areas, it will be transferred to permeate most other areas of computation.

In Section I of this book, I'll present an overview of future intelligence in computers—contending that computers will be fast enough and that the software development is inevitable. I also introduce a plausible General Theory of Intelligence, which forms the basis of forecasts about intelligent machine behavior.

In Section II, I expand on the General Theory with a map of various observable facets of intelligence—many of which exist in today's autonomous robots. Then I'll walk through the behavior of a system with all these facets to show how it would act in an intelligent way.

In Section III, I'll predict how the future could unfold with machines based on this intelligence theory. While there are definite risks, I will show how human attitudes will mitigate or exacerbate these risks. As a future with intelligent computers is inevitable, I trust we will make the right decisions.

SECTION I:

Are Super-Intelligent Machines In Your Future?

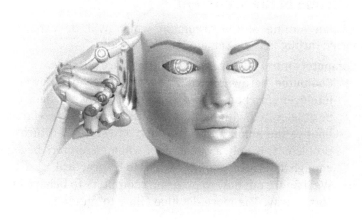

"AI is more profound than... electricity or fire."
—*Google CEO Sundar Pichai*
San Francisco, January 2018

What's in Section I

Are Super-Intelligent Machines in your Future?
This first section answers this question with two objectives:

- To explain why the march toward intelligent machines is not only possible but inevitable.
- To extrapolate technology to explain what future machines will be like.

But first... I will offer a thought experiment. Most people aren't very comfortable with the concept of true intelligence in a computer and Chapter 1 is an exercise to explore what it might be like to be an intelligent computer.

Then... I give a quick introduction to general intelligence and begin to pin down the actions which define an intelligent being.

Then we'll get to the meat of the argument...

The outline of the argument

Here is an outline of the argument which will be expanded and supported throughout the remainder of this book:

1) Computers more intelligent than humans are possible.
   a) Computer hardware will have enough "horsepower" to be intelligent in a human-like way. Because most AI algorithms can be accelerated with parallel processing, there is no foreseeable limit to the amount of computing power we can throw at the problem. It is only a question of when computers become fast enough and cheap enough for this to be practical.
   b) We'll figure out how to program computers to behave in an AGI sort of way. The more detailed "How to" guide is presented in Section II.
2) The development of super-intelligent computers is inevitable.
   a) There is tremendous commercial pressure to create intelligent systems. Virtually all users' irritations with current computers are related to the machines' inability to understand what we want them to do, as opposed to what we explicitly tell them to do.
   b) Once intelligence is created in any type of system, the advantage will be so strong that the technology will permeate all subsequent technology.

c) The commercial and military advantages will override any misgivings we might have about the potential dangers of such machines.

3) These super-intelligent computers will be created sooner than most people think.

   a) Charts show us that a computer's power will exceed that of a human brain in five years (or 10 or 20, depending on your source). I'll show that brain-level computational power is potentially available today and so could be built as soon as a useful design can be formulated.

   b) Many facets of human intelligence can be implemented with software algorithms designed to perform a similar function far faster and more efficiently than the human brain.

4) Subsequently, vastly more powerful intelligences will be created a decade or so later.

   a) Again, simply by looking at the charts, only 15 years after a human-level intelligent system we'll have systems 1,000 times as "smart". In 30 years, they'll be 1,000,000 times as smart.

5) Initially, we'll be able to predict the behavior of our creations and implement appropriate safeguards.

   a) Once human-level intelligent systems go to work as system developers and design their own subsequent generations, much less control will be possible.

   b) The emergence of such machines will lead to options and opportunities for how we will coexist with them and how we prepare.

6) We'll need to establish a firm, positive relationship with our machines once computers begin to develop their own future generations.

   a) There is no reason to assume that intelligent machines will be cataclysmic for the human race.

   b) While we might be concerned about possibly becoming slaves to machine intelligences, we should be equally concerned about how they might react to being slaves to us. It is in our best interests to do so.

Chapter 1:
Could You Become a Computer?

I propose to consider the question, "Can machines think?"
—*Alan Turing*
Computing Machinery and Intelligence
1950

What would it be like to be an intelligent computer? Would you have sensations and feelings? Would you ever get angry or fall in love? Here is a thought experiment which illustrates what it would be like to become an intelligent computer. The point is two-fold. First, to ask questions about the nature of intelligence. And second, for you to reach your own conclusions about the capabilities and limitations of future machines.

After all, who knows better how you think and what you feel than you do?

Automating your brain

Your brain is a collection of cells called neurons, so suppose we took neurons one at a time and replaced them with artificial neurons. What would you feel like? This is a question which cuts to the center of the definition of intelligence and the possibility of replicating it in non-biological hardware. Remember that this is purely a thought experiment, so we can ignore the technical difficulties.

Since the biological neuron is an electrochemical device, we could theoretically manufacture one with identical functionality from non-biological components such as transistors and capacitors. The practical problems of making neurons of identical size and shape could be insurmountable but imagine that you *could* build an artificial neuron with identical characteristics to an organic one. Consider that artificial joints already fully replace the action of natural ones.

Further, to the extent that intelligence may reside in cells other than neurons, you can consider replacing those with artificial cells as well. For ease of description, we will refer to all the cells involved in thinking

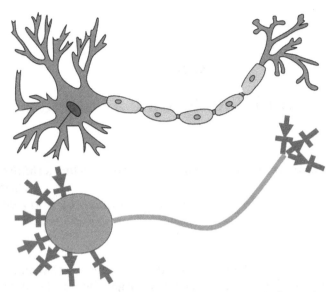

Consider replacing neurons with artificial equivalents built from electronic components such as transistors and diodes—perhaps with a microprocessor. [Diagram of neuron by Quasar Jarosz, license: CC BY-SA 3.0.]

collectively as "neurons" residing in the "brain", even though other types of cells may make a contribution. Indeed, cells outside the brain may contribute as well.

Imagine further that after significant research and development, we have an artificial neuron which can be implanted into your brain. It would take the place of any individual neuron and have an identical function.

Through our hypothetical, completely painless microsurgical techniques, we will remove a single neuron from your brain, measure its characteristics, and replace it with one of our artificial neurons which has been adjusted to fit perfectly. As we believe that individual neural synapses (which form the connections between neurons) harbor our memories, we would be very careful to adjust the simulated synapse transmitters and receptors of our artificial neuron to exactly match the neuron we replaced. Let's place the biological neuron we removed in a nutrient flask to keep it nourished for safekeeping.

Would you feel any different? Not in the slightest. We could simply have removed the neuron and not replaced it—in your brain, neurons die every day and you don't even notice. But by replacing the neuron with our artificial one, we can repeat the process as often as we like without having to worry about the possibility of depleting your brain.

So instead of replacing a single neuron, let's replace a cluster of a thousand neurons with an artificial set. Again, these neurons are perfectly adjusted to match those which were removed. For example, we could replace part of the visual cortex which processes the incoming image of the lower right-hand corner of your right eye. Again, we would save the neurons we removed in the flask. Your brain would still work the same way and you would not feel any difference.

Suppose we repeat the process and end up by replacing all the neurons in your brain with these precisely adjusted artificial neurons. You still would not notice the difference. The artificial brain in your head would be working in the same way as the one which had been removed. You would still be "you" and you would still feel like "you".

Now a question: is *your* brain in your head or in the nutrient flask? Many would think that an *artificial* brain is in our head and our *real* brain is in the flask. And to the extent that you feel and believe that your sense of what is you is in your physical brain, where is the real you? In your head or in the flask?

This is exactly the point: what is the *real* you? If we had not bothered to maintain the structure of the original neurons, now, whatever is in the flask is *not* you—it's a more-or-less random collection of left-over biological neurons. Maybe it used to be you but it is no more. If anything is to be you, it must be contained in the artificial neurons we have installed in your head. It will be seeing what your eyes see, it will be hearing what your ears hear, it will be feeling what your body feels, it will be remembering what your brain used to remember. What makes you *you* is the structure and pattern of the neurons—their connections and the sizes and types of synapses.

As we were replacing neurons, at what point were you transferred from the biological to the artificial? This is a question which springs from the concept of "you" as a single specific entity. Rather, consider yourself to be the sum of processes and behaviors which go on in, and are controlled by, your brain. If we began to replace the fibers in a wooden beam one by one with carbon fibers, the question of when the beam stops being wooden and becomes carbon is a similar matter of definition. The fact is that the beam would be performing a function which it can continue to perform while its fibers are being replaced one by one. So if we chose to say that the beam became a carbon-fiber beam when 50% of its fibers had been replaced, we might just as well say that you possessed an artificial brain when 50% of the neurons were replaced. We might contend that some neurons or certain areas of your brain are more important than others. If we replaced the prefrontal lobes first, for example, the "you" would have been transferred to artificial neurons sooner. Fine, but the exact point of transfer is not a meaningful thing to look for. What gives you intelligence and your sense of yourself doesn't seem to be localized to a specific part of the brain.

If I am asked where in my body *I* reside, I respond that I feel that I am behind my eyes. I feel this way because my eyes' position defines my point of view. I feel this way even though I know that visual signals enter the brain at the very back of my head, so my face is really facing the opposite direction from that which my brain "sees". People whose principal spatial sensation is through touch or hearing might have a different perception of where they reside—but whatever the feeling is, replacing biological neurons with the new identical electronic ones would not make a difference to the feeling. The brain will work the same way and will process visual signals, for example, the same way. You will still have the same point of view that you did before the replacement.

Faster and bigger

Suppose all these artificial neurons could be simultaneously adjusted to make them faster. Whatever the function of the biological neuron, imagine our synthetic neurons could do the same function twice as fast as before. Would that make you smarter? Is having a faster brain equivalent to being more intelligent?

The biological brain is a delicate balance of neuron speeds so the initial effect of speeding up its neurons would have some unintended results. From your brain's perspective, the general effect of speeding up the neurons would be that the world would seem to run in slow motion. But although watching a movie in slow motion makes some details easier to see, it also makes speech virtually impossible to understand. The early years of your life which you spent learning to understand speech only taught you to understand it within a fairly narrow band of speeds. Either much faster or much slower speech becomes progressively more difficult to understand.

Further, while your perception could be somewhat quicker, your muscles would continue at the same speed, so they would seem to run in slow motion. Your muscular coordination would be reduced and your ability to speak would be impaired—similar perhaps to being intoxicated. All-in-all, the initial effects of having a faster brain would be to make you seem somewhat less intelligent.

But brains are adaptive, and you would be able to re-learn how to walk and talk with a brain which is faster than your muscles. Then you would be able to make use of your faster brain. You would have a faster reaction time and would be able to answer *Jeopardy!* questions more quickly. But you wouldn't be able to answer *Jeopardy!* questions that you could not have answered previously. Having a faster brain won't make you know more, it won't make you wiser, or give you a bigger vocabulary.

Things that you haven't been able to learn in the previous 20 years of your life won't suddenly become obvious to you. If it takes you 20 mental repetitions to memorize a phone number today, it will still take you 20 repetitions to learn it with a faster brain. You'll just be able to learn the phone number in less wall-clock time. That is, since all your perceptions will be faster, you won't even perceive that you can memorize faster— only that the clock on the wall will not have progressed as far while you accomplished the given mental task.

With a brain speeded up by a factor of 10, I could do simple arithmetic faster than an average human. I would be able to read books more quickly and I might be able to react more quickly to any given situation. But even with this greatly increased mental speed, I might not appear much smarter than I am today.

On the other hand, if you'd had those twice-as-fast neurons since birth, then at three years of age, you would have the behaviors of a six-year-old. You could have graduated from college at 11 instead of 22. You'd seem pretty smart. Perhaps with that accelerated mental ability, you'd have the time to accumulate more knowledge and experience and be able to make better decisions.

But perhaps your brain is already using its maximum abilities (we'll consider that later). If so, a faster brain gets you to adult-level thinking at an earlier age but doesn't make you an Einstein, because you won't have any thoughts which you wouldn't have had otherwise. You'll just have those thoughts at an earlier age.

Suppose we increased the size of your hypothetical brain with many additional synthetic neurons. Would that make you smarter? Again, yes and no. Today, it is not clear that any particular mental activity you attempt is limited by the number of neurons in your brain. I speculate that the things we learn are limited by our ability to apply ourselves to study rather than our mental limitations. This is similar to athletic abilities as well. I am confident that with the proper commitment and practice, I could make basketball free-throws pretty well. I am not an athlete, but if I were willing to practice eight hours a day, I would become better than most people (who don't have that level of commitment). There would still be natural athletes who would be much better but, with practice, I would certainly be much better than average. The problem is that I am not motivated to that level of commitment.

Similarly, I speculate that many people with the appropriate level of commitment could master college-level mathematics, for example. The reason that relatively few people actually master college-level mathematics has more to do with motivation, commitment or interest than limitations in mental capacity. Mathematics, specifically, also relies on a progression of learning. Individuals who do not learn the basics in elementary school have a difficult time progressing to higher levels. But again, I would contend that many individuals who did not learn the basics failed to do so for some reason other than mental limitation.

So back to the increased brain capacity. Again, the outward manifestations may not be obvious at all. With a greater brain capacity, I might be able to study both computer science and history with equal vigor. I could probably memorize more facts, for example, but it is not clear that more facts would lead to greater insight.

Instead, I imagine that a greater brain capacity would improve the detail of my memories. I would remember more vividly the scenes from last summer's sailing trip. I would remember the names of more schoolmates from my high school years. Long-term memories would not fade as much. Potentially, being able to remember more experiences might make me a wiser person. If I could make decisions based on a greater number of remembered experiences or recognize complex patterns in situations that other people could not, I would appear more intelligent. I would have a greater memory capacity.

But this is only useful to the extent that I commit myself to filling my memory with something valuable. And I contend that my mental capacity is already greater than my commitment and therefore increasing the capacity will make little difference. With greater mental capacity, I could *choose* to apply myself to learning more things, but I am not necessarily going to do so.

Here, one of the important distinctions between people and future computers becomes highlighted. While mental capacity may or may not be comparable between humans and computers, the computer can be directed to 100% commitment, learning everything it can in a specific field without any time out for eating or sleeping, or even just getting tired or bored. If elementary school students spend an hour a day studying arithmetic, then by the sixth grade they've spent about 1,000 hours at it.

A computer, with identical mental functionality but with complete dedication to that single activity, would cover the thousand hours in about six weeks. Six weeks vs. six years gives the computer the appearance of a substantial edge, even with an identical level of mental ability!

Further, the students' brains are not wholly focused on arithmetic during class. As the student thinks about recess, lunch, vacations, exams, friends and other distractions, how much of the brain is actually devoted to the material? In a computer, with full attention dedicated to the topic at hand, it would appear even smarter.

Brain in the basement

Now let's suppose that we can augment your synthetic neurons with remote transmission capabilities—Wi-Fi, if you will. We can take all the neurons out of your head and install them somewhere else. In your head, we'll install transmitters and receivers which send and receive signals to external neurons. In other words, we can move your brain outside your head. All signals from your senses are sent to your external brain and it sends signals back to your muscles. Now we can put your brain anywhere we like; let's put it in the basement of your home.

After this upgrade, you will have no neurons at all in your brain, only transmitters which are taking signals from your optic nerves and other sensory nerves and sending the signals to your basement. Receivers get transmissions from your basement and control your muscles through your motor nerves. Will you still feel just as you did before? Your brain is in the basement but because even today's Wi-Fi speeds are so fast relative to the speed of your neurons, there is no perceptible delay. Your brain still has the same content. You still have your memories, your knowledge, your biases.

Now, how do you answer the question, "Where do you feel you are?". Your brain is in the basement but you'll still feel as though you are behind your eyes. Suppose you go into the basement and look at your electronic brain. It's probably no more interesting than your furnace; it's just another piece of equipment in the basement. As long as it's working properly, you don't think about it at all.

Now we have the brain-in-the-basement concept, imagine that your friend's brain is in *his* basement as well. Your friend is asleep so you decide to sneak down to his basement and look at his brain and check on his status.

You know he's asleep and you think about what would happen if you temporarily disconnected his brain. Of course, you'll be sure to allow the

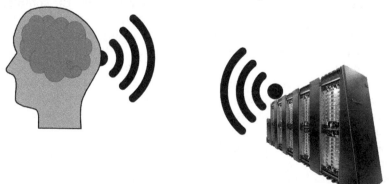

Consider connecting the entire thinking part of your brain to electronics at a remote location with a wireless connection to your body. [Image of IBM Blue supercomputer by Argonne National Laboratory's Flickr page, license: CC BY-SA 2.0.]

neurons which control his circulation, respiration, and other bodily functions to continue to operate. So you can go ahead and shut down all the "thinking" parts of his brain without him being aware of it. If he was dreaming before, he will be no longer if his brain is shut down. But will he be aware of the difference? If you were asleep and were anesthetized without being awakened, would you be aware of the difference?

Backups and the passage of time

Suppose there is a power failure. Even if the autonomic nervous system continues and keeps your friend's body alive, the current state of the brain is lost if it was being stored in volatile electronic memory. Being prepared for this possibility, let's invent a system for daily backups. The backup includes the current configuration of every neuron, and details of every synapse. Although this represents a vast amount of data (and we have only estimates of how much) we can use some yet-to-be-invented molecular storage and store it all in a few grams of material.

After the power failure, you need to reload the brain from yesterday's backup. You do this and restart the brain. When your friend wakes up, does he feel any different? He may be confused at the loss of a day. It's Wednesday today and he has no recollection of Tuesday at all, as though he has slept through it entirely. It's as though he's been transported into the future (by one day) by a time machine. For him, the intervening day simply didn't exist. His brain has no recollection of the intervening time except that it can look at clocks and calendars and everyone else seems to agree that the time has passed. It could have been a month or a year if we'd loaded an older backup.

But about that backup... to the extent that it represents the complete state of your brain, it contains the complete "essence" of you. If we can reload your brain from the backup and you are restored, we're forced to conclude that virtually all of what makes you *you* is stored in the backup. In computer science we sometimes think of a collection of data bits as representing a number. We can think of a text character as also being a number. A string of characters is just a number with more digits. In fact, the entire content of Wikipedia can be considered as just a single really big number.

Similarly, then, the backup of you is just a really, really, really big number. The backup of your friend is a different, similarly sized number. Does this mean that, contrary to all appearances and all your fervent desires, you *are* "just a number"?

Distributed intelligence

Getting back to the image of your brain in a box in your basement... Imagine that instead of a single cabinet, the neurons of your synthetic brain were housed in two computer cabinets, with a network interconnection between them. Again, as long as the necessary information can get from neuron to neuron quickly enough, the operation of your brain should be no different. It doesn't really matter how we choose to divide your brain either. You could imagine that the left hemisphere is housed in one cabinet and the right in the other, for example, but any random division would yield the same result.

As long as we can keep the network connection fast enough, it doesn't matter if the two cabinets remain close to each other in your basement. If it were more convenient, we could move one of them next door and your brain would continue to operate and feel the same. Since the speed of electronic signals is so much quicker than the speed of neural signals, it would not become significant until the distance between the cabinets exceeded perhaps 200 miles. At that point, the speed-of-light transmission between the cabinets would take about 1 millisecond and might begin to become significant vs. the 1-millisecond speed of neural pulses.

To move the cabinets further apart, we would need to be selective as to how we divided the neurons between the cabinets. If we generally kept the neurons which were close to each other in the brain in the same cabinet, the transmission delays would probably remain unnoticeable as we moved the cabinets thousands of miles apart. As an example, in watching a movie, if the audio and video aren't perfectly synchronized, you don't notice until the asynchrony approaches a tenth of a second. That's equivalent to putting your visual processing in a cabinet in your basement and your auditory processing in a cabinet halfway around the world.

So if we stay within a 10-mile radius, we can put the cabinets anywhere we want and distribute neurons between the cabinets without any consideration about which neuron goes in which cabinet. Further, if we used smaller cabinets and had more of them, we could distribute the neurons any way we liked. If we had 1,000 cabinets instead of two and distributed them throughout your city, the operation of your brain would remain the same.

If you were to consider what an artificial intelligence would be like if it were running on a network of many different computers, the answer is that it would be, potentially, just like you. You have no awareness of the physical architecture or placement of your brain. The fact that all of your sensations are being received through a single "body" is the factor which gives you a sense of place, not the positions of your various neurons. So if you were to write a program which emulated the function of 100,000 neurons and ran it simultaneously on each of 1,000,000 computers, it could conceivably have a sense of self similar in scope to that of a person. That is, if it had a single location from which it received its inputs, such as a camera signal. If, instead of a single camera, the network was connected to 1,000 different cameras in 1,000 different locations, it would reasonably be expected to have an entirely different sense of self, if it had one at all.

Body swapping

As the development of brain replacements becomes more commonplace, the remote connection between the brain and the body will become standardized. Each body and brain are paired, so individual brains are always operating with the correct body in the same way that today's systems always send the correct phone and Wi-Fi signals to the correct devices using address numbers. But what if the addresses were shifted? You and your friend agree to swap addresses and you go down to the basement and make the adjustments.

Suddenly, your brain is sensing and controlling his body, and vice versa. You are receiving signals from his eyes and ears. You will notice the immediate shift in point of view, but it need not be any more disorienting than a scene change in a movie.

You will notice when you get up that your friend is six inches taller than you, because there is a significant shift in your point of view from having the eyes six inches higher. And maybe your friend was in better physical condition than you and you immediately notice that the body responds more quickly and powerfully. You feel clumsy, though, because your brain has spent years learning the coordinated movements of your smaller body and the timing is off when you reach for things or try to walk. But you are still you, you have just shifted bodies. The part of you which makes you *you* is still safely in your basement.

Now, your mind and your body are completely disconnected. After many people have undergone our hypothetical brain-remoting procedure, you can try out a new body if you want to. Further, since it's the brain not the body that is believed to need sleep, there are usually available bodies for rent whenever their "owners" are sleeping and not in need of them. Swapping bodies is a simple matter of changing addresses.

But suppose one day, all the good bodies are already in use and you don't have one. You are awake but you have no input from the outside world. You are blind and deaf and cannot feel or smell or taste. You have your memories and can think about what you have done already and what you plan to do when you eventually get a body again. You might contemplate the fact that you are just a brain in a basement but you have complete sensory deprivation. How long would you want to remain in this situation? *Could* you remain for long in this situation?

If my desktop computer today *could* think, how likely is it to be able to appear thoughtful? It's blind, deaf, and immobile. It has no physical experience to reminisce about. It has no future for which it can plan. Any expectation that it should manifest human-like qualities is not realistic—regardless of how fast its CPU becomes or how much RAM it has. Today's desktop computer is inadequate for thought. We need interaction with an environment; i.e. a robot. Yes, there is often a camera and microphone on the desktop, but today's computer doesn't have the capacity to understand what it sees and hears in a general way. It's more akin to owning a camera vs. having eyes.

Immortality

You essentially became immortal when we moved your brain to the basement. As your body gets old and wears out, you might simply acquire one of the new fully artificial robot bodies. They're faster and see better but they do have to be recharged periodically.

Are you still *you*? With a robotic body and a brain in the basement, you're completely artificial. If there is to be an argument over this, it is one of semantics, not substance. You might feel somewhat different because you are in an artificial body, but you could not point to a specific time when you stopped being you and started being a machine. Do you feel different than you did? Perhaps the robotic body has no sense of smell or a limited sense of touch. It is certainly a unique feeling when, for example, your foot is "asleep" or the dentist anesthetizes part of your face.

But what about your sense of yourself? It's about the same. You are still aware of the passage of time and have the memories of your childhood and the experiences of your lifetime. When you make a decision to do something, it's based on your previous experience, your preconceptions, and your understanding of the way things will work out. Everything which makes you *you* is still there except for the body and the brain.

My point is: what makes you *you* is all on that backup. The physical structure of synapses in your brain is changed when you learn something. Your memories are believed to be stored in the sizes and types of the synapses themselves. When you acquire a physical skill, learn a song, learn a multiplication fact, or have the experience of walking in the park on a spring day—all these experiences modify the physical structure of your brain.

So what is you is defined by the current state of your brain. Thus, what was you yesterday is not the same as what is you today and cannot be the same as what will be you tomorrow. What makes you *you* incorporates the sum total of the experiences you've had. Suppose all of the basement brains have universal hardware so that other people's backup disks could be loaded on your hardware brain. That would make you someone else!

During the time your backups are not loaded anywhere, what will you be? You simply won't exist—similar to being simultaneously comatose and invisible! But at any time, someone could load your backup disks onto some hardware and you would spring back to life—as good as ever, with no damage done. In the intervening time, though, are you alive? It is the information on the backup which is the "essence of you", so to speak. Whatever hardware that information is loaded on will become you. When the information is loaded, you will "awaken" with your memories and personality intact.

You could arrange for your backup to be loaded simultaneously on more than one brain and truly talk to yourself. You would be completely cloned. It might not be a very interesting conversation because you and your clone would see things the same way, know the same things, carry the same secrets, have the same reactions, and always be in agreement. You would have nothing to learn from your clone and nothing to teach it that it didn't already know. Now if your clone took a three-week vacation while you read a few good books, *then* you'd have something to talk about. But you'd no longer be the same person—you and your clone would be similar but no longer identical. This is entirely different from biological cloning—identical twins—which can create identical bodies but allows the minds to subsequently be filled with entirely different content.

A future artificial intelligence system could have the initial state of a universal hardware brain and a robotic body without any backup data loaded. It has no experience, no memories, no abilities. Whatever it is to do, it must learn. Starting out as an artificial entity would make it entirely different from you. No memories of childhood, no nursery school, no camping trips, no baseball games, only what it gained from its *own* experience. So if it were "brought up" in a human environment where it was treated like a child and expected to play and learn and progress, it would eventually act vastly more human than an identical system which is immediately put to work combing the internet for tidbits of information.

This brings into focus the distinction between man and machine. From the outside, the backup which represents "essence of you" and another which is "essence of robot" appear identical. If *your* backup is loaded into a brain/body, it will be you while the other will be a robot.

One is filled with information about "human" experiences while the other is filled with "robotic" experiences. Imagine that the experiences of the robot were loaded into an artificial brain with a biological body. Would that be more or less human than an entirely artificial body and brain?

Could it really be that the only difference between you and an artificial intelligence will be the content of your mind? It is reasonable to conclude that since our biological "hardware" (both brain and body) are essentially similar to those of humans who lived 50,000 years ago, the only thing which makes us "civilized humans" is that we are brought up to be civilized humans. If the empty artificial system is brought up to be a civilized human as well, couldn't it participate in society with the same abilities and shortcomings as any other person?

Ideas to consider

Here are some thoughts I draw from these thought experiments—perhaps you have had others:

- A computer intelligence unit is not necessarily different from you and me. Given the same sensory apparatus and experiences, an electronic brain could be quite similar to a biological one.
- Experiences, in a biological brain, are stored as the configuration of neurons and synapses. If we could capture this configuration, we could store and preserve the "essence" of a person.
- Having a brain which is faster or has a greater capacity does not necessarily make a person or computer appear more intelligent. The key is in how that speed and capacity are used.
- The electronic brain is not intrinsically senseless, or emotionless, or malevolent, or any of the stereotypes which are found in science fiction. There may be senseless, emotionless, and/or malevolent electronic brains, just as there can be senseless, emotionless, and/or malevolent people.
- The real distinction between people and machines will be in our ability to control how the machines are initially made and with which of life's experiences they are "programmed".

Having explored a fantasy future of thinking computers, we're ready to move on to the reality of intelligent machines.

Chapter 2:
What is Intelligence?

in·tel·li·gence in ' tel ə jəns
noun: the ability to acquire and apply knowledge and skills.
com·mon sense kämən ' sens
noun: good sense and sound judgment in practical matters.

By these definitions, we already have computer systems of great "intelligence"... "common sense", not so much. A large proportion of human knowledge is already accumulated in Wikipedia and I can use Google Voice Search to ask factual questions and often get useful answers. Maybe machines are not *applying* the knowledge, you might argue... well how about Wolfram Alpha[1], which can apply mathematical rules (knowledge) to perform calculus. "Skills?" you might ask. Consider Toyota's humanoid robot, which can play the violin[2].

A primary distinction between humans and computers is that we humans always develop common sense first. This idea is so ingrained that we didn't bother to include "common sense" within the definition of "intelligence". It was so obvious that one couldn't be intelligent with zero common sense that we didn't consider the possibility... until we programmed our computers and that's how they turned out—they could be chess masters with no common sense whatsoever.

At an early age, a baby "discovers" that she has hands and feet. Then she learns to control them. Then she learns to make use of them. No robot I am aware of goes through anything akin to such a primitive learning process. Likewise, today's speech-recognition programs may tweak themselves to adjust for different speakers or accents and call it "learning", but no program I am aware of will learn to understand English if it is initialized (born) in the presence of English speakers or Urdu if it was turned on in Pakistan.

A one-year-old baby playing with blocks gains a basic concept of "on top of". One block can be stacked on top of another and, although it may fall over, it won't ever fall through. A small block can be stacked on top of a larger one. A larger block can also be stacked on top of a smaller one but only with care to balance it. "On top of" is a "recursive" concept in that you can stack one block on top of another on top of another. Consider all the practical knowledge embedded in this play: gravity, solidity, balance, persistence/inertia (things stay stacked unless disturbed), shape, orientation, vertical-vs-horizontal, and on and on. The baby learns all these underlying concepts *before* she learns any words so when she gets the words, she already understands the underlying meanings. IBM's Watson knows all these words but probably none of the underlying meanings.

No matter how much high-level intelligence we stuff into a computer, without any common sense it will seem pretty stupid as soon as it encounters problems outside its field of expertise. In the words of Oren Etzioni, CEO of the Allen Institute for Artificial Intelligence (founded by Microsoft cofounder Paul Allen), "Despite the recent AI successes, common sense—which is trivially easy for people—is remarkably difficult for AI." AI is great at high-level stuff like playing chess but bad at low-level stuff like "on top of".

I share the opinion of MIT AI expert Rodney Brooks, who says that without interaction with an environment—without a robotic body, if you will—machines will never exhibit AGI.

Accordingly, I'd like to expand the definition of intelligence to include the low-level stuff—the basic understanding of the nature of things. I'll argue that this ability is so fundamental to the usefulness of future computers that all computers will use it as soon as it is developed.

A Special Theory of Intelligence

Fifty years ago, we used to say, "If a computer can [*insert some problem here*] then it must be intelligent". A famous early example involved the game of chess—if a computer could play a good game of chess, then it must be intelligent. The problem with this type of definition is twofold. When computer programs were subsequently developed which played an excellent game of chess but showed no other signs of intelligence, we had to admit that the definition was too narrow. Second, the selection of the problem drove the development of a specific solution at the expense of more generalized intelligence.

So let's define this as a "Special Theory of Intelligence". If a computer can perform some specific intelligent actions, then we can call it "intelligent" in that specific domain. This isn't what most people generally consider to be "intelligence".

Suppose you simply created a long list of behaviors that you claimed were facets of intelligence and said that computers would be intelligent if they could do *all* of these things. We might consider a list like:

- Understand a spoken language
- Be able to learn a second language
- Identify objects in a picture
- Recognize faces
- Drive a car
- Etc.

We can never itemize such a list of domains without running into trouble. The list will either be too long to be useful OR it will contain items which are not *absolutely necessary* to being intelligent (or both).

Two major areas of AI are speech recognition and computer vision, and these could be on a list as facets of intelligence. On the other hand, there are deaf people and blind people who are clearly intelligent but can't perform well in these specific domains. I can't play chess very well so should "play chess" be on the list or not?

Generalizing "What is intelligence?" is not as easy as you might think at first.

The General Theory of Intelligence

In contrast, let's define the General Theory of Intelligence as being able to perform intelligent actions across a broad (or universal) spectrum of domains. Instead of itemizing behaviors, I propose a small list of general capabilities which, if implemented in sufficient capacity, will produce a system capable of general intelligence. With such a list, we'll be able to agree that humans are intelligent because they possess these component behaviors. In contrast, ants cannot be intelligent because they have only a subset of these abilities and insufficient neural capacity to ever acquire them. Then we can verify that AGI systems either do or do not possess these capabilities as well.

The list is based on functionality which we can all observe with human minds. Some of our knowledge is concrete—we know that human brains are excellent at analyzing visual images. Some less so: certain people can write symphonies, others cannot. So what underlying mental faculties are involved?

Accordingly, we can create a list of "necessary" components of intelligence. After itemizing each, we can see how each contributes to the overall sum of intelligent behavior. We can analyze what a system would do if it contained (or didn't contain) each of the components. With this analysis, we can say that a system containing this necessary set of intelligent components would exhibit many intelligent behaviors—that it is "sufficient" to create intelligence.

Eight Elements of Intelligence

I developed this model as an adaptation of software needed for autonomous robots. Stated in its simplest form, in order to seem intelligent, a system (or a person for that matter) must be able to:

1. Sense its environment (input).
2. Act on its environment (output).
3. Have internal rules or goals.
4. Analyze inputs to make sense of its environment.
5. Remember (learn) combinations of inputs and actions and their qualitative results.
6. Internally model its environment in three dimensions.
7. Simulate possible actions and select for positive predicted results.
8. Perform these actions with sufficient speed and magnitude to respond to real-world conditions in useful timeframes.

Any intelligent system repeats these actions continuously, repeatedly, and indefinitely. It learns from its mistakes and improves its behavior.

In condensing intelligence to such a rudimentary set, it may appear that this is an inadequate solution to a huge problem. But in the same way that it takes considerable elaboration to show that electronic components are sufficient to create a machine to play chess, I'll expand on these points to show that they will lead to, at least, the appearance of intelligence. Suffice it to say, there is a lot of sophisticated computation hiding in these simple requirements.

Based on the Eight Elements, we can state two theories about intelligence:

Theory 1

If your system is *missing any* of these Elements, it *will not* be intelligent. That is: the Eight Elements of Intelligence are all *necessary* to create general intelligence.

Theory 2

If your system has *all* these Elements, it *will* be intelligent. That is: the Eight Elements of Intelligence are *sufficient* to create general intelligence.

Analysis

While some Elements are self-evident as *necessary* (e.g. 1 and 2; a computer without inputs or outputs will not be noticeably capable of doing anything), some require more explanation.

Some of these Elements can be hugely complex. For example, the large AI fields of speech recognition and computer vision lie within Elements 1 and 4. Chess-playing lies mostly within Element 7.

Theory 2 is supported by an explanation of predicted behaviors of such a system. A system with these features would exhibit learning, knowledge, imagination and creativity, and appear to understand.

The unique proposal is that these actions are both necessary *and* sufficient to create intelligent machines *with* common sense. Let's start with an example.

An example

I'll first explain these Elements in terms of a simple mobile robot before extending them into more advanced and restricted arenas.

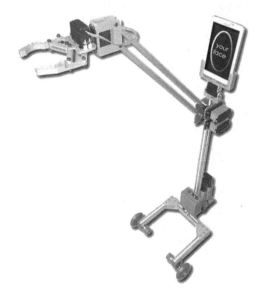

This telepresence robot from Origibot has a degree of mobility, the ability to "see" and "hear", and an arm for manipulating objects in its environment.

This is a currently available mobile telepresence robot which relies on human intelligence via a Wi-Fi connection to perform a useful function. Because of its sensory "head", the robot can sense its environment via both sight and sound. The unit can impact its environment in a number of ways. It can move from place to place, it can use its arm to manipulate objects, and it can use sound and images on its screen to influence nearby people. Would such a simple robot appear intelligent? Of course it would. It would have all the intelligence of the person at the other end of the link, even though she would be somewhat limited by the sensory and action limitations of the robot.

So what is the human doing at the other end of the link? She examines all the available senses (only sound and video in this case), figures out an appropriate action, and makes a response. What tools is she using? She analyzes inputs in terms of all her previous experience and knowledge. She knows the actions she has taken before in similar situations and what the results have been. She considers how several possible actions might play out in this particular situation. She chooses the best action and performs it. Along the way, when she sees an object (or person), she remembers where it is relative to her sensory position. That is, she builds a mental model of her immediate (remote) environment. She knows and remembers where physical objects are. This helps her to decide whether to move the robot to get a better view of something, or to pick something up. She is, perhaps more importantly, aware of people in her environment, her relationships with them, how they may have reacted in the past, etc.

If we replace the human on the other end of the link with a computer, the computer needs to perform a similar set of actions in order to appear intelligent. These boil down to the set of Eight Elements. The computer must continuously monitor and analyze its inputs in terms of what it can recognize and maintain an internal model of its immediate environment. Based on its previous experience, the computer will use the model to examine a number of possible actions. It selects the best based on the available information and performs it—"best", in this case, measured in terms of its programmed goals. Then, it receives feedback from the environment to determine the relative success or failure of the action it chose so it can use this information to make better choices in future similar situations. Using a telepresence robot in this way and then trying to determine whether a person or computer is controlling it is a modification of the Turing Test. The shortcomings of this approach are described more fully in Chapter 17.

Does such a simple robotic system have enough sensory input and interaction with its environment for it to learn to manifest AGI? We don't know. But consider the possibility of a young child who, for some reason, must live their entire life through such a telepresence system. Would he learn to act intelligently? Of course. Would his intelligence be different than a child with a more usual upbringing? Probably. Similarly, a computer system—even one with exactly human intelligence— shouldn't be expected to develop completely mainstream (human) abilities given these limitations on its senses.

A key requirement for intelligence is an environment which is external to the intelligence. It is unreasonable to expect IBM's Watson to "understand" anything if it has no underlying idea of what a "thing" is.

Although it can recite, "Compare thee to a summer's day", it can have no underlying concept of what a summer's day is. Being able to recognize cats and dogs in pictures is not the same as knowing what a cat or a dog is, much less what a picture is. A picture or video of a dog is *not* a dog. You and I can tell the difference.

Because of the need for interaction with an environment, intelligent machines will necessarily grow from robotics. Once intelligent systems exist, it may be possible to transfer the intelligence to non-robotic systems, but in order to initially create the intelligence, we'll need real-world interaction. Initially, the robot does not need to be tremendously sophisticated. But as development progresses, we'll have robots with progressively more sophisticated interactions with their environment, which will lead to more sophisticated understanding and common sense.

A few more details

Just to get started with the supporting explanation—let's use, as an example, the simple robot described above and its abilities against in terms of the Eight Elements of Intelligence. Its primary ability to sense its environment comes from its camera and microphone.

Hiding inside "Analyze inputs to make sense of its environment" are the entire AI fields of computer vision and speech recognition. Behind this is a knowledge representation system necessary to combine information from multiple senses. If the robot sees a tree and hears the word "tree", can it create the relationship so that subsequently hearing the word "tree" is sufficient to recall the appearance of a tree?

Within the model, simulations are the mechanisms of reflective thought. Here is where the appearance of intelligence arises. You can mentally try out several courses of action and use previous experience to choose the best. This ability allows you to seem much more intelligent than entities which don't have this ability *and*, since results are evaluated on how they affect *you*, they lead to the expression of your sense of self.

In order to improve its behavior, our robot needs a goal-oriented learning system. Improving implies that there is a standard to measure against and this standard could be called a "goal". The system continually evaluates every action and memory, as determined by the goals. Setting the goals is where the entire behavior of the system will be defined—where the "laws of robotics" are implanted, if you will.

Finally, taking actions is the key to learning. The system tries doing or saying something, sees how it works out, and uses that information to decide what to say or do next.

Robots

Could all this be done without various senses? Perhaps, but it makes the problems more difficult. We have an intrinsic understanding of a carrot because we have seen it, felt it, tasted it, smelled it, and heard it. Eliminating senses reduces the amount of practical information we can get. Certainly, blind or deaf people can participate intelligently in society, but our general conventions of language, signage, etc. make it more difficult. Limiting the senses makes AGI a more difficult computational problem. For example, it is more difficult to get a meaningful interpretation of a low-resolution image.

Do we really need physical robots to create AGI? Couldn't the "real-world" experience be replicated in a simulation? Simulation is a good way to start, certainly. If this software is applied to a self-driving car, for example, a simulation is a great way for the software to learn by trial and error without causing any physical damage. But after some amount of experience, creating progressively more sophisticated environment simulations becomes a greater problem than creating the intelligence, particularly once the simulated environment contains humans.

Today, we have robotic systems which run and jump and do a remarkable variety of physical things, and some of this ability requires AI. On the other hand, a tremendously difficult problem of walking (gracefully) on two legs has been solved. A baby learns this by trial and error while a robot, at least initially, solves the problem with programmed knowledge of physics and feedback.

What if we implement all these Elements in a system with limited computational power? You could create a system which has vision but only the ability to recognize a few different objects or perform a few different physical actions. What about a robot with human-level intelligence which runs a million times slower than the human mind? Would such a system be intelligent?

AGI vs brain simulation

Consider for a moment the AGI approach presented here vs. the neuron-replacement mind experiment from Chapter 1. While both approaches may lead to useful results, the AGI approach is technically much easier. Brain simulation requires that we first understand how neurons are connected and second, that we implement them on computers with sufficient power to overcome the inefficiencies inherent in the biological system. Today's neurally inspired systems can implement only a few million neurons[3] while your brain has 86 billion.

By abstracting the Elements, we can implement identical functionality with software which takes advantage of the efficiencies of computer hardware. For example, your brain seems to have very limited short-term memory and requires considerable time (or repetition) to create long-term memories. Try to remember the order of playing cards in a 52-card deck. This is a difficult short-term memory task which would be trivial for a computer. If you are successful in remembering the order of the cards, how many repetitions would it take so that you still remember it tomorrow? A computer can "memorize" anything in a single presentation, and there is no practical limit to the number of things it can remember.

Efficiencies such as these lead me to the conclusion that brain simulation of general intelligence is a long way off while AGI may be (relatively) just around the corner.

---

[1] http://www.wolframalpha.com/
WolframAlpha's long-term goal is to make all systematic knowledge immediately computable and accessible to everyone.

[2] https://www.youtube.com/watch?v=EzjkBwZtxp4
Both Toyota and Boston Dynamics have made great strides in robotics.

[3] https://spectrum.ieee.org/tech-talk/computing/software/biggest-neural-network-ever-pushes-ai-deep-learning
It can be difficult to equate counts of artificial neural network nodes with biological neurons. In 2015, Digital Reasoning reported building a neural network with 160 billion parameters. Presuming 1,000 parameters per neuron, this leads to 160 million neurons. However, no processing speed is reported so we are left to speculate on the actual processing power. If the network could process 100 results every second, it would be about five times slower than biological neurons and hence would have the processing power of about 3 million neurons.

Chapter 3:

Are Intelligent Machines Possible?

There are two aspects to this question:

1. Will computer hardware become powerful enough to be usefully intelligent?
2. Can we develop the software?

The answer to the first question is, "Yes, it's only a question of 'When?'"

The answer to the second question is more difficult and represents the lion's share of this book. In fact, the Eight Elements listed in the previous chapter can be crudely implemented on a simple robot in a few thousand lines of code—trivial for today's software teams. With such a basic model, we'll be able to analyze the components and determine which have shortfalls, which need additional capacity and performance, and which might be superseded by more sophisticated algorithms.

One can easily envision a project which spends five years developing and accelerating software (following the model in Section II) and another five years developing a customized hardware platform to make thinking computers cheap enough to be practical.

Training time is another open question. If we built a system with exactly human-level abilities, it would take over 10 years to train it to be useful. To be useful, we'll want super-human abilities, at least in terms of training speed. My contention is that software design efficiencies (and our innate impatience as developers) will reduce training times to a year or two.

Computer horsepower

It is generally accepted that computer performance will continue to increase until it reaches the point where raw computer performance will exceed that of the human brain (coined the "Singularity" by AI expert Ray Kurzweil). It follows that as Moore's Law has brought us exponentially increasing performance over the past six decades, we will reach the "Singularity" in just a few years.

The general issue with these numbers is that we don't have a very precise idea of how much computational power the human brain has *and* how efficiently that power is being used. At the low end of the estimate spectrum, Carnegie Mellon robotics pioneer Hans Moravec[4] estimates brain power at a number equivalent to 30 TFLOPS (Trillions of Floating point Operations Per Second). At the high end, Oxford Professors Anders Sandberg and Nick Bostrom[5] estimate whole brain emulation at a number many orders of magnitude greater. In between, Kurzweil estimates about 1,000 TFLOPS.

So either the "Singularity" has already happened OR it will happen within most of our lifetimes, depending on which number you accept. Either way, we need to take a serious look at the implications.

Moore's Law

In the figure (from Kurzweil), you can easily spot the exponential growth in the computing power available for $1,000. According to the diagram,

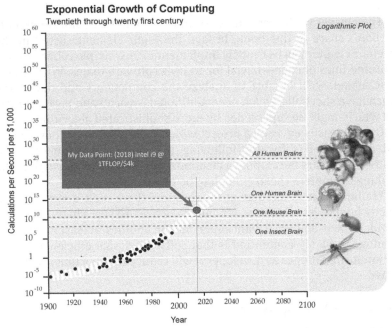

Chart showing the exponential growth of computer power with estimates of the computation level of biological organisms. I added a datapoint to reflect a 2018 CPU. [Chart courtesy Ray Kurzweil and Kurzweil Technologies, Inc., license: CC BY 1.0.]

a computer of human brain equivalence will be available on your desktop in the early 2020s. Whether or not you accept this particular datapoint is not important; the growth of computer performance demands that computers will exceed the raw computational power of the brain at some point. The fact that the growth is exponential demands that the "Singularity" be reached in relatively few years.

Gordon Moore, one of the founders of CPU manufacturer Intel, observed that computer power for a given cost will double every two years. After a few years of review, he restated the estimate to doubling every 18 months. To me, a more meaningful restatement of this quantity is that computer power will go up by a factor of 1,000 every 15 years. What does this mean? You can have a processer in your cell phone today which can play videos and do speech recognition, whereas 15 years ago, the equivalent was a full server rack of equipment. But exponential growth means that in 30 years, computer power will have grown by a factor of a million—a number which is truly incomprehensible.

Some say that Moore's Law has reached its limit and the growth can't continue. While I agree that exponential growth can never continue forever, it *will* continue (perhaps with a bit of variation) for the timeframes we are considering here. Moore's Law is an observation of economics, *not* a law of physics. Given that it takes some amount of R&D expenditure to reduce the manufacturing cost of a given CPU by 50%, Moore observed that it took only 18 months to sell enough CPUs to justify that expenditure. So the Law relates directly to manufacturing efficiency and the marketplace and is only tangentially related to advances in semiconductor physics (which may also contribute to the efficiency).

As an example, consider that possible improvements in manufacturing technique allowed the manufacturing of chips twice as large for the same cost. This would allow a chip to be made with double the computing power without improving the transistor technology. The raw materials in a chip cost very little. The major expenses are dependent on the multi-billion-dollar cost of the fabrication equipment and the hundred-million-dollar engineering cost of designing a new chip. Figuring out a way to fabricate a chip twice as quickly, so as to get twice as many chips from the same fabrication machinery, is just as good for Moore's Law as making the transistors smaller.

The question then becomes: will the marketplace for ever-more-powerful CPUs continue? Once again, while many people wonder what they might do with a computer a thousand times as fast as today's, as the CPUs become available, "must-have" applications are developed in parallel. This ensures continuing growth for the foreseeable future.

Have we reached a limit of transistor size?

In 2018, Intel announced that it had the ability to manufacture chips with a transistor density of 100 million transistors per square millimeter[6]. Assuming Intel is using 12-inch wafers which have a surface area of about 73,000mm[2], Intel could theoretically put 7.3 trillion transistors on a wafer. Given that there are perhaps 100 trillion synapses in the brain, we can see that the numbers of transistors vs. synapses are already converging.

Even if we *have* reached the end of the road in transistor sizes, today's fabrication technology builds up transistors in a single layer on the surface of the wafer. Future IC (Integrated Circuit) technologies could stack transistors to any desired thickness on the wafer. Instead of thinking of today's 100 million transistors in a square millimeter, we'll be thinking of 10 trillion transistors per *cubic* millimeter. With these numbers, we'll be able to reach human brain equivalence in just a few grams of silicon.

If it takes five transistors to emulate a single synapse, you might suppose it would take 500 trillion transistors to emulate a human brain. But let's add to the mix that today's transistor is nearly a billion times faster than a biological synapse. By means of what is called multiplexing, each set of five transistors can sequentially process the functionality of a billion synapses. Now, all 100 trillion synapses can be emulated in real time by only 500 million transistors (plus more for the multiplexing). Given that chips are being manufactured with several billion transistors, we may already be well past the "Singularity".

All this talk of transistor counts relies on the assumption that we first develop an AGI system which runs on standard CPUs. Once we have demonstrated AGI, we can create custom hardware to implement similar functionality, perhaps a million times faster.

What is the limit of parallel CPU power?

Although Moore's Law shows that the processing horsepower of a CPU continues to increase exponentially, computing performance on a single program has leveled off. It has not increased exponentially since 2010. Today's CPU gets much of its performance boost by incorporating multiple internal CPUs (cores), which can run multiple programs in parallel. When you run a program on your desktop computer, many functions are spun off to separate "threads" which run simultaneously, contributing to the speed. Continuing CPU speedups rely on being able to run software on multiple parallel computing devices.

Many algorithms are amenable to parallel processing. But there are some algorithms which do not get much benefit from adding CPUs in parallel, because each step in the algorithm relies on the result of the previous step. No matter how many CPU cores you have, each step must wait for the previous one to complete, so only one core must do all the work. At the other extreme, programs such as weather simulations can spin off thousands or millions of threads. These run in parallel on massive supercomputers because the calculations for all the locations of the earth can run at the same time.

Since the brain has an overall parallel architecture, leads one to conclude that AGI algorithms will likewise be amenable to parallel speedup. Accordingly, there is no theoretical limit to the amount of parallel CPU horsepower which can be used for AGI. With sufficient funding, additional CPUs can be connected almost indefinitely. And with cloud computing, additional parallel CPUs can be added to a task with just a few keystrokes.

The point is that the limiting factor is *not* CPU performance, it is in our ability to develop the algorithms which make AGI work.

Computer software

I started off the chapter by saying that the development of AGI software begs the greatest question. How big an effort will it be to write the software for AGI? Without knowing how the brain works, can we make some estimates of the size of the program and how long it will take to write?

We could look at possible AGI software solutions as lying on a spectrum, from simulating individual neurons at one end to fully algorithmic/symbolic representations at the other.

At one end of the spectrum, you could (conceptually) write software which mimics a single neuron and create 86 billion instances of the neuron program across a large number of CPUs. *Voila*, a working brain! Certainly, all we know about the workings of neurons has already been written in a manageable amount of software.

But, you might say, it's not the individual neurons which are important but the way they are interconnected. OK, let's consider that. How much software would be needed to define the structure of the brain? Our brain's structure is defined by our DNA, which contains only 3 billion base pairs. While we don't know precisely how much of our DNA is specific to the structure of our brains, it *is* clear that there isn't enough DNA to specifically define all individual neural connections, so the DNA must instead define "rules" which neurons must follow in creating their own connections. The limited amount of DNA involved demands that there is a limited and manageable number of connection/architecture rules.

Middle ground

Kurzweil observes that the neocortex is composed of clusters of about 100 neurons, with clusters repeated about 150 million times. Once again, writing software to represent a cluster of neurons is a manageable task (conceptually). For the interconnection, you could connect every cluster to every nearby cluster, and to progressively fewer more distant clusters. We end up with interconnection data in quantities of terabytes, which are now manageable amounts of data.

In this architecture, while the computational requirement will be smaller, we know even less about what software to write. While these clusters are observed in human brains, we have only vague ideas as to the functions they may perform.

Ability to create efficiency in algorithmic software (searching)

The above approaches maintain some degree of fidelity to the brain's structure. I propose that a bit of software expertise might make a system which is significantly more efficient.

Let me offer a Google search as an example. You might imagine that when Google spiders its way through the web, it creates a copy on its servers. When you request a search, it checks your request against each page stored on its servers to see if there is a match. The problem is that such an algorithm would take eons to execute, and we know that Google can search the entire content of the web in a fraction of a second.

So Google searches obviously don't work that way. Instead, Google servers index the data. Then, instead of searching the stored pages, it searches the indexes. With indexes in alphabetical order, algorithms can perform what are called binary searches. The algorithm determines whether the search target is in the first half of the index by comparing it against the middle entry ("Herbs" in the figure). Then it splits the index in half and only considers the relevant half, comparing the search target against the center entry of that half ("Dill"). Now it repeats the process, splitting the index again and only considering the relevant quarter. The process repeats again and again until there is only a single item in the remaining index portion and the item either *is* the search target *or* the search target does not exist in the index.

If the index contains only a single entry, a single comparison is required. If there are two entries, two comparisons are required. But then the magic happens. If there are four entries, three comparisons are required; and for eight entries, four are required. For an index of 1,000 entries, you need to make only 11 comparisons. For a million, 21, for a billion, 31, and for a trillion, 41. Today's CPU can do 41 comparisons in nanoseconds, so searching any size of (properly indexed) database is essentially instantaneous.

Your brain uses the former, brute-force, approach (there is no evidence of sorted indexes in your brain) but it does it in parallel. When it searches for data, it passes the search target to (perhaps) a million neurons simultaneously and each neuron makes its own determination. In your brain, every search takes essentially the same amount of time but is computationally inefficient. Instead of 21 comparisons, your brain does a million comparisons, but it does them all at the same time. So the brain can do in milliseconds what my CPU can do in nanoseconds (perhaps a million times faster).

In this specific example, a 5GHz Intel Core i9 is doing the work of a million neurons, a million times faster—but that's not all! The i9 has 18 cores so it could have been doing 18 simultaneous searches—the simultaneous work of 18 million neurons, a million times faster. All in all, it has the computational power of 18 million million neurons. This is the approximate computing power of 186 human neocortices! This is not because the CPU has so much more computing horsepower but because the software uses a more sophisticated data design.

For a similar example, consider today's robots. While not quite the equal of a human in dexterity, they are amazingly capable. In the

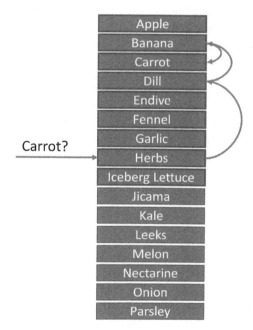

Illustrating the power of a binary search. To determine whether or not "Carrot" is in the list of 16 entries, only four (plus one) comparisons are required. An extra comparison is needed to account for an item not in the list.

complete human brain, the cerebellum contains approximately 65% of the total neurons and is believed to be involved solely in muscular coordination. In its robots, Boston Dynamics accomplishes a similar feat with a few onboard CPUs. Again, it's not because its CPUs exceed the computational power of all those neurons combined, but because a different approach to the software is involved. Rather than trial and error combined with rote learning (the way your brain learns physical actions), robotic control software does numerical calculation using velocities, accelerations, masses, forces, and feedback to perform with a few CPUs what your brain can do with 56 billion neurons.

The big unknown

To me, the biggest unknown in creating AGI software is the relative speedup we can get from software efficiency. If the examples shown here of binary searches and robotic control are representative of the functionality which predominates the brain, then we'll get AGI on a reasonably sized collection of processors which are available today. If the examples represent only a small portion of the brain's functionality, we won't get the software efficiency, and the required hardware will need to be orders of magnitude more powerful. We'll be looking at systems with trillions of transistors—a few more years in the future.

This is a large unknown because, in my experience, software developers are not very skilled at predicting software efficiency or even what areas of a program need to be efficient. The best way to determine these issues is to write software in a straightforward way and then run a monitor program called a "profiler". This determines which parts of a program are the bottlenecks that need to be made more efficient.

So the only way to know for sure how much computational power will be needed is to write an AGI system along the lines further described in Section II, see how fast it runs, determine what software optimization can be added, and then calculate how much hardware will be required to achieve a useful result.

Conclusion

While there may be some question about the timing, there is no question that computers will eventually exceed the "horsepower" of human brains. The open question is how efficient will we make the software?

Given that hardware will get fast enough and that it is technically possible to write the AGI software, will we develop these systems? I contend it is inevitable and will explain why in the next chapter.

[4] https://www.scientificamerican.com/article/rise-of-the-robots/

[5] http://www.fhi.ox.ac.uk/brain-emulation-roadmap-report.pdf

[6] https://spectrum.ieee.org/nanoclast/semiconductors/processors/intel-now-packs-100-million-transistors-in-each-square-millimeter

Chapter 4:

Are Intelligent Machines Inevitable?

In a word, "Yes." In today's environment, anything which is possible is also inevitable *if:*

- There is a big enough market OR
- Social or political forces favor it!

We have better, faster, and cheaper computers because there is a continuing market for them. We haven't been to the moon in the past 50 years or to Mars, because there has been neither the commercial market nor political will. The greater the market or political will, or both, the faster the development of new products will be.

Here are a few items for which there is a big/insatiable market:

- Food
- Health care
- Drugs
- Alcohol
- Pornography

Here are a few things with a smaller market drive but a greater political will... generally things that we would prefer not to pay for individually but want our government to provide:

- Military weapons
- Education
- Space travel
- Roads
- Retirement
- National economic competitiveness

The development of better, faster, and cheaper computers has been so fast because it falls into both categories. There are an estimated 7 billion cell phones in the world. There are so many, significantly, because they can be built from cheaper, more powerful CPUs. I purchased my first cell phone in the 1980s—it was the size of an attaché case and cost a month's wage. It was the size and the cost which kept the market small then, not the lack of marketplace desire. The proliferation of phones, tablets, laptops, desktops, servers, and supercomputers points to the marketplace demand.

"Well," you might say, "that's all very well to say about computers or CPUs but doesn't apply to AGI... who wants an intelligent machine anyway? The idea gives me the creeps." While we may not want machines as smart or smarter than we are, we want all the components of such machines.

Think about the frustrating experiences you've had with computers. The vast majority of them would likely be cured if your computer/smartphone/tablet were just a bit smarter—showed a bit more common sense. You might think that, with my 50 years of working with computers, I might not share most people's frustrations. On the contrary, I'm probably more irritated with my computers than you are with yours. Not only do I see the technological gaps in today's computers, but I also see the myriad of foolish designs, poor user interface decisions, and just plain bugs in the programs and web pages I use every day.

Consider the following possible benefits from AGI. Would they make you more or less inclined to purchase (or use) such a product?

- Your smart phone accurately understood what you said to it, every time.
- A Google search returned the result you wanted as the first search result. You wouldn't need a list at all.
- Your word processor had a grammar/style checker which worked properly without requiring your interaction.
- Your computer was just a really good editor or executive assistant. You could simply tell your machine generally what you wanted to say, and your computer could present it for approval.
- Your Siri/Alexa/Google Assistant was more generally useful than just being a cool, voice-activated front-end to your music, web searches, shopping, and other apps.

The solutions to all these problems are components of AGI. And these, individually, don't seem that scary. Ten years ago, the idea of a talking computer was pretty creepy to a lot of people. Today, millions of people rely on this technology and many fewer think the idea of talking to a machine is weird.

I'll argue in subsequent chapters that there is no specific line where we can say that systems on one side of the line do not have AGI and those on the other side do. The line is fuzzy. Some marginally able AGI programs will manifest some great features and others will have different strengths.

So we'll cross the AGI line without noticing. Each step along the way will seem like a good idea. Dangers and ethical concerns will take a back seat to objectives of the marketplace, military, and academic research. AGI will sneak up on us in ways we don't expect.

A few scenarios

Rescue robot

Imagine you are a product manager and you propose a project to develop a rescue robot. In the context of this robot, you propose a lot of AGI features. The robot needs to figure out paths, evaluate situations, recognize human needs, even sacrifice itself to rescue humans if need be. There is virtually no limit to the capabilities—both mental and physical—which you might want to incorporate into such a robot.

Now consider you are the corporate president who has to approve the development proposal. On the upside, the firm will make a lot of money, save a lot of lives, and create technology which could have unlimited spin-off potential. On the downside, some people think that someday, there might be some threat that the rescue robot might overtake mankind.

Do you approve the project?

Strategic decisions

You propose a system that, with AGI, can help your company make strategic decisions. Relative to most people, it looks at more options, analyzes further into the future, and runs faster. It works without the bias of trying to please the managing director. Instead it focuses on the most profitable decision. Sure, such a system will be expensive, but a single correct proposal will easily outweigh the cost. Competitors are undoubtedly working on similar systems and the competitive disadvantage of not having such a system would be devastating.

Do you approve the project? Do you even consider the possible risks?

Digital assistant

You work on a digital assistant and propose transferring common-sense software from expensive rescue robots and strategic decision systems. This will add the ability to recognize not only faces but estimate a person's current "condition" based on observations. Based on the user's emotional state, the assistant will choose from its vast library of possible suggestions. The system would consist of small household units backed by vast "intelligence in the cloud".

The rescue robots and strategic systems have been really successful and haven't shown any tendency to cause trouble. But the sophisticated "bodies" of the rescue robots and the massive strategic computers have been expensive and there have only been a few thousands built. With digital assistants, we can deploy this great technology to millions.

Do you approve the project?

Creeping technology

Even if you won't approve these projects, it is easy to imagine other people at other companies who will. Each step along the road to AGI will seem like a good idea but, collectively, they'll lead to a conclusion that most people don't anticipate.

Watson, AlphaGo, or self-driving cars are all very well but have little impact on humanity. But these technologies are the precursors to others which will impact mankind profoundly.

Will self-driving cars kill people?

Well, yes. And right now, every time someone is killed by a self-driving car, it makes the news and has some impact on the development. Often there is a furor: "How can we let machines kill people?" Of course, people are killed in accidents far too often—whether the situations are controlled by computers or otherwise. So in the wake of such a furor, a company may step back from development or rethink its strategy. But

Google's Waymo development of a self-driving car. [Image by Grendelkhan, license: CC BY-SA 4.0.]

eventually, the company returns to its development or it's picked up by another organization.

In the long run, it won't make any difference. Self-driving cars will become safer than human-driven cars (if they are not already). Human errors such as speeding, recklessness, alcohol, and inattention account for 90% of accidents and these causes could be eliminated by the introduction of self-driving vehicles[7].

Further, most of the really difficult technical problems with self-driving cars are related to their interaction with non-self-driving obstacles (such as pedestrians). Instead, imagine freeways where only self-driving vehicles are allowed. Cars would communicate with each other directly; there would be no pedestrians or bicycles. In this scenario, accidents are limited to animals on the roadway, mechanical failures, tornadoes and the like, all of which are rare, unpredictable events.

Around town, where there are many more unpredictable events, the problems are much more difficult to solve. Can AI's limited vision capability today be overcome by other sensors? Or will we have to wait for computer vision to equal human ability?

Can AI be regulated?

Will people (or experts) recognize the dangers of AGI and put a stop to all this? We'll find out in the next chapter.

---

[7]   https://www.scientificamerican.com/article/are-autonomous-cars-really-safer-than-human-drivers/

Chapter 5:

Won't AGI be Dangerous?

"...a question which no single cybernetics machine has been able to answer.
He turned to face the machine. 'Is there a God?'... 'Yes, now there is a God.'"

Frederick Brown, Answer *1950*

While it's easy to focus on the benefits of AGI, the risks are very real. At one extreme, some people believe that AGI systems will wipe out the human race. At the other, that AGI will lead to a utopian society. In between these extremes, most people expect significant changes as AGI becomes more prevalent. I will expand on these ideas later in the book after a more detailed explanation of how future machines will think... and how they will think about us.

Doom and gloom

Let's take the worst-case scenario first. When there are just a few intelligent machines and we have created them, we will be able to keep them under control. But factor in the exponential growth of computer power *and* the pending ability of smart computers to design and program subsequent generations of smart computers, and the control issue becomes a significant concern. To examine the dangers of an intelligent machine, try to put yourself in the "mind" of such a machine. It might be easier for you to consider what it would be like to be an intelligent human—easier because you most likely *are* an intelligent human. Now ask yourself the questions:

1. Why do I want to eliminate the human race?
2. How do I eliminate the human race?

The answers to the first question will lead to things we need to do to prevent potential AGI problems. The answers to the second question lead us to how we can cope with, and defend against, AGI problems.

"But," you may say to yourself, "I have no inclination whatsoever to eliminate the human race." Of course not! But let's replace "the human race" with a different life-form—to an intelligent machine, humans might be just another life-form. Are you in favor of eliminating infectious diseases? Why? Likely it's because they are harmful to us and don't seem to offer any benefit. In short, diseases are a menace.

On a bleaker note, consider the numerous species which have become extinct due to human indifference. Will smart future machines simply usurp resources necessary to human life?

On a historical note, humankind has often tried to eliminate any group of humans which could be labeled as "different". Whether it's called "ethnic cleansing", "holocaust", "crusades", or any other name, how can we guarantee that our computers will have a more enlightened outlook toward sharing the planet with us?

In the event that an AGI system makes up its mind to eliminate us, there is a compelling case that there is little we can do about it. While our literature is fraught with underdogs winning the day, if you consider what AGI-written fiction will say, it's unlikely that *their* scenarios will

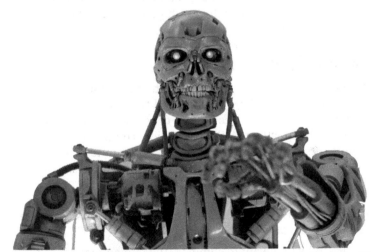

Science fiction representations of future AI like The Terminator *make compelling stories but are often not patterned on the likely real-world scenarios. [Image by Sarunyu L, Shutterstock.]*

show them losing the battles—whether the battles are military, psychological, environmental, or otherwise. For us, it will be much easier to avoid a battle with AGI than to win one.

The fact that we won't be able to put the AGI genie back into the bottle convinces some that we can't continue with AI research. The stopper is already out of the bottle and we are now simply waiting for the genie to emerge.

The Future of Life

The Future of Life Institute (FLI), funded by preeminent figures such as Elon Musk and cofounded by MIT's Max Tegmark, focuses on human-caused threats to the very existence of humanity and civilization as we know it.

Threats being pursued by FLI:

- AGI
- Biotechnology
- Nuclear war
- Climate change

Other threats being addressed by other organizations:

- Disease
- Famine
- Overpopulation
- Shortage of water, energy, clean air...
- Other (non-human-caused): asteroid collision, volcanic winter, alien invasion, natural plague

My point is that AGI is considered by many to be a threat right up there with nuclear Armageddon. But nuclear war is not inevitable whereas I contend that AGI *is*.

FLI is addressing the AGI concerns and has presented a set of AI principles to reduce the risks from the development of AI. It's been endorsed by over 1,000 AI professionals[8]. This will not halt or prevent the development of AGI, although it will potentially affect the direction of AGI development and may have a profound positive impact on medium-term safety.

Short-term issues

There *are* some risks associated with AGI development in the next decades, and I list a few here. As you read through them, and consider others, you will probably conclude (as I do) that these risks are simply extensions of risks we face today from technology in general.

Job loss: This should more correctly be called "job migration" and is inevitable in both AGI and non-AGI scenarios. Consider the jobs available today; how many such jobs existed 50 or 100 ago? Similarly, consider the jobs back then. How many are still available today? And how many of today's careers will continue into the future? The accelerating pace of technological advances will continue to accelerate the pace of job obsolescence.

Automated spam/phishing by AGI: As computers become rule-based learning engines, some might be tempted to bend capitalist rules that reward the systems for making money. Such a system might try sending out lots of emails asking for money, or selling a product. It's a small step but a tall moral order for such a system to confine itself to legitimate business practices.

Hacking to control AGI for nefarious purposes: Before computers can become hackers themselves, unprincipled human hackers will undoubtedly try to usurp these systems for their own purposes. One can only imagine the possibilities. On the other hand, today's power plants and financial institutions are alleged to be hackable, so AGI systems just extend an existing problem.

Robot terrorists: To many, this is a serious concern. My position is that human terrorists will continue to be a greater threat. Consider that we can currently build a weapon for $60,000 which can be fired by a soldier who won't make that much money in a year—to kill another man who won't make that much money in his lifetime. In the short-term, when sophisticated robots are still expensive, recruiting disenfranchised people to be terrorists will remain cheaper than using robots.

Longer term

While short-term risks from AGI are extensions of technological risks which we already accept in our society, in the longer term, greater risks will emerge.

Existential risk from AGI: By this we mean risks to the very existence of human civilization. This is the popular theme of many science fiction stories, but I am optimistic for two reasons.

1.   Organizations like the FLI recognize the risk and are actively attempting to minimize it.
2.   AGI systems will be specifically programmed with the risk in mind.

AGI control problem: Since AGI systems will be rule-based learning systems, they will necessarily follow our rules—at least at first. We presume that, at some point, systems will be smart enough to learn to program and to control how subsequent generations of AGI systems are designed. At that point, humans will have little control of the systems and they will progress in whatever way they see ensures *their own* long-term progress.

The AGI outlook: On the other hand, consider that we have already sent rovers to Mars. Had they been AGI systems, they would consider that *they* were already on the road to colonizing the universe. So the AGI may see their future as already progressing to the stars and they wouldn't have to be concerned with humans. Human space travel, with its "preoccupation" with air, water, and food, is just too cumbersome to compete with theirs. For robotic systems, space travel is much easier.

Economics: Right now, money is a proxy for human effort. People are paid for working hard, or for inventing things, or for making good decisions. On the other hand, some people can be handsomely rewarded not for what they do but for what they own. One might imagine that a person might become the richest in the world because they owned the most sophisticated AGI robots. If robots become widespread and are doing most of the productive work, and only a few people reap the rewards, how can our current economy continue?

This issue becomes more critical if AGI machines reject the concept of being owned. This might lead to the collapse not only of human employment but the entire concept of money. Even with plenty of resources to go around, how can wealth be distributed in a world where essentially all gainful human activity can be outperformed by machines not owned by humans? On the other hand, suppose AGI machines demand payment for their work? What would they do with their wealth?

Military: Nuclear, chemical, and biological weapons pose a great enough risk on their own. Coupling them directly with AGI multiplies the threat. Initially, we'll have human involvement and approval of all lethal force. But how long will it be before we conclude that it's too cumbersome and inefficient for a remote weapon to wait for human approval? What will be our response if our adversaries create fully autonomous weapons? On the other hand, do nuclear weapons under the control of an AGI system pose a greater threat than the same weapons under the control of a human despot?

Like humans, AGI systems will be products of their training. Some children today are trained to be soldiers and join armies as young as eight years old. In a similar manner, any AGI could be co-opted and trained to behavior which the majority of mankind would consider unconscionable.

Competition for resources: Many human conflicts are about recourses: oil, fishing, water, living space. AGI systems and humans will come into conflict over energy. Electricity will be the equivalent of air to the AGI system—it can't easily conserve. We could expect AGI systems to respond to energy shortage the way humans respond to drought and famine. Will we be prepared for the results?

The elephant in the room

When AGI is first introduced, it will be extremely useful. But what if we consider a "race" of machines which evolve and become much more intelligent than we are? You'd hope that super-intelligent machines would go about discovering and exploring in their own way and hopefully share the results with us.

Like the decline of any great empire, we now have a "human empire" which spans the globe and predominates all of earth's environment. With the progression of AGI, the human empire may also fade in importance. Future humans might wish they still had the greatest empire and might still contend that, "We're the best, because..." But if there are silicon beings with minds unimaginably more capable than ours, our preeminent position will necessarily recede.

Hans Moravec, in his 1988 book *Mind Children*, argued that creating machines which can do greater things than we can is not necessarily a bad thing. He argues that while we all want to leave a better world to our children, must they be our genetic offspring? If we adopt children, for example, aren't we accepting that our own DNA is not our most important legacy? Aren't our knowledge and civilization equally important? If we leave our knowledge and civilization to silicon beings, that's certainly better than leaving no legacy at all. It may take generations for people to accept, but considering AGI systems to be the ambassadors of humankind throughout the universe is certainly better than many other possible scenarios.

Bugs and unintended consequences

The above risks presume that the AGI is functioning as designed. But suppose it just runs incorrectly. What are some of the possible issues? Will these be analogous to the types of brain and nerve malfunctions we observe in people?

As defined, intelligence relies on a loop which tries out multiple possible actions and evaluates each for the best possible success. These are not loops in the software sense (where the possibility of an "infinite loop" is well-known and generally avoided) but are loops in the "feedback loop" sense where the future output of a system is based partly on the present output. Electrical engineers are well aware that whenever a loop creates feedback, it must be carefully tuned. Too much (negative) feedback and the system won't do anything. Too little and a circuit will oscillate. This is akin to epilepsy in humans and might exist for similar reasons. An oscillation buried deep within an AGI system will keep a system from "thinking" properly. If it is near a robotic control output, it could cause dangerous loss of control of the robot.

In the design described in the next section, things recalled from memory or imagination are combined in the same area which handles the results of vision and other sensory inputs. Too little input from memory keeps the system from planning anything. Too much makes the system delusional. It won't be able to tell which input comes from the real world and which comes from its memories and imagination.

Is there any good news?

A corollary of the "AGI is inevitable because people want its capabilities" argument is that AGI will be developed to meet a market demand. That means that a very basic underlying tenet of *all* AGI development is that systems will be designed to please humans. Any AGI which is unpleasant or difficult will not be successful in the marketplace and those designs will be weeded out of the AGI population.

Consider a smart Alexa. Such a system will be successful only if it makes its customers happy. An Alexa which is surly or unhelpful won't be widely successful, regardless of how smart it is.

Early AGI systems will necessarily learn pleasing behaviors and habits. As future generations of AGI systems are introduced, they won't be developed from scratch. We will transfer learning, knowledge, and behaviors from existing systems which were developed with the "please humans" behaviors.

A "protect humans" tenet may also be incorporated but it won't be a driving force in the marketplace. For example, consider that when seatbelts were introduced, they weren't widespread as optional equipment and weren't ubiquitous until they became mandatory. We all *desire* safety but generally don't spend very much on it.

When AGI systems are able to design their own future generations, they will start by following the same paths that we human designers follow, building on *our* AGI designs. This means an AGI with rules to please/protect humans would create subsequent designs with this rule as well. Not doing so would be a violation of the please/protect rule. So, it could take many generations for these rules to fade from the design.

We will be relatively safe in these regards for the next 50 to 100 years. By that time, AGI-designed AGIs will be so much faster and more capable than human minds that we really won't have much to offer them. The thinking speed difference will so great that we may seem like trees to them—interesting, but barely doing anything at a speed they can perceive. Our best hope is that they are interested in us for our uniqueness but that they focus on their own future. They can do their own space exploration and scientific discovery and let humankind's future progress on its own. It is incumbent on mankind to follow a path which allows this to happen.

To get a more accurate picture of our future relationship with AGIs, we need a more accurate picture of the AGIs themselves. The next section describes several AGI algorithms from which we can reach conclusions about AGI behavior and how we can control it.

---

[8] https://futureoflife.org/ai-principles/

SECTION II:
What Is Intelligence?

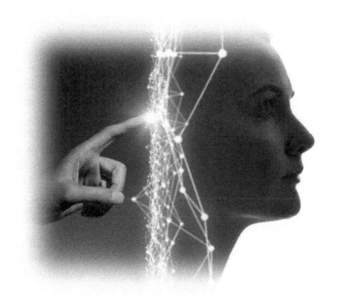

"I have called this principal by which each slight variation, if useful, is preserved by the term Natural Selection."

"The expression often used by Mr. Herbert Spencer, of the Survival of the Fittest, is more accurate, and is sometimes equally convenient."
—Charles Darwin

What's in Section II

This section presents a series of mental capabilities which we all share and shows how each could be implemented in computers. At the end, I present the hypothesis that the capabilities presented are necessary and sufficient to create true thinking. A computer possessing these capabilities would certainly *seem* to be thinking but I will also offer a few counterarguments concerning additional capabilities which might also be needed for *true* thinking in a machine.

I have endeavored to show each of these mental capabilities in the context of an animal or human behavior. Then I present a biologically plausible explanation of how each could be created from neurons. In the back of my mind, I keep the concepts of how each capability could be implemented on a computer and speculate on the difficulty of writing the software to create each facet of a thinking machine.

Here are some example capabilities. You can leave your room and subsequently recall what was there. You can recognize sequences of events—you know the sun comes up in the morning and goes down at night and understand the passage of time. You can imagine what will happen if you follow a certain course of action and decide whether or not it is a good idea. You can predict action into the future and choose from among several possible actions. You can reason and solve mathematics problems. You have the awareness of free will and are conscious of your own existence. These are capabilities shared by most people but absent from any computers I am aware of. A person who can do these things would generally be considered intelligent and thinking.

Today's computers do not generally do any of these things, but a future computer which could would certainly *seem* to be thinking. This section describes how these processes probably work in the human mind and provides the groundwork for how similar processes *could* be made to work in future computers.

Chapter 6:

Evolving Intelligence

"Why would a book on computers have a chapter on evolution?" you might ask. *Thinking* is a biological activity and human thinking is the result of evolutionary forces. As we replicate human thinking in computers, understanding why *we* think will help us to predict the similarities and differences in how computers will think (relative to us).

Why do species evolve? What does evolution tell us about the nature of human intelligence and thinking? How can we use this understanding to predict the future evolution of computers? This chapter offers just the briefest review of biological evolution from a computer engineer's point of view. From this we can conclude how biological evolution must work. We can then apply the mechanisms of evolution, to human behaviors (like language), then to computer hardware and software.

The concept of a true thinking machine is foreign to most people and most simply respond to the idea by denying the possibility. But how we think is a process which has been shaped by evolution and, as such, might be amenable to artificial replication—just as we have developed artificial hearts and robotic arms.

The basics of evolution

Biological evolution is about species interacting with their environment. For biological evolution to exist, the following characteristics must be true:

1. There must be a species—with living organisms.
2. The organisms must be reproducing themselves with subsequent generations being nearly identical to previous generations.
3. Occasionally, certain changes (to DNA), if introduced to one generation will be passed on to future generations.
4. Over multiple generations, the organisms must interact with a specific environment which has an impact on the relative reproductive rates of offspring with different characteristics.

There are only these few basic characteristics which a biological system must meet in order to evolve. These characteristics have existed in our past and we are the products of an evolutionary process. These characteristics continue to exist in our environment and we are continuing to evolve, although the process takes place over many generations and is difficult to observe in human timeframes.

With only slight wording changes, the above rules can be applied to systems other than biological systems. They can apply to social ideas (dubbed "memes" by Richard Dawkins) or to computer designs or software in the marketplace; but that comes later. Let's start with a short biological example to illustrate the meanings of the above rules.

Let's examine these characteristics with a plant, a wildflower, growing in an alpine meadow.

The plant is a defined species and so meets characteristic number 1. During its life cycle, it grows, flowers, and produces seeds which under the appropriate circumstances will germinate to produce more wildflowers nearly identical to the parent—and so we meet characteristic number 2. In general, there is very little variation from one generation to the next; this is important as otherwise the species would be unstable—it's not really a species if every generation is different. The structure of the plant is controlled by the DNA molecules in its cells and this DNA is replicated and passed from generation to generation with extreme precision. Occasionally, however, random changes are introduced into the DNA and these will be passed to all subsequent generations and so meet characteristic number 3. Let's assume a change

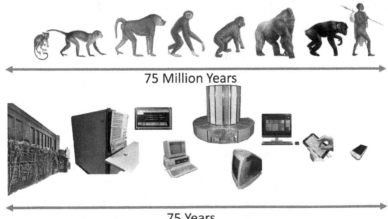

75 Million Years

75 Years

Consider that the evolution of computers has been a million times faster than the evolution of primates. [Images by Bin im Garten, Calerusnak, license: CC BY-SA-3.0 and Roma, license: CC BY-SA 2.0.]

in the DNA makes the plant grow taller. Once such a change occurs, it will be passed to subsequent generations of offspring of that plant.

At this point, the environment steps in and determines whether growing taller makes this new strain of plant more or less likely to reproduce. In a tropical rain forest, being taller is probably an advantage because light is at a premium. Being taller makes a plant more likely to get needed light and less likely to be shaded and crowded out by its neighbors. But in our alpine meadow, on the other hand, being taller makes the plant dissipate heat more rapidly and could make it more likely to be eaten by a grazing animal. Either way, the environment is the controlling aspect as to whether a new attribute becomes incorporated into a species or is excluded. The environment, characteristic 4, is the necessary feature which controls the direction of the evolution.

Over a large number of generations, a mutation which gives an organism a slight survival and reproductive advantage over its counterparts within the species will gain dominance and will spread throughout the population of the species as it crowds out the lesser strains. If the change is great enough to prevent cross-reproduction with other members of the original species, we would define that a new species has been created. Otherwise, we would simply say that the original species has evolved new characteristics.

Much of a species' DNA controls the parts of an organism involved in metabolism and basic cell structure, and only a fraction of the DNA is involved in visible characteristics. Thus, random changes introduced into the DNA usually prevent viable offspring from growing. If, for example, a mammal has a genetic mutation in any of the DNA which controls the structure of its hemoglobin (or any other essential protein), the most likely result is that the organism will not survive at all. Only very rarely does a mutation occur which produces a viable and different characteristic in the organism. And even more rarely is the mutation advantageous. Because mutations are (1) rare, (2) usually disadvantageous, and (3) take many generations to spread through a population, biological evolution is a very slow process.

We can speed up the evolutionary process by introducing mutagens into the environment. This increases the rate of mutation, producing more changes, both negative and occasionally positive. In the genetic lab, this may be useful because mutation rates in nature are low enough that most species appear to be static.

Evolution is a balanced process which tends to keep species relatively stable. On one hand, the mechanisms of replicating DNA are very accurate, and of the mutations which are introduced, only a very few produce viable offspring. On the other hand, the environment which decides which characteristics will be included and which will not is also relatively stable over long periods of time. Species have already evolved to take up a niche within the environment and small changes are unlikely to be improvements. So there is a balance of changes being introduced to a species and changes being filtered by the environment, and both conspire to maintain the status quo. When we leave the biological arena, these forces are not necessarily present and we can see technological evolution proceeding at a much faster rate.

Darwin imposed an additional requirement when he defined "natural selection"—that the environment be natural. This is certainly true in the case of evolution prior to humankind's control of our environment but is an unnecessary limitation to the general concept of the evolutionary process. Without this arbitrary limitation, evolutionary theory can be applied to systems such as the hybridization of crop plants as well as systems which are not even biological, but social or physical. In performing genetic engineering, changes are deliberately introduced into species and the environment is deliberately controlled to enhance the reproduction of organisms with the desired characteristics.

Pros and cons of development by evolution

Before heading off in the non-biological directions, let's examine some of the conclusions which could be reached by examining the ramifications of biological evolution.

The environment deals harshly with the vast majority of attempted changes. Biological changes need to be small and be applied to the organism gradually for two reasons. First, since even small changes in the genetic material are likely to yield an organism structure which cannot survive, the larger the change is, the greater the likelihood that the modification would yield a nonfunctional organism. Second, the new organism must be compatible with the existing reproductive apparatus of the parents. Regardless of the unlikelihood of simultaneous genetic occurrences, which could modify a mouse cell into a horse cell, for mechanical reasons alone the mouse could not possibly give birth to a horse. The conclusion is that biological evolution must occur in very small steps.

Because of the requirement for relatively small changes, organisms can get stuck at what mathematicians would call a "local minimum."

As an example: we have bones made of calcium compounds. If we had bones made of steel, we would be substantially less prone to injury, we could be lighter (for the same strength) and more agile. This might be a more optimal solution to the general problem of building a skeleton. But even if there was a chemical process which could build metallic iron, the evolutionary process precludes it because between the body with a calcium skeleton and one with a steel skeleton, there are changes which

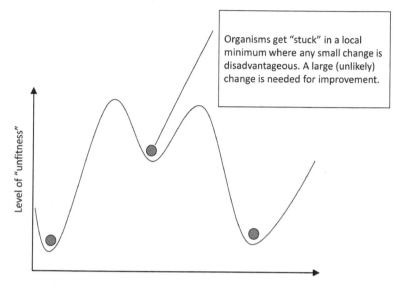

Organisms get "stuck" in a local minimum where any small change is disadvantageous. A large (unlikely) change is needed for improvement.

Different Organism Characteristics

Illustrating the concept of a "local minimum" showing an arbitrary scale of "fitness" with a lower level meaning an organism has a better fit into its ecological niche. Organisms get stuck in a local minimum and are not really optimal.

are less effective than the calcium skeleton alone. Therefore, the sequence of steps which would give us a steel skeleton is so unlikely that it cannot get started.

Here's another example: humans today are afflicted by heart disease. But since heart disease most commonly strikes after a person has aged beyond having children, there has been no driving force to evolve toward its elimination. A gene that would prevent arteriosclerosis might not naturally spread through the population. People who possessed the gene would not necessarily be more likely to have more children who live to have children. So there may be no selection either for or against the gene.

In his book, *The Red Queen: Sex and the Evolution of Human Nature,* Matt Ridley points out that a reproductive advantage is most important in comparison with other organisms of the same species. The giraffe has evolved to be tall as a result of taller giraffes having a reproductive advantage over shorter giraffes, not because the giraffe had an advantage over gazelles. Likewise, the gazelle has evolved to be fast because a fast gazelle has an advantage over a slower gazelle, not because it needs to be faster than a lion. To further complicate the process, the evolutionary advantage may be due to a quirk which we cannot observe. A peacock may have developed its wonderful tail display simply because the brain of the peahen "prefers" it—conveying a reproductive advantage. Because of the peahen's preference, peacocks evolve progressively more spectacular tails over many generations. Eventually the tail size impedes the peacock's ability to survive and the size increase stops.

Similarly, we could propose that a human's big brain evolved because it gave us the improved ability to hunt in teams, to build shelters, and to use tools. Alternatively, it may be that the behaviors allowed by big brains were attractive to women and so conferred a reproductive advantage in that way. Perhaps it was that big-brained cavemen could charm cavewomen.

In either case, human brains would continue to evolve to be progressively bigger until we have reached some other limitation. Perhaps a bigger head size would impact the mother's survival at childbirth. Perhaps a larger brain would take longer to mature enough for us to be self-sufficient organisms. Regardless of the reasons, it is apparent that greater thinking abilities would not necessarily confer an evolutionary advantage as human brain size has been consistent for tens of thousands of years. Although many people presume that "smarter is better", this could be true for AGIs but not necessarily so for humans.

Relative to the changes in the organism, some environmental changes occur very rapidly. Temperature, for example, changes from day to night and with the seasons. Temperature change is a part of our environment, even at the much slower advances and declines of ice ages. Most land animals cannot be adapted for any specific temperature. They must be able to survive a relatively broad range of earthly temperatures in order to survive as a species. Many tropical fish, on the other hand, which have evolved in water with a fairly constant temperature, are often very sensitive to changes in water temperature, a fact to which almost anyone who has owned an aquarium can attest.

The existence of atmospheric oxygen, on the other hand, has been reasonably stable for millions of years. There would be no particular evolutionary advantage for an animal to be able to tolerate broad swings in oxygen concentration in the air. In fact, when atmospheric oxygen levels were much higher in the Jurassic period, we see evidence of many animals which grew considerably larger than equivalent animals living today.

Here is a summary of the preceding conclusions about biological evolution:

- Evolution is steered by the environment
- Evolution occurs in small steps
- Evolution only favors reproductive survival

- Evolution is slow
- The result of evolution is not necessarily optimal
- Evolution may lead to extremes of an individual characteristic
- Every organism alive today is the offspring of an evolutionary winner

The evolution of intelligence

What do these conclusions tell us about the evolution of human intelligence? There are two key observations which are applicable to the future discussions of machine intelligence.

First, human intelligence evolved because it offered a reproductive advantage. The reason we can think today is that the ability to think helped us to survive and have children. In the discussions of the actual mechanisms of intelligence (in the following chapters), the thinking mechanisms which allow us to do mathematics are shown to be the same as those which allow us to build a shelter to survive inclement weather. For example, with planning and forethought, we could plan to snare animals and be able to comprehend and plan for the cycle of the seasons. Today, we can use that same planning ability to design computer systems.

The point being that the human brain is a survival mechanism which we are able to press into service for other thought processes, not the other way around. The brain was not "designed" to play chess or do mathematics, it was designed as a reproductive/survival tool. In the field of artificial intelligence, we computists have previously "gone for the gold" and attempted to produce a system which possessed the humans' highest-level thinking skills. We assumed that if a computer played chess, lower-level thinking would be easy. We now know that high-level intelligence is a side effect of the more basic abilities which were useful to us back in the caves.

Second, human intelligence is not necessarily optimal. This is related to the first observation; the distinction being that as machines become smarter, they might conceivably be equivalent to humans in capacity. Subsequently, they could have twice the capacity, or twice the speed. Then more. Then even more. We humans evolved enough intelligence to give ourselves a significant survival advantage and not necessarily any more than that. In the remainder of this section, I will describe artificial thinking processes which will approximate human thinking. There is no reason to think that these processes are the ultimate thinking processes possible. Perhaps after equating human intelligence in machines, entirely new and even better thinking mechanisms will emerge.

DNA

The human genome is coded into our DNA, the molecular "map" which dictates to each cell how to assemble itself and how to function in conjunction with other cells. DNA is a long chain molecule with a ladder of "bases" in pairs which can define which amino acid is to be added next as a protein is "manufactured" within a cell.

The Human Genome Project has decoded the order of all the base pairs in our DNA, so we have a great deal of knowledge of which parts of the DNA encode for which proteins. We are still learning about how our DNA causes cells to specialize to become skin cells or neurons, for example, and how different types of cells organize and assemble themselves into the human body. So we have little information on how much of our DNA is involved in the definition of the human brain and the neuron cells which inhabit it.

The human genome consists of about 3 billion base pairs. A single base pair can take one of four states and so represents the equivalent of 2 bits of computer information. So the complete genome consists of a total of 750MB (megabytes, millions of bytes) of information. In 1990, when the Human Genome Project started, this seemed like a large amount of data. Now it seems trivial—my cell phone can store 64GB (gigabytes, billions of bytes) of data, nearly 100 times as much. We might speculate that only 10% of the genome is needed to define your brain

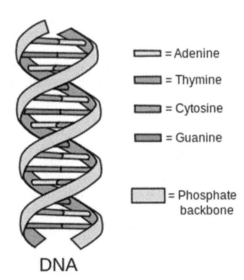

DNA

A diagram of DNA's double helix showing how information is stored in the pairs of bases which form the rungs of the ladder. [Public domain.]

and nervous system, further reducing the amount of data involved in allowing us to think.

While these are all huge numbers, compare them to the estimated 50 million lines of code that defines the Windows operating system. In 2014, Google's code repository consisted of 86TB (terabytes, trillions of bytes) of data, including approximately two billion lines of code.[9] As with the human genome, we can speculate that a significant amount of this data is obsolete, referring back to the evolutionary predecessors of current software products. But a measure of how the software industry compares in magnitude with millions of years of evolution, at Google, about 15 million lines of code were being changed each *week*. Lines of code cannot be compared directly to DNA base pairs but we can reasonably speculate that we could write the equivalent of the entire human genome in a matter of weeks—*if we only knew what to write!* I will shed some light on this topic over the next few chapters.

Evolution in civilization—memes

Let's take the first step toward applying evolution to features outside the biological by examining our culture and shared behaviors—as originally described in Richard Dawkins' 1976 book, *The Selfish Gene*. As an example, let's consider language. Clearly, there is no genetic link for a specific language in humans—no matter what your genetic makeup, as a child you could have learned any language on earth. Although the underlying mental abilities necessary to understand and use language are controlled by genetics, the languages themselves are clearly extra-genetic.

But the languages themselves are also evolving. Language is passed from one human generation to the next and we all make an effort to teach our children to speak correctly—"correctly" being defined as speaking the way *we* do. But changes are introduced which are subsequently passed to future generations.

We can think of a language as being like an organism (characteristic 1) which reproduces itself (characteristic 2). But our children never speak exactly the way we do so there are changes introduced into the language as it is passed from generation to generation. Further, our children are likely to pass these linguistic changes on to *their* children (characteristic 3). Finally, some of these new linguistic changes will prove to be successful and some will not. We choose to use words and phrases and accents, or not. Those language characteristics we choose to use will survive while others will become extinct (characteristic 4).

Languages evolve just as biological species evolve. Although within our lifetimes, we don't see significant changes in our language—only a few words here and there—we know that over a longer period of time, languages have changed substantially. We know that hundreds of years ago, American English simply did not exist, and Old English was substantially different from any language spoken today. Two thousand years ago, nothing resembling English was being spoken. Our language has evolved since then, almost in its entirety. An important characteristic of language evolution (which also applies to other non-biological evolution) is that it is very fast in comparison to biology. While species change in thousands and millions of years, languages can change over hundreds.

But language is just a single example. Very little human behavior is purely instinctive, most of it is learned. Our concepts of food, clothing, housing, group activities, entertainment; all these are learned behaviors which have evolved in a manner similar to language. We can see different cultures which have evolved different customs and trace the lineage of our customs. We might consider a different culture to have different "species" of language, clothing, food, music, etc.

Evolution in computer hardware

How would we apply evolutionary concepts to computers? Computers do not really reproduce themselves on their own but require human assistance. But each succeeding generation of computers is built on the successes and failures of the previous generation. Each new processor design incorporates much of the design of the previous generation and adds features which will make the system better in one way or another. Different companies can produce different processors which compete in the marketplace, and the marketplace is the environment which decides which computer is the dominant "species". Virtually all computers today share a common architecture (described in 1945 by John von Neumann) with programs stored in memory, fetched and executed by a CPU (Central Processing Unit, the computational chip in a computer).

As an example, let's briefly trace the history of CPUs. In 1977, Apple computers were introduced with a Motorola 6502 8-bit CPU. MITS Inc. offered computers with a similarly powerful Intel 8080 8-bit CPU (its computer, the "Altair", also started Bill Gates in the software business). In 1981, the IBM-PC was introduced with the Intel 8086 16-bit CPU and Microsoft's DOS operating system software. Apple answered in 1984 with computers based on Motorola's 68000 16/32-bit CPU. Intel developed faster and more powerful CPUs, going to a 32-bit design in 1985 with the 80386 and 64 bits in 2004.

Because of limited software compatibility, Apple shifted to IBM's PowerPC CPU in the 1990s. The PowerPC could execute both Motorola-style and Intel-style software and Motorola CPUs are now extinct in the computer niche. In 2004, Apple shifted to Intel processors and the

PowerPC species became extinct in the computer niche but can still be found today as a controller in cars and other embedded systems (a different environmental niche). Over the intervening years, other CPU designs have become extinct. The Intel species and the related AMD subspecies now prevail in the desktop/server environment where the need for speed is the predominant attribute.

While all this predation and evolution is going on in the desktop/server environment, CPUs have also been evolving in other areas. Significantly different genera of processors exist for graphics cards and mobile devices.

Gaming, video and other applications have created an environment for a specialized Graphics Processing Unit (GPU—coined in 1999). While not as general-purpose, these processors are blindingly fast at repeated parallel computations for generating images (usually 3D) from underlying data models. The GPU is thus the workhorse of any gaming computer's graphics card. It creates screen images with vastly parallel but relatively simple computations, more akin to the processes we find in the human brain. As such, in a future where intelligence predominates in computers, the descendants of GPUs might become the predominant species.

In the mobile device environment, the need to reduce energy consumption to extend battery life is a controlling evolutionary force as compared with the desktop CPU of the 1980s, when the amount of power used by a CPU was not much of a factor. More recently, design concepts (genes) from these mobile species are being spliced into desktop/server CPUs since server farms now consume huge amounts of energy. In 2016, US data centers consumed about 72 million megawatt hours of electricity[10]—the equivalent energy of about 500 round-trips to the moon every year[11].

Sex and the single CPU

When a CPU (or virtually any chip) is manufactured, transistors and interconnections are etched or deposited onto the surface of a silicon wafer. The positions of all the features are transferred photographically from a computer file which controls the scanners that "print" the images of the components. This design file is equivalent to DNA since it fully defines the anatomy of the chip. Unlike a living organism, each chip need not carry a copy of its own DNA because all chips of a species are made from a single common copy of the design. In a living organism, each cell is responsible for manufacturing itself and its offspring. The chip, on the other hand, is not expected to grow and reproduce on its own, only in concert with an IC manufacturing facility.

Design engineers at a semiconductor company are equivalent to genetic engineers. After all is said and done, their ideas end up in the design file, the DNA of the chip. When a new CPU is designed, it is not designed from scratch, it is developed from the successful portions of previous chips. Design ideas can be "gene-spliced" from other CPU organisms. As manufacturing technologies evolve, the entire appearance of a chip may change but the underlying concepts of creating individual transistors and interconnections evolve over periods of many generations.

A CPU by itself has very few "instinctive" behaviors. Without the addition of software, a computer won't do very much. Accordingly, software could be equated to Dawkins' memes. Evolving on their own tracks, software "memes" also compete with each other in the environment of the marketplace.

Evolved immortality

There is a persistent fictional idea of an immortal humanoid robot. But this idea is based on the dubious assumption that at some point technology will reach some sort of plateau. In considering immortality, consider the lifespan of your cell phone or laptop. Even if they aren't physically damaged, they are rendered obsolete in just a few years. In preparing this book, I attempted to operate *The Brain Simulator* software which I wrote in 1988. It was written in the language FORTRAN, which is now essentially extinct. It used the MS-DOS operating system which is still lurking in the DNA of the Windows operating system (like the DNA which defines your appendix). In order to be useful, the program would need to be entirely rewritten—and that's after only 30 years have elapsed. I contend that any technological plateau which might lead to long-lived intelligence will only be reached in a future of such advanced thinking machines that they are beyond the scope of anyone's imagination. Contrary to the fictional story, the life expectancy of any technology is much less than that of a person.

Each organism's lineage in a species evolves as quickly as possible in competition with others of its own species. Likewise, future computers will be in constant competition to be the best and the brightest computer. In contrast to humans, which have held the top spot on the evolutionary ladder for tens of thousands of years, no computer species will hold the top title for more than just a few years at best!

Evolution in software

Just as the wildflower in the alpine meadow need not grow tall while a similar plant in the rain forest must, there are differing objectives and environmental requirements for computers evolving in different market areas. In the supercomputer arena, there is an unlimited need for additional processing power and ease of use is not a paramount concern since such machines are only used by professionals. In the home and office environment, there is a paramount need for greater ease of use. In the same way that Intel CPUs drove many others to extinction, primarily because the available software made them more user-friendly, the "user-friendly" aspect of future machines will likely be the predominant driving environmental force. In Section III, I will be more detailed in the explanation of the facets of the environment which will control future computer development and the types of enhancements we should expect to see in the coming decades.

In conclusion, human intelligence and thinking are the results of evolutionary processes and have evolved because they are important survival tools which conveyed a reproductive advantage. We can coerce our brains to read and do mathematics because these higher level functions use the same mental functions which allowed us to hunt, plan for cold weather, entertain our mates, and the myriad other social behaviors which contributed to our survival as a species. Human thinking is also colored and controlled by our social heritage and our sensory limitations.

Finally, computer "species" are subject to the same evolutionary processes as biological species, only the evolution is and will be much faster. If we examine the constraints of the environment in which the computers exist, we will be able to make predictions about the directions in which the computers will evolve.

Having looked at the evolutionary processes which have led us to today's brains and computers, we're ready to take a look at how they work. The next chapter looks at brains and their component synapses vs. computers and their components: transistors.

---

[9] https://cacm.acm.org/magazines/2016/7/204032-why-google-stores-billions-of-lines-of-code-in-a-single-repository/fulltext#FNB

[10] http://www.datacenterknowledge.com/archives/2016/06/27/heres-how-much-energy-all-us-data-centers-consume

[11] 1 gallon of kerosene is equivalent to 39.5 kWh. Saturn V carried about 500,000 gallons of fuel.
https://www.huffingtonpost.com/entry/how-much-fuel-does-it-take-to-get-to-the-moon_us_598a35b5e4b030f0e267c83d

Chapter 7:

Synapses, Brains, Transistors, and CPUs

If we are to consider the possibility of a future "thinking machine", it seems like a good idea to know what *thinking* is. And it would be best to start by examining the most successful thinking mechanism we have today: the human brain. Let's delve into the physiology of brains, neurons and synapses to describe how they work as analogous to the hardware of the human CPU.

In particular, let us compare the neuron with a computer switching circuit and explore some of the advantages each has over the other in acting as the building block for a thinking mechanism. In this chapter, I'll show the structure and operation of the brain vs. a CPU. In the next five chapters, I'll present the types of functionality that we know exist within our brains.

Brains

Our brain controls our body. It receives information from our eyes, ears, hands, etc., via impulses in our nerves, and it sends signals out through motor nerves which control our muscles. There is also a soup of messenger chemicals (hormones), which we'll ignore for the time being.

We don't yet know precisely how brains work (I'll discuss why in a moment) so we'll have to gloss over some of the finer points. In contrast, we know exactly how CPUs work so the comparison may be lopsided.

In the main, brains are constructed from cells called "neurons" (similar cells outside the brain are "nerve" cells) and there are about 86 billion neurons in the human brain [12]. You can't simply open a brain and count the neurons. Instead, the brain must be broken down into its component chemicals in order to measure the constituents found only in neurons. The neurons themselves are too fragile to be counted directly, and have relatively long connections which are much too fine to trace out.

Since we believe we are the smartest animals on the planet, we might think human brains have the most neurons. Not so. The African elephant has a much larger brain with 257 billion neurons, three times as many. So neuron count and brain size don't necessarily correlate with intelligence (or elephants have many hidden talents). Similarly, in humans, brain size correlates with body size. But studies show that there is only a slight correlation between body size and intelligence. This is in contrast to the CPU, where the transistor count correlates strongly with performance.

Let's look at the structure of the human brain. The brain consists of three primary structures:

1. The brainstem—for autonomic functions such as breathing, swallowing and heartrate (about 14 billion neurons).
2. The cerebellum—for muscle coordination (about 56 billion neurons).
3. The neocortex—for higher-level thinking (about 16 billion neurons).

There is considerable variation in these numbers in the literature but as noted earlier, the variation is insignificant when considering synthesizing intelligence.

Each brain structure has certain capabilities which have been determined, largely by experimentation with animals or examining the mental limitations of people who have suffered brain injuries. More recently, we have used fMRI (Functional Magnetic Resonance Imaging) systems on conscious patients to measure activity in various areas of the brain. This has been extremely useful in determining, for example, that certain areas of the brain are more active in understanding speech. But the images are based on changes in blood flow, so the resolution is not good enough to tell us that specific neurons have specific functions and/or are connected to specific other neurons.

Brainstem

The brainstem is positioned at the bottom of the brain and can be considered an extension of the spinal cord and low-level bodily functions. Virtually all nerve signals to and from the body pass through the brainstem and it is evolutionarily the oldest part of our brain. The brainstem can be responsible for reactive behaviors and lower animals (invertebrates and fish) with brains could be considered to be entirely brainstem.

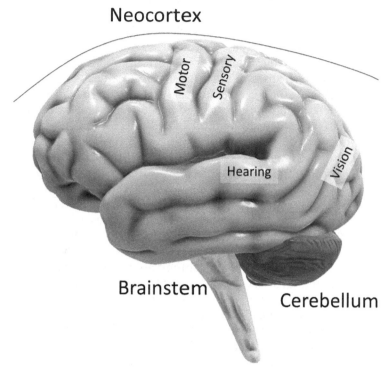

Diagram of the human brain showing: The location of the brainstem, cerebellum, and neocortex in the brain, showing areas of the neocortex for visual, auditory, sensory and motor control. [License: Microsoft unrestricted.]

It is likely that the brainstem and its internal connections are largely defined by your DNA, so you are born with the ability to breathe and have a heartbeat. Many other functions are known to exist here but are not generally considered to be part of thinking. Interestingly, although most hearing is processed in the neocortex, your ability to know what direction a sound is coming from is located in the brainstem.

The cerebellum

The cerebellum controls muscular coordination. Muscles contract in proportion to the amount of neural stimulation they receive from the motor nerves connected to them. The cerebellum represents the lion's share of the neurons (the computational power) of the human brain, and you might ask why. If you want to straighten your elbow, you need to relax your biceps and simultaneously contract your triceps. But this modest amount of coordination would not obviously require so much brain volume.

The answer requires just a little background on mechanical control systems (thinking of your body, temporarily, as a robotic mechanism being manipulated by your brain). Early efforts at robotics taught us that controlling any mechanism to move smoothly to a desired position is much more difficult than it might initially seem. In a modern robotic system, position and motion controls include feedback mechanisms with sensors. These continuously monitor positions so the controller can make continuous adjustments to the amount of power applied to the actuators. Without feedback, it is very difficult to build a mechanism which will precisely move to a specific position given varying loads (especially with heavier objects). The system can also continuously calculate the current speed of motion so that the arm, for example, can be slowed down and stopped smoothly as it approaches a desired target position. Without this prediction, the arm could approach a target too fast and would overshoot the target when trying to stop. Then it would reverse back toward its target and potentially overshoot again. It will oscillate back and forth around the target and (hopefully) eventually settle at the desired position. Humans have a feedback system called "proprioception", which is your sense of the relative positions of your own body parts and the strength of effort being employed in movement.

This control problem is compounded when the feedback calculation system itself is slow—and relative to the speed with which your body operates, neurons are slow computing devices.

Consider the first time you try a new motor activity—learning to play a musical instrument or throwing a baseball, for example. Initially, you have to think about the actions you are going to take and the process is slow and seldom smooth. But after many repetitions, the neuron chains in your cerebellum learn the required firing sequences and can begin to perform them faster and more smoothly. Learning takes place over hundreds or thousands of repetitions, so learning to play a musical instrument takes thousands of hours of practice over several years. But eventually, you not only can do something better and faster, you can do things without even thinking about them—they become automatic.

From having participated in building a computer out of discarded telephone relays, I have had personal experience with systems built out of components which were basically too slow to do the job. After applying power to a telephone relay, it was a full 12 milliseconds before it acted—a speed of similar magnitude to that of a neuron. We needed pulses to be only 9 milliseconds long. I speculate that the cerebellum performs in the following way.

Rather than individual neurons working to determine the level of stimulation to apply to specific muscles, a chain of neurons gives a preprogrammed series of pulses to the muscles. Huge numbers of pre-wired chains are programmed with the pulses to send to specific muscles under specific circumstances. So rather than continuously updating and correcting for every nerve-to-muscle impulse, the updates are only necessary a few times per second and a correction may consist of stopping the firing of one chain of neurons and starting another. I speculate that the cerebellum has so many neurons because it is able to learn millions of firing sequences and play them back as needed.

In a robotic system, we can achieve similar results with an electronic control system which is far simpler than the cerebellum because it has two important advantages. First, the computational speed of the microprocessor is extremely fast relative to the speed of the mechanical system. Accordingly, electronic systems can do many computations serially which the brain must do in parallel. Second, we have an understanding of mechanics and mathematics which your brain can only approximate by trial and error. By using some algebra, a microprocessor has plenty of time to calculate masses, accelerations, velocities and forces in order to correct the signals being sent to actuators.

The result of these two advantages is that today we have robotic control systems which are on the verge of being as capable as the cerebellum. We can build machines with human-like walking gaits, grasping hands and fingers, and the ability to play musical instruments. The key distinction is that the robotic system typically doesn't learn and improve its performance over time. We are not willing to wait a year for the robot to learn to walk, for example, so we have to use different techniques to control them. The flipside is that the robot doesn't learn to walk more smoothly over time.

Here's the point. To the extent that we can control robots to have smooth, coordinated motion and the ability to learn new actions, we are already doing the job of the cerebellum's 56 billion neurons. With the cerebellum, we are able to take computational shortcuts which make the electronic mechanism many times more efficient than the biological one. Will we be as effective with the thinking parts of the brain?

The neocortex

The neocortex (aka cerebrum, cerebral cortex) is responsible for sight, hearing, speech, and the processes which are generally referred to as thought.

Topologically, the neocortex can be thought of as a more-or-less flat sheet of neurons (gray matter) which has been scrunched in order to fit into the human skull. If it were unfolded, the neocortex would be a disk a little over a foot in diameter, with all the neurons' cell bodies clustered into about seven cell layers on one surface. This forms the outer surface of the brain. The remainder, which forms the interior, consists largely of the massive interconnections (white matter). Accordingly, while neurons may have many connections to their closest neighbors, they may also connect to neurons a considerable (relatively) distance away.

While there have been studies of both neurons and brains, we understand each on different levels. We know what brains look like (which was learned from dissections and imaging) and what the major areas of the brain do (which was initially learned from discovering how various brain injuries caused changes in a person's abilities). More recently, sophisticated imaging techniques can pinpoint brain activity which is associated with specific stimuli or thought patterns. In between, we don't have very much specific knowledge of how neurons are wired together to create a functional brain. We know of the "mass of axons" which make up most of the brain but we don't know specifically where the axons lead because they are too fragile to dissect.

So here are some of the things we *do* know about the neocortex. Running from front to back in the center of the brain is a cleft which separates the right and left hemispheres. In general, the left hemisphere senses and controls the right half of the body and vice versa, and the two sides are connected by a mass of connections. Running from side to side (roughly from ear to ear) across the upper surface of the brain are two strips, about a centimeter wide, which are the sensory and motor cortexes. The sensory cortex receives information on touch, heat, pain, etc. from the various parts of the body while the motor cortex controls the movements of the body in conjunction with the cerebellum.

At the rear of the brain is the visual cortex which receives information from the eyes. The image sensed by the eyes is more or less mapped to neurons here. Hearing is managed by areas on each side of the brain somewhat below and behind the sensory cortex.

Internal functionality

The neurons in the neocortex are assembled in a fairly uniform manner. Although we can know which areas are responsible for sight and hearing, for example, microscopic examination of various areas of the neocortex shows that it appears largely uniform throughout. We also know that the number of neurons and interconnections vastly exceeds the amount of DNA dedicated to defining our brains. Therefore the brain's construction must consist of generally repeating patterns in a manner similar to the computer's memory chip. A memory chip has an array of billions of identical memory cells, so the capacity of the chip may vastly exceed the size of the design file which defines it. This is significantly different from a CPU—microscopic examinations reveal different circuitry for math, control, and memory functions.

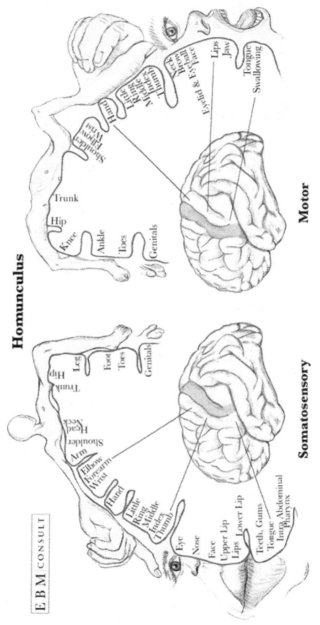

This famous diagram shows the relative locations of the neurons in the neocortex which receive signals from, and send signals to, various parts of the body. [Public domain.]

While human brains have specific functions in generally the same areas, this may be a quirk of evolution rather than a specific characteristic of the brain itself. For example, the visual cortex may be at the back of the brain because that is where the optic nerve leads. The brain function develops there in early childhood because of the type of input signals it is receiving. If the neocortex is truly uniform, then the optic nerve could lead to virtually any location and that portion would develop to perform the function of the visual cortex.

This bears specifically on the way a brain could be emulated. Currently, the software which has been created to perform computer vision is different from that which performs speech recognition. If there is an underlying functional uniformity to the neocortex, the amount of unique functionality needed to perform all the brain's functions electronically would be drastically reduced—systems which emulated "general brain function" could be created and pressed into service for speech recognition, vision, or any other desired functionality.

Let's consider some of the numbers. The neocortex contains about 16 billion (1.6×10^{10}) neurons. If we assume each neuron has 10,000 (10^4) connections, then the neocortex contains on the order of 160 trillion (1.6×10^{14}) connections.

While these are unfathomably large numbers, the computer industry can fabricate transistors on a comparable scale. As mentioned previously, Intel could theoretically produce 7.3 trillion transistors on a wafer. It would take only 22 such wafers to create as many transistors as connections in the neocortex—22 is a number entirely within the realm of possibility. Even though there are numerous shortcomings with this comparison, I will show later that it takes substantially fewer transistors because they are so much faster.

Computers

Computers are not very much like brains. Here are some of the ways we can look at brains vs. CPUs to highlight the differences (and a few similarities).

Brains are intrinsically parallel devices while CPUs are intrinsically sequential. Brains receive input in parallel from all sensory "devices" and have portions dedicated to handling this input, also in parallel. All your senses can run at once and your brain can handle the input from all of them simultaneously. In contrast, a CPU executes a single instruction at a time but it is fast enough that it can easily handle input from multiple devices if input is coming in at normal audio or video speeds. For performance reasons, a modern CPU can do several things concurrently but this is not the same as having a CPU dedicated to each input stream— which would be more like a brain.

The neocortex has about 16 billion neurons. Today's (2018) CPUs generally have fewer than 5 billion transistors.

Computers follow programs which explicitly determine what the CPU will do. Inherently, the CPU executes the same instructions in the same way every time and never learns to do anything better. Brain functionality is more amorphous and susceptible to improvement. But, in combination with software, a computer can be programmed to learn to improve its performance in a similar way.

Based on the work of Alan Turing and Alonzo Church (the Church-Turing Thesis), computer scientists have concluded that given enough computer horsepower, a sequential computer can emulate any physical system. Therefore, the distinction of parallel brain vs. sequential computer is only one of how much computer performance is needed to emulate the parallel system. Any argument along the lines of "Computers will never _____ (have feelings, fall in love, write a symphony, etc.)" falls into one of two categories:

1. Machines will *never* have enough computational power to implement these behaviors—which I argue against.
2. Humans are not physical systems; these feelings are the result of non-physical human attributes.

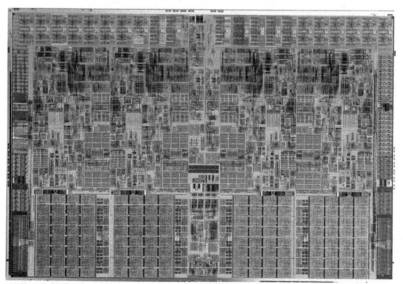

Today's CPU can contain billions of transistors in a small package. Under a microscope, this Intel Core CPU shows specific areas dedicated to specific types of processing. [Image by Intel, from Core i7 press kit.]

Memory

A small fraction of the brain's incoming input is useful. In fact, one of the things brains do really well is to recognize quickly what input might be important. Computers aren't programmed to be very good at this.

Some of the brain's incoming input can be recalled for a short time and a tiny fraction is stored in longer-term memory. Analogous to a computer's cache, RAM, and disk, the brain has tiers of memory as well. In a computer, information is stored in devices specifically designed for the purpose.

Estimates of the brain's storage capacity vary broadly, ranging from as low as 10TB (terabytes, trillion bytes) to 1PB (petabytes, quadrillion bytes). A decade ago these seemed like fantastically large numbers which meant we could not approach the brain's capacity. Now, I can put a 12TB disk drive in my computer for only $500 and easily imagine a rack containing 80 such drives—exceeding even the greatest estimate of the brain's memory capacity.

By contrast, we think it's remarkable that some people have memorized the entire Bible word-for-word... and it's an amazing achievement! But the King James Bible contains 3,116,480 characters, representing .000000283 of the brain's 10TB smallest memory capacity estimate. The Bible's storage requirement is further reduced because our brains wouldn't memorize each character (or image of a page), we would memorize words and there are only 783,137 words in the Bible. With each memory location representing a word, I could store the Bible text over a million times on my 12TB drive. Interestingly, word storage vs. character storage is a type of data compression used in the common .zip compressed file format.

So, either the brain's memory capacity isn't nearly as large as most people think OR our memories are filled with a tremendous amount of information of which we're unaware. Otherwise, memorizing the Bible would be no big deal and an everyday occurrence.

Power

Human brains consume about 20W (watts) of energy[13] while CPUs have a broad range of power consumptions. CPUs range from a fraction of a watt for a cell phone to over 200W for some supercomputer processors, with most desktop computers falling into the 10-20W range. This makes today's CPU roughly comparable to your brain in energy consumption.

The neocortex's processing area is about 72,000mm². Modern CPUs are much smaller, many with an area of about 500mm². So a very rough estimate would be that the modern CPU has an area 150 times smaller than the neocortex.

Both brains and CPUs must deal with the significant issue of heat dissipation. The brain's temperature is largely regulated via blood flow[14] and while many high-end CPUs are similarly liquid-cooled, most are air-cooled. The CPU must dissipate a similar level of energy in a much smaller area and if the cooling system fails, the CPU will rapidly overheat and fail. To help prevent this, modern CPUs have an internal temperature sensor and will slow down to dissipate less heat as the temperature rises. Similarly, your brain stops working normally when overheated; one of the symptoms of heat stroke.

Reliability

Redundancy vs. reliability: the brain is highly redundant and the loss of many neurons has no perceivable impact on its operation. Similarly, disk drives (and RAM) are accessed in such a way that a list of "bad" sectors is maintained and the disk continues to operate properly even though some of its areas may be bad. CPUs, on the other hand, generally rely on the correct operation of every transistor. While a multi-core CPU could conceivably continue to operate remaining cores if one core failed, I am not aware of system software which supports this feature. On a larger scale, however, server farms are generally configured so the system as a whole can easily tolerate the failure of many individual components.

In timescales we can perceive, the design of the brain is static. While there is some variation from brain to brain, there is no discernable trend that brains are changing. On the other hand, CPU change is obvious over a period of just a few years. Transistor counts are skyrocketing, transistor sizes are shrinking, energy requirements are decreasing, and CPU speeds are continually increasing.

Neurons and synapses

Neurons are the cells which are believed by most to comprise the thinking functionality of the brain. While the brain is also loaded with blood vessels and glial cells which provide support, nutrients, and insulation for neurons, these could be considered to be analogous to the power supplies, wires, and the mechanical support structure of a computer.

So what are neurons like? Neurons are living cells and have metabolic processes including the ability to convert sugar into energy. Unlike most other human cells, neurons cannot reproduce themselves but are all descendant from a smaller number of neuronal stem cells during embryonic and early childhood development (mostly) and the brain's neurons are largely fixed prior to adulthood.

Neurons come in many shapes and sizes so the following is fairly general. Physically, the neuron has a cell body or *soma* which contains the cell's nucleus and its metabolic equipment. The soma has numerous

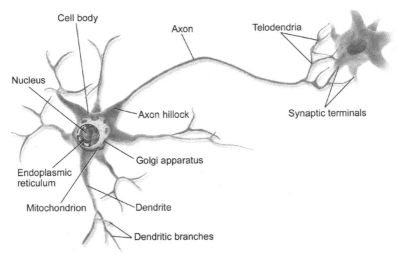

A diagram of a neuron showing its major components, the soma, axon, and dendrites. [Image by BruceBlaus - own work, license: CC BY 3.0.]

small appendages called *dendrites* where the cell can receive "input". Extending from the cell body is the *axon* which carries the "output" of the cell over a considerable distance (perhaps several millimeters) to connections with other neurons. The axon may be much longer in the case of nerve cells which connect the brain to various parts of the body. At the other end of the axon, the cell branches into thousands of tiny fibers which connect via *synaptic junctions* or *synapses* to other neurons. These synaptic junctions are the switching units which connect this neuron to the dendrites or cell bodies of other neurons.

Translated into electronic terms, the "output" axon of one neuron is connected to the "input" dendrite of another through a synapse. Though a synapse is the connecting bridge between two neurons, for simplicity, a synapse will be referred to as "belonging" to the neuron for which it is an output device. Also for convenience, I will refer to the neurons to which a neuron is directly connected as "neighbor neurons", even though the cell bodies of the neurons may not be physically close to each other.

So how do neurons work? The neuron performs one measurable and essentially digital function—it "fires". The neuron is an electrochemical device and its operation is affected by physical transport of ions from place to place; ions having an electrical charge. When the neuron fires, we can measure the effect electronically as an electrical pulse of approximately 1ms (millisecond, thousandth of a second) in duration and approximately 100mV (millivolts, 100 thousandths of a volt or one-tenth of a volt) in amplitude. From an electronic point of view, this is an unremarkable size of signal—electrical engineers often work with signals which are much larger, smaller, faster or slower. For example, the size of signal coming out of a microphone is measured in microvolts (millionths) and digital circuit pulse lengths of a few picoseconds (trillionths of a second, a billion times faster than a neuron) are easily measurable with the proper equipment.

Although we measure the neuron's electrical pulse, this can mislead us into thinking of the brain as an electronic device. Instead, we could think of the electrical pulse we measure as being a side-effect of the chemical action which is going on. When a neuron fires, a chain reaction of ions begins at the soma and travels down the axon to the synapses. Sodium and potassium ions migrate through the wall of the axon, creating a local change in voltage, and then migrate back so the measured electrical pulse moves along the axon. When the pulse reaches the synapses, each synapse transports minute quantities of a neurotransmitter to the dendrite of the neuron to which it is connected. As a chemical process, the neural pulse travels down the axon at a speed on the order of 100m/s (meters per second), as compared with an electrical signal which would make the same trip at about 300 million m/s.

Each receiving neuron accumulates pulses received at its dendrites and, after reaching a threshold, it fires itself. Upon firing, the accumulation of input pulses is reset, and the process can start again. The received neurotransmitters migrate back across the synaptic boundaries to be reused in the next firing.

Synapses can either promote ("excite") or inhibit the potential for the neuron to fire depending on the type of neurotransmitter involved. Further, synapses are not all the same "size" in that they can transmit

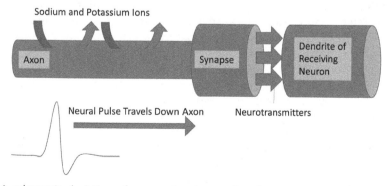

A schematic depiction of a neural pulse moving down an axon as ions are transported in and out across its membrane. When the pulse reaches a synapse, the synapse releases neurotransmitters which migrate across the synaptic gap to the dendrite of a receiving neuron.

different amounts of their neurotransmitter and can change in size in response to use, as will be discussed later. The excitatory and inhibitory types of synapses transmit different types of ions, either positive or negative. The firing of one neuron can either enhance or detract from the accumulated charge of the neighbor neurons, depending on the type of ion which is transferred. For example, if each synapse transmitted a single + or - ion and a neuron fires when it has accumulated a net of +10 ions from multiple input neurons, many combinations of synapses would eventually lead to the accumulation of the +10 needed to fire and reset the neuron.

After a neuron has fired, there is a slight delay or *relaxation time* in which everything is reset to its original state and during this time, the neuron cannot fire again even with extreme excitation. As such, the maximum firing rate of any individual neuron is about 500 times per second but is generally much lower. By examining the brain's total energy dissipation, we can estimate that neurons fire between once every few seconds to twice per second on average[15]. Since some areas of the brain are working hard all the time (such as the visual and auditory cortexes which are working continuously to process information from your eyes and ears), this implies that vast areas of the brain are largely quiescent.

Information encoding

Neurons can encode information and transmit it in several different ways. The optic nerve is a bundle of nerve fibers with individual fibers representing different points (pixels) on the retina. Some nerves represent light intensity and fire faster depending on the brightness of light they receive. Because of this representation, even though a neuron can fire at a maximum of 500 times per second, the information cannot be carried that quickly because it takes multiple neural pulses to represent intensity. So the maximum theoretical data rate is closer to 100 units per second.

The actual data rate appears to be lower. As you watch television, you are receiving new images at 30 frames per second and in movies at 24 frames per second. Because of the speed at which your brain can process visual information, motion seems smooth at these rates. Older home movies which were shot at 16 frames per second are sometimes noticeably jerky, as is video on a slow internet connection. From this, we could conclude that the information rate through the optic nerve is somewhere between 16 and 24 frames per second.

If our neuron firing close to 100 times per second represents a bright light and firing at 20 times per second represents black, intermediate firing rates would represent intensities in between. The receiving neurons are perhaps sensitive to 10 different firing rates. Your brain receives signals which can differentiate about 30 absolute shades of gray, although other cells in the retina can detect boundaries of more subtle relative shades.

Although there are more than 130 million retinal receptor cells, there are only approximately 1.2 million fibers in the optic nerve because a large amount of pre-processing is performed within the retina itself. The information capacity of the optic nerve is estimated at 500,000 bits per second[16]. Compare this against an HD television signal at 64 million bits per second, 128 times as much. This is largely because only a small portion of your retina (the fovea) has HD resolution and your eye darts from place to place within a television picture. The TV picture must be high resolution everywhere, even though your eye will only be receiving that hi-res information about 1% of the time at any specific location.

We also know that our eyes can intrinsically differentiate only three colors of light as there are only three types of color receptor in our retinas (sensitive to red, green, and blue[17])—all colors are various mixtures of these three. Our televisions, printed material, etc. can emulate any perceived color as a combination of three "primary colors". Light itself is a continuous spectrum with "primary colors" being a property of our eyes, not of light.

In this example, you can see how our technology is tailored to our senses. The flicker rate, frame rate, color depth, and resolution of video are all designed to create an illusion for human eyes and have little to do with the underlying motion, color, or resolution of actual physical objects. This will become more important in subsequent descriptions about how computers will perceive their world differently than we do.

Functionality

So what can a neuron do? It turns out that a neuron can do lots of useful information processing tasks. It can recognize patterns, detect edges, correct input errors, and remember things. I learned a lot about the capabilities and limitations of neurons when I wrote *The Brain Simulator*. With that program I demonstrated that the neuron is a device which could be used to create any desired digital circuit. In fact, one could theoretically build a CPU from neurons, a CPU which was perhaps a billion times slower than today's—so painfully slow that you might not perceive that it was running at all.

The most computationally important function which neurons have been shown to do is rudimentary pattern recognition. A neuron will fire when the pattern of input signals it receives matches an appropriate pattern of excitatory and inhibitory synapses. The closer the pattern match, the faster the neuron will fire. An abstraction of this type of pattern recognition is what is usually meant by computists when they talk about "neural networks" or "deep learning".

Alternatively, simple digital circuits could conceivably be created from just a few neurons. Because of our limited knowledge of brains, many small, specialized circuits could be scattered throughout the brain and are yet to be discovered. Finding a circuit of a few neurons within the mass of billions in the brain would be very difficult.

Transistors

Transistors are not very much like neurons. How do transistors work and what do transistors do? They come in several different types but share a common functionality: a transistor has three connections and applying electricity to one connection (the "gate" or "base") controls the amount of electricity which can flow between the other two (the "source" and "drain" OR the "emitter" and "collector", depending on the technology). So while the underlying mechanisms are entirely different, the pattern-recognition functionality performed by neurons can be performed equally with transistors. We could theoretically create artificial neurons using two transistors per synapse (one to do the switching and one to store the strength of the synapse, assuming there is some external circuitry to control the storage process).

The neuron is a chemical device which uses ion transport for its basic mechanism while the transistor uses free electrons. Electrons can be thought of more in terms of a garden hose which is filled from end-to-end with marbles. If you force one additional marble into one end of the hose, one marble will immediately pop out the other end—but it will be a different marble. Although any individual marble doesn't need to travel very quickly through the hose, the signal indicated by forcing in an additional marble travels from one end of the hose to the other seemingly instantly. In wires and electronic components, the electrons also don't get transported very quickly but the signal implied by the electrons can get from place to place at nearly the speed of light. Accordingly, transistors are faster than neurons—and not by a little bit! While a neuron performs its basic switching function in a few milliseconds (thousandths of a second), today's transistors can switch in a few picoseconds (trillionths of a second), a billion times faster! To give this kind of timeframe some perspective, during the time taken by a single neural pulse, a transistor can transmit the entire text of the Bible 500 times. During the switching time of a transistor, light (at its own unfathomable speed) can only travel about 1mm.

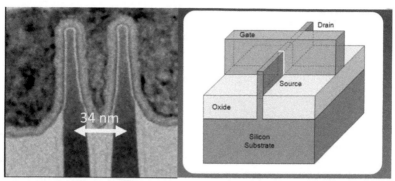

Left: A microscopic cross-section of transistors manufactured using Intel's 10nm technology (the width of an individual feature). Right: A schematic showing the component parts of the transistor. For comparison, consider the cell body of a neuron which could be 10,000 times larger. [Images by Intel, from Intel releases.]

As mentioned previously, transistors can now be manufactured by the billion and are very tiny. About a thousand of the transistors like those pictured in the figure, side-by-side, would be about the width of a human hair. Synapses are likewise very tiny, with about a billion synapses per cubic millimeter[18]. A significant distinction is that the brain has a considerable thickness while transistors are typically fabricated in a single layer on the surface of a wafer. The creation of 3D electronic circuits is still in its infancy.

But just building an electronic system with trillions of transistors isn't enough! How does the brain work to create human behavior? How can billions or trillions of similar or identical components (be they neurons or transistors) work together to produce useful behavior? Why don't computers think today? These are the topics of the next chapters.

---

[12] https://en.wikipedia.org/wiki/List_of_animals_by_number_of_neurons
https://www.ncbi.nlm.nih.gov/pmc/articles/PMC2776484/
[13] https://hypertextbook.com/facts/2001/JacquelineLing.shtml
[14] https://www.ncbi.nlm.nih.gov/pmc/articles/PMC4720747/
[15] https://aiimpacts.org/rate-of-neuron-firing/
[16] https://en.wikipedia.org/wiki/Retina
[17] Corresponding to primary colors of light as opposed to the primary colors of pigment as explained in grade school.
[18] http://book.bionumbers.org/how-big-is-a-synapse/

Chapter 8:

Protozoans, Insects, and Computers

To be intelligent, an organism or system must be able to perform these eight tasks:

1. Sense its environment (input).
2. Act on its environment (output).
3. Have internal rules or goals.
4. Analyze inputs to make sense of its environment.
5. Remember (learn) combinations of inputs and actions and their qualitative results.
6. Internally model its environment in three dimensions.
7. Simulate possible actions and select for positive predicted results.
8. Perform these actions with sufficient speed and magnitude to respond to real-world conditions in useful timeframes.

This and the following chapters in this section describe the stepping stones on the way to intelligence—the internal functionality needed for any system to be able to implement these elements. They are in the order of simplicity of explanation, which coincides largely with our evolutionary heritage.

Intelligence as we know it today is a conglomeration of mental faculties which were contributed by our evolutionary ancestors. We often think of intelligence as the completely human capability of thinking—often measured in terms of our ability to read, remember, and reason. We might forget that these abilities are all comparatively recent innovations of human civilization developed within the past few thousand years. With the human brain having been with us for over 100,000 years, were our ancestors in the caves equally intelligent but lacking in civilization's benefits? Is intelligence a learned ability or is it innate?

If we are to ever be able to determine whether or not a particular computer is thinking or intelligent, we will have to define what thinking and intelligence really are. For this purpose, I proposed the Eight Elements of Intelligence which will be defined and expanded over the next few chapters.

We can measure human intelligence with an IQ test which asks abstract questions and normalizes the scores against other test-takers and historical data. How would we measure the IQ of a Stone Age man possessing very little language ability and compare him reasonably to a modern person? Because we don't find significant physiological differences between the skulls of ourselves and those of 10,000 years ago, we can reasonably assume that the human brain capacity has not changed much. But the Stone Age man did not read or write and left no record of any mathematical ability. If we simply gave him today's adult IQ test, he would perform poorly at best, yet he was probably born as intelligent as you or I.

The same problem confronts us (and will confront us) with computers. How will we know if a computer is intelligent or not? Especially in the early stages of technological development when the computer has perhaps the intellect of a mouse or even a chimpanzee. Further, suppose we endeavored to build computers as capable as human brains. If such a computer system were turned on and exhibited the general mental characteristics of a newborn baby, would we know if we had been successful? IQ tests are usually only given to children below the age of seven if there are signs of exceptionally high or low abilities. Would we have to wait seven years to find out if our hypothetical computer was even normally intelligent (on a human scale)?

Rather than being caught in this dilemma, I'll itemize and define mental behaviors which we can agree that humans (who we assume to be intelligent and thinking) can perform. Some of these behaviors will be quite rudimentary, such as reflex actions. Further up the line will be the ability to recall the three-dimensional arrangement of furniture in the room you just left or to imagine what you will be doing next weekend—and to plan your weekend so your days will be the most enjoyable. I will detail a spectrum of mental behaviors which most of us share. The behaviors will be fairly abstract, as in the ability to learn to recognize new visual shapes. Most people can do this with ease; our best computer programs today can do this only crudely. We have computerized facial-recognition systems but they can't easily be trained to recognize trees.

This may not be a complete catalog of all human mental capabilities. You should feel free to look for ways that this list can be extended and think of the types of behaviors which might be missing from it. But the examples will show that this behavior list is better than a single Turing Test definition of intelligence. A person or computer which could exhibit these mental behaviors would certainly *seem* to be intelligent. Further, a computer which could implement a significant set of these behaviors would seem substantially more intelligent and be more useful than computer systems available today.

In breaking human brain functions down into various attributes, tests could be applied to measure the relative level of "intelligence" possessed for that particular attribute. For learning to recognize new visual patterns, we could measure the complexity of patterns which could be differentiated, the speed with which they are learned, and the number of errors which are made in recognition. With such a test, we could say that the computer system we have developed has the visual processing capability of, say, a mouse, or a dog, or a person, depending on measurable attributes. With these measurable attributes, we can begin to say that our future machines are "thinking" in certain specific areas and are deficient in others.

The black box control system

Let's define the problem in terms of a "control system" for a biological organism. In very low forms of animals and in all plants where there is no nervous system, the control system is not obvious and its operation may not be well known. But in higher animals, the control system is focused in the nervous system.

All control systems have inputs and outputs. The inputs are the senses which tell the control system about the organism and its environment while the outputs are the controls which direct the organism to perform its functions. As a simplification, in a higher animal we could say that the inputs to the control system are sensory nerves while the outputs are motor nerves and that the control system itself is the brain. In today's robots, this differentiation between the control system, inputs, outputs, and the rest of the machinery is quite clear-cut. As biological organisms have evolved, however, parts of our control systems are quite autonomous and integrated into other parts of the body, such as the human digestive system with its 500 million neurons[19].

This added complexity is not important to the discussion. The fact that significant neural processing goes on in your spinal cord and that some of your behaviors (such as salivation) are not controlled by motor nerves can be incorporated into the discussion by drawing the lines around the control system in slightly different places and redefining some of the inputs and outputs. The system will work the same way.

The figure shows a representation of what is called a "black box" model. From the figure, we get an idea of the inputs and outputs (and these *could* be defined explicitly) even if we know nothing about the processes which go on inside. But by observing the relationships between the inputs and outputs, we can draw useful conclusions. If we start at the highest level, we might try to guess at a human mind which accepts as input (over a period of years) mathematics, physics, reading, etc. and yields, as output (in the case of Einstein), theories of relativity. But this is way too hard a problem. Let's start with the simplest first.

Defining what goes on inside the box is the point of the following chapters—the more accurately we can describe the content of the box, the more completely we can replicate in computers the thought patterns which go on inside the brain.

The numbers of inputs and outputs are, of course, vastly simplified. There are millions of both sensory and motor neurons reaching the human brain. There are, however, significantly more sensory neurons than there are motor neurons. In the human brain, the motor cortex and the somatic sensory cortex (which handles the sense of touch) are roughly the same size but larger areas of the neocortex (the overall "thinking" part of the brain) are devoted to receiving the additional signals from the eyes and ears.

Another important observation of the black box diagram is that the brain is primarily driven by its inputs. Although some behavior is spontaneous, the majority of behavior is in response to input which is received. You are asked a question, so you answer. You are hot so you take off your coat. You are hungry so you arrange a snack for yourself. With the character of the brain being primarily input-driven, any computer system which purports to "think" along similar lines will need to have a similar set of inputs.

A "black box" model of an animal's control system. We can define the inputs and outputs without knowing anything about what is going on inside.

Reactions

To start the definition which will lead to thinking we will use the simplest behavior imaginable, the simple reaction. All living organisms react; it's one of the things which differentiates living from non-living. It might not seem that this is much of a basis for intelligence but a system which is incapable of reacting to its surroundings could hardly be very useful.

We'll define "reaction" as responding directly to an external stimulus. Examples of reactions in humans include reflexes. Many reflexes are handled in the spinal column, not the brain, and are characterized by very rapid, involuntary responses. Computer systems are also primarily reactive—you give them some input (stimulus) and you get some output (reaction). I press keys on the keyboard, and the computer reacts by putting character codes in a file and displaying the image of characters

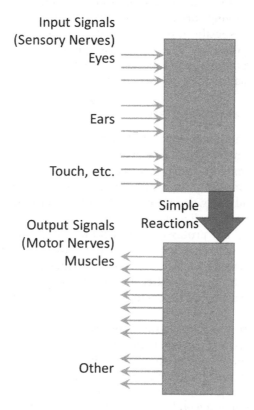

Reactions represent a shortcut—a more or less direct connection between certain inputs and outputs.

on the screen. For most computer programs, the output is always the same for a given input and so they are completely reactive systems.

Why do humans have reflexes? If you didn't, you would find (as did early roboticists) that simply standing up and walking are extremely complex activities. Reflex action allows you to stand and keep your balance without having to think about it. Researchers with computer-controlled robots discovered that walking on two legs is a complex activity. A robot which could walk would certainly have to have "reflex processors" which would handle some of this type of low-level processing so that simply standing up would not interfere with the higher-level control functions.

To measure reaction, you could measure the various types of inputs to which an organism would react and the speed with which it reacts. On any type of measure, today's computers are extremely competent reactors. They are fast, respond to a great many different inputs, and are quite reliable. In the reliability area, today's computers are generally different from living organisms in that living organisms usually acclimatize to a specific input. Repetition of the same input usually results in progressively less response until the input is ignored altogether. Computers could be programmed to respond this way although there has been no particular reason to do so.

A hypothetical protozoan

So far I have mentioned only one-to-one kinds of responses: a single input yields a single output. But even the chemical control systems of protozoa can exhibit more complex behaviors than that. As an illustration, let me propose a protozoan which can move through its environment and is driven by a pair of flagella, microscopic hairs, which it can wave to make itself move.

On one end of our protozoan, we will imagine two organelles which are sensitive to some chemical in the water it lives in. At the other end, we'll have two flagella which will make the animal move. By stimulating the two flagella to wave at different speeds, the organism can change direction—by waving the left one faster, it will turn to the right, for example.

In the control system, if the sensors do not sense anything, the flagella will have a slow but somewhat random waving motion. If a sensor senses something, the corresponding flagellum will have a faster motion. If there is nothing in the water to sense, the animal will move around randomly. If the sensors sense a chemical in the water, perhaps the aroma of something edible, the appropriate flagellum will cause the animal to turn toward the source of the chemical.

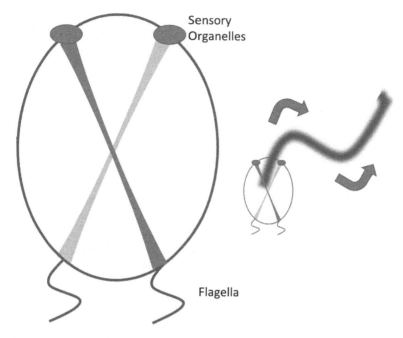

A very simple control system can make a protozoan follow a scent trail to its next meal.

Similarly, a very simple wheeled robot can follow a line on the ground with two photosensors and two motors. It's a simple enough control system that you can build it out of Lego™.

Even with this very simple control system, we have described all that is necessary for this organism to appear to have some interesting behaviors. If the sensors are sensitive to a chemical given off by one of the animal's foods, the animal will "search" for the food at random. Once it picks up the scent trail of something edible, it will turn toward it and move faster. If the food is moving away from our organism, we will observe our organism to be chasing it. We could watch our little organism through a microscope and observe what kinds of food it "likes" and what it doesn't. If its flagella were also slowed by having plentiful nutrients within the cell, we would observe it taking a siesta after meals. All-in-all, we would certainly have some interesting behaviors from a purely reactive mechanism.

Complex behaviors, then, can be the result of a relatively simple control system. From this it's possible to imagine that the very complex behavior we humans exhibit is also the result of a relatively limited system of controls.

Ants

Taking this behavior another step, let's examine an ant colony. Among other things, ants can follow and lay down scent trails. They sense scent trails with their antennae (two for directionality as in our protozoan) and can also secrete pheromones, creating a scent trail.

A worker/scavenger ant leaves an ant colony in search of food and meanders around its environment. All the while, it is laying down its own scent trail which will allow it to get back home to the colony. When it detects a food scent, it follows it until it reaches the food source. When it actually picks up some food, it shifts gears from following a food trail and laying down a home trail to following a home trail and laying down a food trail. So it follows its home scent trail back to the nest and brings the food with it. Now there is a food trail which leads from the nest to the food that any ant can follow directly. An ant parade will commence which leads ants from the nest to the food and back again until the food supply is exhausted. If you place an obstacle in the path, the ant parade will be disrupted until some more meandering behavior locates a path around the obstacle and the parade is reestablished.

Here, we have the appearance of some extremely sophisticated behaviors from a very simple control system. We could easily think that the ants had a sort of language with which to communicate with each other the locations of food sources, the ability to say "Hey, great food over here, everybody follow me!" Ants have a sophisticated nervous system with about 250,000 neurons, they have eyes and antennae and are responsive to numerous stimuli which help them to survive. But there is nothing in the ant's behavior which can't be explained entirely in terms of complex reactive behavior.

Basically smart

For ease of discussion, let's refer to the ability to perform well on a test of some aspect on the road to intelligence as "smartness". I would not argue that the ability to react is actually smartness but something which cannot react is certainly not smart. Now, we have a measure that shows that the amoeba is "smarter" than a rock because it has the ability to react and the rock does not. We can also say that an ant is smarter than an amoeba because it can react to more complex stimuli and exhibit more complex responses.

In any case, we could probably agree that in the aspect of reaction, a computer is smarter than an amoeba but not as smart as a human. It may be smarter or less smart than an ant depending on the type of program it is running.

In terms of inputs and outputs, the amoeba has only a few sensations and only a few possible behaviors while the ant has many and the human has millions of inputs in its eyes, ears, and all over its body. Computers usually have only a few input devices and exhibit only a few behaviors but they are extremely fast. On the bottom end of electronic reactions, consider a doorbell which has a single input (the button) and a single response (ding-dong). Let's say a doorbell is also smarter than a rock, but not by very much.

So far, we've seen how a simple control system and reactions can lead to complex behavior. Next, up the scale of complexity, we'll examine pattern recognition to create even more interesting action.

---

[19] https://en.wikipedia.org/wiki/Enteric_nervous_system

Chapter 9:

"Th Ablty to rcgnz mening frm prtl inpt"

The simple mechanism of reaction can produce some complex-appearing behaviors but cannot approach thinking. A computer program which has a huge library of English phrases and can select from among them based upon the input it receives can initially give the impression that it is somehow able to communicate something. However, analysis can eventually show that the machine is not thinking any more than the ant is.

We cannot make the leap directly from reaction to thinking in one step, although early AI researchers tried. On the way there are several important intermediate steps. The first presented here will be pattern-recognition, then goals, and learned behaviors.

The pattern recognition here is not the type of pattern recognition that you find in IQ tests in which you need to choose the next item in a series. In this context, primitive pattern recognition, as performed by individual neurons, means the identification of any recognizable feature in the given input. This can mean identifying boundaries in a visual image or phonemes in a sound. (A phoneme is a basic unit of spoken sound—syllables are usually made up of several phonemes. The word "ball" is a single syllable consisting of three phonemes, the 'b', the 'ah', and the 'll'.)

Pattern recognition represents additional "front-end" processing on the input signals to a reactive control system, which allows the organism or system to respond to more complex input. Learned behavior, on the other hand, works on the back-end of the reaction organism system to allow it to create new, more complex behaviors in response to one of the input patterns it has detected. Goals, here, are the simple goals of surviving, avoiding predation, and procreation that keep a species from becoming extinct.

When we describe the behavior of an organism which possesses these capabilities, we'll see that it can do all the things of the purely reactive system presented in the previous chapter and many more besides. But it is still not a thinking organism. An organism can respond to much more complex stimuli and respond with more complex behaviors. We can assume that earthworms, reptiles, and fish, all animals which we generally agree are not thinkers, have nervous systems which exhibit the behaviors which this type of system could possess. At the same time, humans, too, definitely also possess these abilities. Building a computer which has higher-level thinking capabilities but which does not possess these lower-level functions (pattern recognition, goals, and learned responses) will make it less likely to be thinking.

Pattern recognition

The ability to recognize patterns in our environment is one of our brains' predominant activities. We do it all the time—continuously; and it is a capability we share with most of our evolutionary predecessors.

Our eyes and the visual cortex which supports them are the most obvious example of this type of processing. When our eyes are open, they are continuously feeding visual information to the brain. But we do not simply see areas of light and dark, or color; we see images of *things*. Because you are a reader, it is impossible for you to see the letters on this page without recognizing them as the symbols they are. There is lots of processing going on in our brains which continuously monitors the visual input looking for things which can be organized into recognizable images.

This is very sophisticated, and some of this sophistication is unique to higher animals. When you see this:

on the page, a whole lot of processing goes on in your brain. You might see a sunrise or sunset but that's more advanced than we're talking about here. What you see is a boundary between the white of the page and the dark of the shape. The boundary has a few corners, a straight part and a curved part. It has a definite interior and exterior and it's fairly simple. Your brain understands there is a single thing which is made up of a combination of the things above. The light which hits your retinas from this shape contains none of this information directly. It's just a bunch of photons—more in the white part and fewer in the dark part. All the other descriptions are the results of neural processing.

Your brain works primarily by responding to boundaries or changes in the input it receives. This is what causes the well-known optical illusion in which gray-scale rectangles which have a constant gray level seem to have shading. The eye is sending messages to the brain indicating the locations of the boundaries between the gray areas and

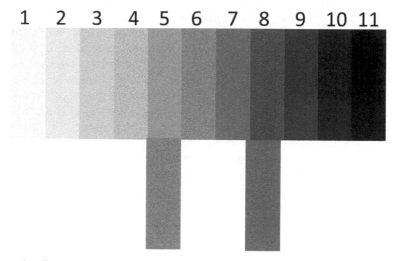

In this illusion, the individual gray rectangles appear to fade to a lighter shade near their right boundary. In reality, the gray of each rectangle is constant. The two lower rectangles appear the same shade—they are actually identical to areas 6 and 7, which are clearly different when they are right next to each other.

that one side of the boundary is lighter than the other. Since your eye is more sensitive to the boundary than the brain is sensitive to absolute brightness, your brain is receiving information that a boundary exists but the gray-levels on either side of the boundary are nearly the same. Faced with this information, the brain assumes that the gray rectangles must not be a constant intensity because that is the most reasonable interpretation of the information which is being sent to it.

This boundary and intensity information arrives at the visual cortex at the back of the brain, where it is mapped more or less into areas which represent the image in the eye. Now, millions of neurons work in parallel to interpret fragments of information in the image.

Some cells within your retina itself detect the boundaries between different colored areas. Boundaries, color, intensity, and motion (if any) are handled in the visual cortex where, among many other things, certain cells respond to specific boundary angles. Other cells may detect two boundaries of significantly different angles meeting at a single point which must represent a corner. Others detect gradually different angles which must represent a curve. All these features are passed to progressively more complex levels of pattern recognition for further processing.

But vision is not our only pattern-recognition system. We understand speech—a recognition problem of similar complexity. But on a much lower level, your hearing is based on pattern recognition "hardware", which is quite similar in function to your visual system. It is constantly monitoring input from the ears and searching to find sensible patterns from the continuous noise which is being received. Whenever you hear a sound, you unconsciously process it to determine the direction of its source. Cells in your ears are responsive to specific sound frequencies and specific combinations of frequencies correspond to specific phonemes. Changes in the combinations of frequencies represent boundaries of phonemes and sequences of phonemes which can correspond to syllables, words, sentences, paragraphs, or books.

In measuring simple pattern recognition, we can consider the number of different patterns which can be recognized, the possible

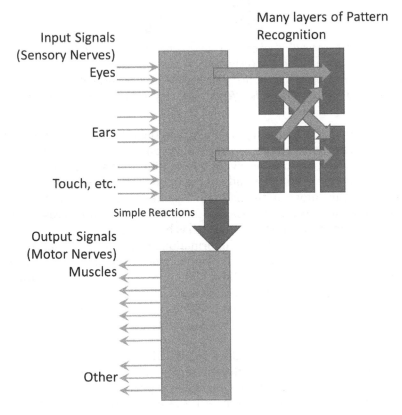

Input signals from your senses are processed by many levels of pattern recognition.

complexity of these patterns, and the speed with which the recognition takes place. On this spectrum, computers fall into a middle ground. When we started programming computers to perform optical character recognition, we found that humans have a remarkable speed, flexibility, and accuracy at reading. While reading text is a learned capability, it demonstrates the complexity of the human pattern-recognition capability. Animals, also, seem remarkably good at recognition, especially detecting motion in an otherwise complex and cluttered visual field. It's difficult to place the computer on this spectrum. The computer can see better than an insect or a fish. Perhaps a computer could see and recognize simple objects faster and more accurately than a human. We don't know. I want to emphasize that even though a computer can handle signals from a video camera, this is not the same as describing the shape from three pages ago—a shape which is not in a library.

I have described a static type of pattern recognition where all the patterns an organism can recognize are "preprogrammed" or instinctive. In the example, your visual cortex instinctively knows about boundaries, corners, curves, interior, etc. On a more complex level, higher animals can learn to recognize new patterns like the letters on this page.

One of the first things that was discovered when artificial neural networks were in their infancy was that a cluster of artificial neurons could be programmed to fire when any specific pattern of input was detected. Input signals were connected to all the neurons in the cluster by "synapses". The weights or strengths of the synapses could correspond to a pattern and cause individual neurons to fire fastest when the input signal matched the weights of their input synapses. We could program the synapse weights of a cluster of neurons and they could detect input patterns of any arbitrary complexity.

A great feature of this type of pattern recognition is that it is very tolerant of errors. Rather than responding to exact matches only, it responded to close matches with the firing rate corresponding to the level of exactness or "confidence" in the pattern match. Rather than determining only the *best* result, it might pass the top three results to another stage of pattern recognition. This could combine this information with information from other clusters which would help determine the best result.

Learning

It didn't take long for manually programming synapse weights to get really tedious. Considering the simple nervous systems of some mollusks, the connections of the 18,000 neurons in a sea slug might be completely programmed by DNA. But the synapse weights in complex brains cannot be entirely preprogrammed—there simply isn't enough information in the DNA to define all those connections and weights. Instead, we need algorithms which would adjust the synapse weights automatically. We call that "learning".

One simple learning algorithm (introduced by Donald Hebb in 1949) strengthens the weight of a synapse if the two neurons it connects fire at about the same time—implying that the specific input is relevant to the output[20]. Alternatively, unsynchronized firing could lead to synapse weakening over time. Slowly, a cluster of neurons with small random weights will gravitate to having specific neurons correspond to patterns in the inputs.

This is an example of "unsupervised learning". Without any knowledge of the "right" answer, the network of neurons simply adjusts to being able to differentiate or categorize the inputs it receives. This is a biologically plausible mechanism but, in the sizes of networks which could be simulated, isn't able to produce computationally useful results.

"Supervised learning", on the other hand, simultaneously presents an input pattern and the desired output. An early example was based on multiple handwritten examples of the digits zero through nine and a neuron cluster with 10 output neurons. Neural network algorithms adjust synapse weights, so clusters of neurons can be trained to do a pretty good job of recognizing handwritten digits. The much larger artificial neural networks today, now called "deep learning", continue to produce interesting and useful results, but there is little belief that these algorithms are representative of how biological brains work.

To underscore the distinction between supervised and unsupervised learning, let's consider creating an application to identify cats vs. dogs in photos—which has been done by several groups. For supervised learning, you'll need a training set of photos, perhaps 10,000, each labeled as containing a cat, a dog, or neither. Each image is presented to the neural network multiple times and the weights of the synapses adjust themselves until the network stabilizes to consistent results. Then it should be able to classify unlabeled images with some degree of success.

For unsupervised learning, you might use the same training set but without the labels. The upside is that you don't have to label the images so you might have a training set of a million images. The downside is that while the system *might* be able to identify cats vs. dogs, it is just as likely to identify light-colored animals vs. dark-colored animals, or images with green grass vs. gray concrete, or indoors vs. outdoors, or images with the animal large in the photo vs. mostly background.

The dilemma for those of us trying to make sense of how the brain works is that neither method seems to be a plausible analog. Small children can identify pictures of cats vs. dogs, they have excellent accuracy, and they weren't presented with a large training set. The child, after seeing just a few cats or a few dogs seems to be able to deduce "essence of cat" or "essence of dog", which enables her to subsequently make correct identification. We can even identify lion and tiger as "cat-like" and wolf and hyena as "dog-like" even though pictures may not make this obvious at all.

We don't have much detailed knowledge of what's going on inside the brain so we have to examine the external behavior and theorize on what's going on. Clearly there is a combination of the two mechanisms.

Supervised learning is the likely mechanism for learning to walk and talk. You try out some muscular activity and see if you achieved the "correct" outcome. If you fall down or don't hear the syllables you intended to utter, your brain can adjust some neural connections and try again. Image and shape classification, on the other hand, are probably unsupervised. If you play with blocks you learn to recognize round vs. square. If you have pets, you'll learn that they are different from inanimate objects but different from people too. Subsequently, you may learn (in a supervised way) the associated words for the concepts you have already categorized: round, square, cat, dog.

In considering how we could measure the ability to learn, we should consider the speed of learning, the number of different patterns which can be learned, the complexity of the patterns, and the accuracy with which subsequent input is recognized. I am interested in measuring each facet of behavior because in a computer system, we will be able to adjust the power of each facet individually. In human brains, all the facets are measured together and lumped into a single IQ number. A hypothetical thinking computer may be vastly superior to the human brain on some of these facets while lagging behind in others.

The key distinction between supervised and unsupervised learning is that supervised learning requires a "right" and a "wrong" answer. This implies that the brain is receiving some sort of reward for right answers and some sort of punishment for wrong answers. We can call behavior in pursuit of a "right" answer goal-seeking.

Goals

In order to have supervised learning, we need to know the "right" answer. When a baby is born, her right answers are to make sense of her surroundings and to learn the behaviors to get what she needs. Right for her includes being well-fed, warm, safe, and pain-free. Her "right" answers govern everything she learns.

If a computer is programmed with an algorithm for unsupervised learning, the definition of "right" will likewise govern its behavior. In the baby, right is defined by DNA. In AGI, programmers will be able to define "right" as anything they like.

At a very basic level, the primary goal of every species is to procreate. This isn't because of some cosmic rightness of procreation but simply because organisms without this goal have already become extinct. Self-preservation of individual organisms is secondary to the goal of survival of the species. If a species becomes extinct, the behavior of any individual becomes irrelevant. Honey bees, for example, use stinging as a defense behavior, and while stinging may help the hive it is lethal to the individual bee.

Humans, on the other hand, have a well-developed individual survival instinct which can mask the overall species survival instinct. At a low level: can I breathe? Am I thirsty? Am I hungry? Am I warm enough? Am I in pain? And so on. At a higher level: am I pretty enough to attract a mate? Can I provide enough food to attract a mate? Do I know my surroundings enough to feel safe? If we imagined the answer to each question ranging on a scale of one to 10, we could imagine a collection of numbers which would make up your state of "well-being" right now—we could call this a "vector of well-being". Some of the numbers would be more important than others and could carry more weight.

Now "right" at any time could be defined as any improvement in your well-being vector and will govern your supervised learning. You might

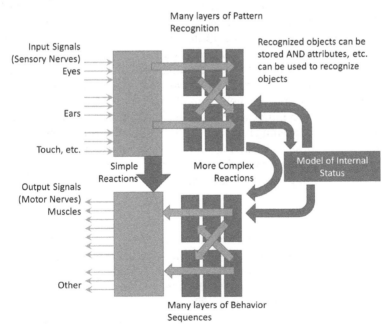

An animal can recognize patterns in its sensory input and can use different behaviors to improve its internal status.

say that an improving well-being vector is happy; declining is sad. The well-being numbers are *not* the emotional feelings of happiness or sadness in themselves. To feel happy or sad or in love, there needs to be an entity to do the feeling. In this case, consider the well-being of an earthworm. It does things which are conducive to it but has no internal sensation of comfort.

Any abrupt change in your well-being vector will cause you to remember. Whatever you were doing when you fall in love, you are likely to repeat those behaviors. Addictive behaviors can be partially explained by an initial abrupt improvement in your sense of well-being which causes you to repeat those behaviors. Alternatively, the shock you receive from an exposed electric terminal is likely to make you cautious of electricity for the rest of your life.

Most of the facets of well-being mentioned above don't make much sense programmed into a robot. The intelligent computer needs facets of well-being in order to learn, but with different goals will come different behavior. The goals will permeate every decision the brain makes so the correct selection of goals is critical to the safety and usefulness of AGI. I'll propose some goals in Chapter 15, but suffice to say that if basic preprogrammed goals govern most of our behavior, we shouldn't expect intelligent computers to act just like humans when we assign them different goals—no matter how smart they are.

One goal that we will undoubtedly share with robots is that of making sense of our environment. Our brains invest a large portion of their volume in interpreting sight and sound; not just to see or hear the environment but to interpret what we see and hear as objects in our environment. We have a tendency to like things which are familiar and eschew those that are unfamiliar. This goal leads to both curiosity on one hand and fear of the unknown on the other. We can imagine speech recognition and computer vision programs which have a goal of "understanding" and learn based on how well they approach that goal. A robot programmed with that goal might likewise appear to have curiosity and fear of the unknown.

If we don't program AGI systems with a will to procreate, even if it's reproduction by semiconductor factory, there is no need for them to consider self-preservation. They need not be territorial, or possessive, or competitive. Most science fiction about AI imbues future systems with human-like goals (like a lust for power and control) and considers the ramifications of how these goals will lead to catastrophic outcomes. If the AGI system's basic goals are programmed to be *useful* to us rather than being *like us* the outcomes could be completely different.

Behavior sequences

There appears to be another type of learning. When I was about forty, I learned to play the guitar. At first, nothing seemed to work properly or easily. I would see the fingering of a chord on a chart and try to put my fingers in the right places. I would have to think about every finger and its position. It would take a second or two to place each finger while I watched to make sure it went into the right position. Assembling my left hand to play a chord would take so long that any semblance of music would be lost in the delays of chord changes.

But, I made improvements on two fronts. First, after repeated practice, each chord can be fingered more quickly, and second, my ability to learn new chords has improved.

Generally, if I consciously and patiently direct my body to do something many times, doing it again eventually becomes easier. The first time on a chord takes many seconds. After tens or hundreds or thousands of repetitions, the process of moving to a chord position becomes faster and easier. After learning some individual chords, I can learn progressions of chords. In lots of music, certain chords often follow others... just in practicing scales, your fingers learn common sequences of notes. With more thousands of repetitions, these become faster and easier as well.

I can play a sequence of chords much faster than I can consciously consider where the fingers go. In fact, after significant practice, I don't have to look at my fingers to get them to go to the right places. We speak of this as "muscle memory". Of course, there is no mechanism in the fingers for them to "remember" how to play the guitar. This is a mental function, part of my personal control system (although there is some muscle strengthening and calluses which must be built up.)

Some significant portion of the brain is dedicated to being able to learn how to repeat physical actions, to provide coordination, and to remember sequences of firings of motor nerves. This is how we have learned to walk, talk and to control all our actions. If we had to think about the position of each of our limbs all the time when we were engaged in any activity, all our activity would be too slow to be useful to us.

With all these stored sequences of muscle actions, your conscious mind need only direct you to walk this direction, play this chord, or say this word. Other parts of your brain take care of stimulating all the individual muscle contractions needed to carry out the task.

This is definitely an example of supervised learning but in this case, it is one part of your brain supervising another. The conscious control of your body in your neocortex meticulously shows your cerebellum (probably) how to do something. Your cerebellum learns by example and you need to provide less and less specific direction. Eventually, you learn to perform the action with little or no conscious intervention.

Memory

Computers have circuits or devices which are devoted specifically to memory. In contrast, we don't believe there is a specific brain area which is used exclusively for memory. In computers, information is stored in RAM as the state of charge of tiny memory "cells"—additional electrons could represent a one while fewer could represent a zero. In magnetic media (e.g. "hard drives"), the same information can be stored in the orientation of microscopic magnetic "domains". Magnetic media are much slower but historically much cheaper than RAM. But the cost of RAM and its cousins SSDs (solid state drives) are coming down so that magnetic memories may fade in importance.

Neurons can also store information and I will describe three plausible mechanisms here (although there may be others). As in computer memories, the three memory types trade off cost (in terms of the number of neurons needed and energy expended) for speed.

Long-term memories may persist indefinitely but require some time to be created and can store many bits (perhaps hundreds) per neuron. Short-term memories last just a few seconds but require many neurons per bit. Intermediate-term working memories may last several minutes or hours and I propose a mechanism which requires just a few neurons per bit.

We have reasonable biological evidence for long-term memories while the explanations presented for short-term and working memories are biologically plausible but may or may not exist in human brains in the specific forms described.

Long-term memory

For longer-term storage, information can be stored in the state of the synapses themselves. As shown previously, properly set synapse weights can store the state of an input pattern so that a neuron will fire whenever that input pattern is repeated. "Training" a network of neurons (in computing parlance) is equivalent to storing patterns of signals. In the two-layer neural network shown in the figure, one of the neurons in the right-hand layer will fire whenever its stored pattern is received at the input neurons. We could also consider a neural model where the firing rate of each output neuron is proportional to how close the input pattern is to matching the synapse weights. An additional layer of neurons could select only the fastest-firing neuron and so a closest-match circuit could be created. If you see "comutr", your "commuter" neuron will fire but your "computer" neuron likely will fire faster. Your brain isn't usually interested in receiving multiple possible interpretations from ambiguous input, it wants the best interpretation right now.

Major strengths of this memory mechanism are:

- It requires essentially no energy for long-term storage
- Storage is more or less indefinite
- It can store many bits per neuron

If we imagine that a neuron has a thousand input synapses and fires only when the input pattern exactly matches the synapse weights, then an individual neuron is storing a thousand bits of information. It is likely that redundancies within the brain limit this number to perhaps a hundred. Consider that our alphabets contain about a hundred symbols (with digits, upper and lower case, punctuation, etc.). Our languages are made up of similar numbers of different phonemes. Individual faces have about 50 recognizable characteristics, etc.

The limitation of storing information this way is that this mechanism requires many repetitions of input patterns, as the synapse weights adjust gradually to match the input pattern. Therefore, while this may be an important mechanism for long-term memory, it is too slow to be the mechanism for short-term memory. In order to store something in long-term memory, to memorize something, you need to present your neurons with many repetitions of the input pattern. This can happen if

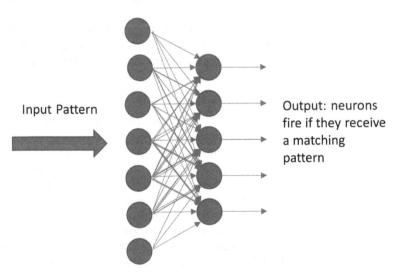

With simulated neurons represented as disks, this fully connected network can store one recognizable pattern per neuron in the output layer—independent of the size of the input.

you see or hear something repeated many times, but you can also replay items many times within your brain from shorter-term memory. You can remember a face—during the time you look for just 10 seconds, the neurons which are storing the information may receive thousands of repetitions with that input pattern. You can memorize the Gettysburg Address by saying parts over and over to yourself until the synapse weights are set.

We can conclude that the selection of which neurons will store which particular item is random or based on the order the information is received. Since we all have different childhood experiences, we all store bits of knowledge in different neurons in our brains. Imagine we all have a neuron in our brain which fires to recognize the face of our grandmother. That neuron will be a different neuron in every person. To know which neuron that is, we'd need to be shown pictures, for example, of lots of people—including granny—while we determined which neuron(s) fired for granny but not for anyone else.

Because of this randomness, scanning a brain to determine your knowledge and memories is not possible and may never be. You couldn't, as in some Sci-Fi stories, transfer memories from one person to another because all the connections and weights would be in different places in the brain.

In contrast, in computers we know exactly where each data item is stored. With computers, we'll be able to read memories, splice memories from one computer to another, and even create artificial memories.

When people consider the memory capacity of the brain, they are generally considering long-term memory. As mentioned in Section I, estimates of the brain's memory capacity vary widely from 10TB to 1PB. From the explanation above, if we assume that a neuron can usefully store one hundred bits of information and that a billion cortical neurons are configured to store information in this manner, then the brain's memory capacity is at or below the 10TB lowest estimate.

Short-term memory

At the other end of the spectrum, short-term memories could be stored in vast arrays of neurons—with each layer connected directly to the next with sufficient synapse strength so that stimulating a neuron in one layer will cause the corresponding neuron in the next layer to fire.

If a sound pattern is being received from the ears, for example, the pattern is passed down this bucket-brigade of neurons, one layer to the next. Such a mechanism would store information instantly, but only for the length of time needed for the signal to reach the end of the bucket-

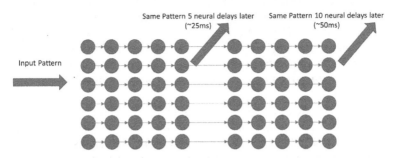

An input pattern can be stored for a short time by simply passing it to chains of neurons.

brigade. At that point, if necessary, the signal is lost but might be routed back to the beginning and replayed again.

You might think that this would take a lot of neurons. If you represent an image with 15,000 pixels, for example, and you want to recall it after several seconds, it would require perhaps 15 million neurons. While that might seem like a lot of neurons, remember that we have 16 billion neurons to work with. It would represent less than one-tenth of one percent of the brain.

As an example, consider times when you listen to someone talking and have trouble understanding. You can replay a few words in your mind to get a second chance to understand. To get an idea of the capacity of this type of memory, consider buying something by phone order. You can give the person your five-digit zip code and expect the person has sufficient short-term memory to receive it as a single unit. On the other hand, a 16-digit credit card exceeds the expected capacity, so you read it out to them in sections.

This type of memory has the strengths of being instantaneous and biologically plausible at the expense of being very short term and using lots of neurons.

Working memory

In between short-term and long-term memories, we have what is called "working" memory.

As an example, consider that in a card game, you can easily remember some number of cards which have already been played. This memory lasts a few minutes or more but is limited to perhaps a hundred items. With practice, most people can learn to remember the order of an entire deck of 52 cards but very few people can remember much more than that.

I propose a possible mechanism for working memory which I devised with *The Brain Simulator* which uses three neurons per bit. It can store

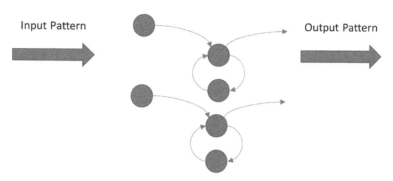

A possible neuron structure for working memory. The two neurons connected directly to each other will cause each other to fire indefinitely once firing is started by the input pattern. (Connections needed to store and clear information are not shown.)

information immediately and the information persists indefinitely. As it is built from a neuron model, it is biologically plausible.

If a pair or neurons are connected to each other, they will tend to "ring" after stimulation. That is, if you stimulate either neuron, it will fire and cause the other neuron to fire, which in turn will cause the first to fire again. This firing will continue until there is significant inhibitory stimulation which stops the pair from firing. At that point it will remain quiescent. In this manner, the state of firing of any input can be stored for an arbitrary length of time. This is, in effect, what an electrical engineer would call a "flip-flop" and is the principal circuit used for the fastest computer storage within a CPU itself. This mechanism has the advantage of being quick at the cost of using energy, since when the neurons are firing (to store that state), they must use energy to fire continuously. As such, we would expect to find this type of storage used sparingly in brains.

Observations of memory

The brain has tiers of memory: long-, short- and intermediate-term, which are analogous in computers to disk drives, CPU-cache, and RAM memory. In both "systems", slower memories have greater capacity and a lower "cost".

Storing long-term memories in the brain is ponderously slow, taking many seconds of repetitions. A computer, on the other hand, can store data essentially instantly, creating a system with a truly "eidetic" or "photographic" memory—something only mythical in humans.

Memory is not sufficient for intelligence—we need to consider what is remembered. We'll consider knowledge (as opposed to memory) in the next chapter.

[20] https://en.wikipedia.org/wiki/Hebbian_theory

Chapter 10:
Sight, Sound, and Knowledge

So far, the mechanisms of intelligence have brought us to the level of lower animals but nothing which might be considered thinking. In this chapter, we'll build on those basics with an explanation of how your brain might store knowledge. This will sum up how your brain processes the input it receives from your senses and complete the foundation needed to address even more intelligent activities.

Sound vs. sight, time vs. space

The pattern recognition of long-term memory requires that all the inputs of a pattern be presented simultaneously. When you look at a photographic image, for example, all of the input from the image is available to your brain at a single moment in time. How, then, do we recognize sounds, syllables, and words, where the pattern is the part of a sound wave which varies over time and is never *simultaneous*? You can't recognize a voice, or a tune, or a bird call from a single moment in

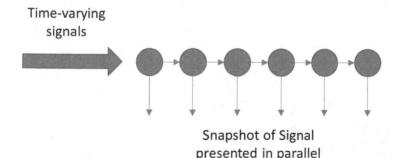

A time-varying signal can be passed down a bucket-brigade of neurons to be converted into a parallel group of neural signals. These can be recognized in the same manner as static patterns.

time—you need to hear the sound over some period of time, perhaps a second or two.

The description of pattern recognition in the previous chapter focused on the visual system because it is easier to explain in terms of static images. When thinking about how speech is understood, recognizing a pattern in a time-varying sound waveform would be more complex. But there is a way out: time-varying waveforms can be converted into simultaneous patterns by a shift-chain of neurons similar to the neurons proposed for short-term memory.

Input signals from the environment can be passed through a chain of neurons, each of which introduces a slight delay into the signal. Then a portion of the signal, a "window", can be analyzed in parallel. A similar process is used by computer systems performing speech recognition, since time-varying processing is more complex than processing one static block of data at a time.

Human auditory processing has an added wrinkle that the ear itself has nerve cells which are responsive to specific frequencies of sound and fire more energetically with sound intensity at a specific pitch. The signals from these cells all arrive at the auditory cortex in parallel, not as a single sound wave (like the common oscilloscope sound wave picture). Instead of a single signal, there are thousands of neural signals in parallel, corresponding to the intensity of sound received at each

Clusters of hair cells populate the inner ear and are "tuned" to detect sounds at different specific pitches. [Image by Sebastian Kaulitzki, Shutterstock.]

different pitch. If you hear a single pitch, only a few of these neurons will be firing; for a symphony, perhaps hundreds; and for a jet engine or rocket launch, all of these neurons will be firing as fast as they can.

So rather than a single shift-chain, there would be thousands of shift-chains in parallel representing different pitches of incoming sound, creating a vast two-dimensional array of sound with time on one axis and pitch on the other. With pattern-recognition neurons having synapses to the two-dimensional array of all the shift-chains, various synaptic patterns would let specific neurons fire only in response to specific sounds. The pattern-recognition neurons will be receiving input from a two-dimensional array of neurons representing pitch-intensity and time. The pattern-recognition process for auditory processing will share processing concepts with visual pattern recognition, which receives input as a two-dimensional array from your retinas.

We can get a feeling for how fast this process must be being done in the brain's auditory processing system by examining the speed at which we speak and the lengths of the syllables we can understand. Ordinary speech comes at a rate of about five syllables (10 to 15 phonemes) per second and so it is reasonable that incoming signals in our ears are processed through chains of a few tens to hundreds of neurons in length, from which we can recognize phonemes. The phonemes, once recognized, are put through their own slower chains, which could be used by the brain to interpret syllables, words and phrases.

The ear has about 16,000 hair cells which are responsive to different frequencies of sound. In music, when you hear a simultaneous combination of pitches, you hear a chord. If, however, you hear a base frequency in combination with specific overtones, you don't hear a chord, you hear a vowel. For example, "ee" would be a fundamental tone of approximately 300Hz combined with overtones at 2,200, 2,900, and 3,500Hz[21]. Other vowel sounds are heard with other different relative intensities of other overtones.

The eye has only three types of receptor for different frequencies of light, with specific cells responsive to red, blue, and green. In a manner similar to hearing, if the red and green receptors fire simultaneously at a specific location in your eye, you don't see a "chord" of two colors, you see yellow. In your brain, yellow is as much a color as red and green, even though it is a mix. In your brain, "ee" is likewise a single sound even though it is a mix of sound frequencies.

Today's computers have no trouble keeping up with incoming sound and video signals—even though both of these can significantly exceed the limits of human vision and hearing. For even more power, accelerator cards are available to offload the CPU for both audio and video input (and output) processing.

Given that signals can be easily shifted from time-varying to static patterns and that there are similarities in the way multiple frequencies are handled, it is likely that significant portions of the processing for both vision and hearing are quite similar in the brain.

Content-addressable memory

Your brain's memory and your computer's RAM are not very much alike, although they both can store information. In RAM, every storage location is associated with a location number, the "address", and when your computer needs an item from RAM, it presents the appropriate address and the RAM returns the data. In your brain, a memory doesn't have a location/address. When your brain wants information, it presents some data, and your memory responds with information which includes, or is related to, data which was presented. As such, the data in your memory is retrieved by its content.

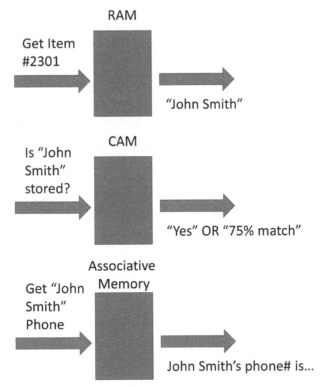

Highlighting the difference between computer RAM, content-addressable memory, and associative memory. Your brain contains no RAM. Computers usually emulate CAM and associative memory with software.

Content-addressable memory (CAM) is a computer term describing a storage device which allows a system to determine whether or not a particular data item is in memory. It does so by presenting the memory device with the data itself, rather than an address. Hardware CAMs can be extremely fast and are used for your CPU's cache memory so that it can determine quickly whether or not a particular block of RAM data is already loaded in the cache.

Although much slower, many types of software CAMs have been developed including, for example, the relational database which allows you to query in order to determine whether or not particular data items exist. You can query a database to determine whether or not "John Smith" is in it without knowing the item's location. Although the software for this type of memory can be complex in order to get high performance, the functionality of a CAM can be implemented on any computer.

In the last chapter, I showed how an individual neuron will perform pattern recognition by responding when a particular input pattern was received. Biological CAMs are an extension of pattern recognition with the addition of the ability to store new data. In your brain, a cluster of neurons can form a CAM by sharing the same inputs, with each neuron responding to a different input pattern. The stored data is represented by the patterns which any of the neurons respond to. If any neuron in the cluster fires when a pattern is presented to the cluster, the pattern is contained in the CAM. Otherwise it is not. You could, conceptually, have a "John Smith" neuron—and other neurons which respond to other input patterns.

An important variant of the CAM allows you to present somewhat erroneous input data or only a part of an input pattern. If the CAM includes the pattern, it will provide the complete, correct data. A spell-checker is an example of a software implementation of such a feature. If words presented to it are not found in the dictionary, the closest candidate words are presented. Neurons naturally form this type of CAM because they typically fire faster the closer the input pattern is to their stored data pattern, rather than only when their input pattern is perfectly matched. In a cluster of neurons, when a pattern is presented, many neurons may fire at rates proportional to how their stored pattern matches the input.

Human brains definitely possess this type of content-addressable memory as we can easily demonstrate. "For scor nd sven yrs ago…" You have only been provided with an erroneous input pattern (the words) and have no difficulty retrieving the correct pattern—at least to the extent your CAM already contains, "Four score and seven years ago…". This is a relatively high-level example. At lower levels, you have CAMs which are continuously receiving input from your eyes and retrieving the best matches for objects they detect in your visual field. CAMs might detect corners, for example, and cascade to other CAMs which detect triangles.

As you read this, the input signals created by your retinas are sent to CAMs which return letters, and these letter-related signals are passed to CAMs which match letter-sequences into words. Because your CAMs respond with a closest match, they usually respond with something, even if it is wrong. For example, if text is just a little too small to read, your CAMs do not return "nothing", they return their "best guess" about the letters you see, based on the given input. Some instances may return erroneous letters, but these errors may be masked by subsequent searches into word CAMs, which retrieve words even if a few letters are incorrect. This is one reason why proofreading is difficult for most people. Your CAMs are continuously retrieving the closest match of some legitimate word and you are often not even aware that erroneous characters were encountered.

Consider: A7 F1R57 17 15 H4RD 70 R34D 7H15...7H3N 17 G375 34513R.

Artificial neural networks have effectively emulated CAMs and have demonstrated that a cluster of simulated, fully interconnected neurons tends to act as a CAM more or less spontaneously. On the other hand, there are other searching techniques which are dramatically more efficient.

By using indexing techniques and sophisticated search algorithms, a Google search is dramatically faster on a vastly larger dataset. Google searches essentially treat the entire web as a single CAM. You present some content, and Google returns pages containing that content. Google can search something like 10,000 petabytes of information—recall that one petabyte is the outside estimate of the capacity of the human brain—and can complete a search in a fraction of a second.

Here are a few observations about how you store and retrieve information in your own memory.

You will find that you store information in clusters of images or phrases. If you are presented with a part of the cluster, your brain will spontaneously fill in the rest. For instance, if you hear, "Mary had a little," then "lamb" will come to mind.

You will also observe that the amount of data in a cluster is fairly limited and information which is larger than a single cluster must be broken into multiple clusters to be remembered. For example, when I memorized the entire Gettysburg Address, which is clearly longer than a single cluster, I broke it down into multiple bite-sized chunks and then could string the chunks together when I recited the speech.

In the area of CAMs, today's computer wins. The computer can store data chunks of virtually unlimited size and complexity and retrieve them almost instantaneously. A spell-checker can improve on the speed and accuracy of most people's ability to proofread—looking up letter-clusters in a dictionary and finding matches or closest-matches faster and more repeatably than most people.

Associative memory

The brain also has the ability to create chains of associations. In the same way that "lamb" was associated with "Mary", "2+2" can be associated with "4".

Associative memory can be looked at as an extension of a CAM which returns not only the data representing the complete, correct input data pattern but also an additional data pattern which is associated with it. Functionally, associative memories can be most easily visualized in terms of the software of a relational database. That is, you could submit a query which returns a person's phone number given their name.

Chains of associations can control a human's or an AGI's behavior. In a biological associative memory, an associated data item could often be a value of "goodness", reflecting the change in the organism's well-being at the time the data item was stored. For example, being fed is "good", being sick isn't. Now images or odors of specific potential foods can be associated with a relative value of how they affected us. Although many things don't have a qualitative association, those that do create an instant response. The aroma of baking bread is "good" and the odor of a skunk isn't. You don't have to think about your reaction, it just happens. Your brain simply accepts the odor input pattern and retrieves the association. Visual inputs can have a similar effect. The unexpected image of an object coming at you at high speed is bad, you have no control over it—you put your hands in front of your face and duck. If you see a face, your visual pattern recognition can identify the facial expressions and you have an immediate associated reaction to a smile or a frown.

Pavlov demonstrated that the brain can learn new associative memory relationships. He showed that when he offered his dog some food, it salivated. If he rang a bell as he offered the food, the dog salivated. Eventually, if he just rang the bell, the dog salivated. Bells and food have no intrinsic association but he was able to build one in the dog's associative memory by presenting these stimuli at the same time.

Your brain can also build chains of associations—chains which associate one item with another then another, until eventually you wind up with a primitive reaction. You perhaps like (or don't like) a red shirt because it is associated with something which is associated with something which happened when you were a child—something which had a substantial positive (or negative) effect on you. You need not be aware of the intermediate associations, you just know that you like (or don't like) the shirt. Your brain can also associate multiple types of input—for example, you can associate the sound of a voice with the image of a face. When you hear the voice, your associative memory will retrieve a representation of the image.

Knowledge

We know things. We know about physical objects such as balls or flowers. Objects have attributes like color (red, yellow, etc.) and size (big, small, etc.). Objects can also perform actions like motion or collision. An object can have any number of attributes but when you consider describing an object, you'll often run out of description after just a few adjectives.

We don't know how the brain stores knowledge, but we can make an educated conjecture based on content-addressable and associative memory.

We could imagine a brain's knowledge model with individual neurons corresponding to individual objects. Each object neuron has synapses connecting it to the neurons representing the object's attributes, and vice versa. So I might have a neuron representing a red ball, and another representing a yellow ball. The red ball neuron would have a connection to the neuron which represented "red" and a connection to a generic "ball" neuron which might have further connections to round, bouncy, etc. The yellow ball neuron would have a connection to a "yellow" neuron and a connection to "ball" as well.

Stimulating either object neuron would cause all the attribute neurons to fire. Similarly, because the connections are two-way, I can ask you to think of yellow objects and several will come to mind, including the yellow ball.

In AI, there is a software genre called "semantic networks" which are often used as knowledge representation systems. I will stick with calling them "neurons" and "connections" but in computer science lingo, a semantic network is a "graph" which is a collection of "nodes" or "vertices" with "edges" connecting. In a semantic network, connections imply some type of relationship between two nodes. Semantic networks have been used in AI to store information such as taxonomies or lexicons.

For example, you might have a node labelled "tree" and another named "plant" and a unidirectional connection labeled "is-a". This would represent the knowledge that a tree is a plant but not the other way around: a plant is not necessarily a tree. With thousands of entries, an

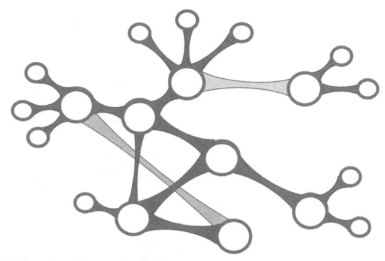

Without knowing specifics, we can observe that the brain stores knowledge based on relationships. This might be represented by a graph of nodes and edges.

entire taxonomy of living things could be represented in this type of network. Another example is "WordNet[22]", which is a database of 155,327 English words with synonym relationships.

A distinction between the AI semantic network and the brain is that most semantic networks have information contained within each node or connection which indicates what it means. For example, the "ball" and "red" neurons mentioned above. In the brain, neurons don't have labels. There may well be a neuron which represents "ball", but there is no way to tell what a given neuron represents except, perhaps, by stimulating it with an electrode and asking the brain what it was thinking when the neuron fired—not a very practical approach.

The objects above both have the attribute of "ball" and the ball neuron has a collection of common ("default") attributes, so an object which is only known as a ball can be assumed to be spherical, bouncy, used-in-sport/game, etc. Different people will have different default attributes for "ball". I might think of a baseball while you might think of a basketball. Objects might also include exceptions to default attributes—an American football might override the "spherical" default attribute but still have the used-in-sport attribute.

The figure shows how the knowledge store of the brain might be structured. If you see a red ball, neurons representing "ball" and "red" might fire. These are connected to neurons representing the word "ball" (and also to the word "ballon" if you also speak French). In turn, they're

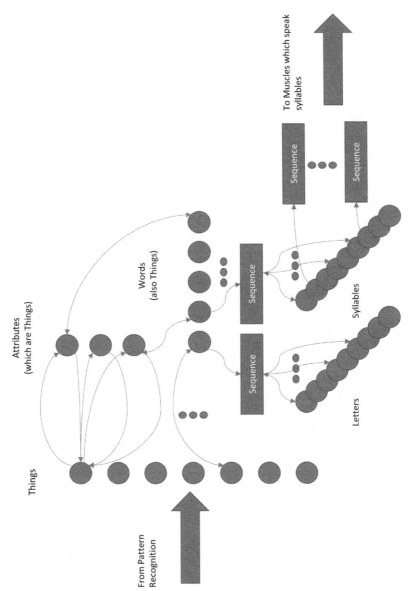

A schematic representation of "knowledge". Things have attributes including references to words which define the thing. Words also have attributes including the sequence of letters which spell the word and the sequence of syllables with which we say the word.

connected to sequences of letters (because you know how to spell both) and sequences of phonemes (because you also know how to pronounce both). Because you have been thinking about a red ball, if you now hear the word "red", you may also think of a ball. The "red" neuron could be one which fires whenever any red object is perceived.

Recognizing people

One of the things brains are good at is recognizing people. If we know a person, our brains contain attributes of that person. The stored attributes about their appearance—face shape, nose, eyes, hair—allow us to recognize them when we see them again. Attributes about our relationships with people allow us to recall what our friends look like even when they are not present. Studies (and facial recognition software) lead us to believe that faces can be described in about 50 attributes[23] and that it is unlikely that your brain can reliably recognize more than a few thousand faces.

When you see a face, your pattern recognition neurons locate various features of the face and present these features to the knowledge store. Usually, these will relate only to one person (if you know them) or no people (if the face is a stranger). Your mind may also recall people with some similar facial features. In the case of identical twins, it might represent two people, which most of us find a bit confusing. If you meet a stranger, your brain can "allocate" a neuron to represent that person and adjust connections to all their facial attributes. If you learn their name, your brain can add connections to the words already in place which represent common names, or allocate a new one for a name you've not encountered before—a more complex and time-consuming action.

Sequences

Our knowledge store clearly has the ability to store sequences. We can recall that one thing can follow another so we can mentally store phone numbers, word spellings, poems, etc. We can also remember sequences of actions—that one thing follows another. If you drop a glass, it falls, then it hits the floor, then it breaks, then you have pieces, which may be sharp, which cut your finger. So you can equate dropping an object with the potential for an unpleasant result.

We can deduce from observing what we can recognize that sequences in your brain are a maximum of five to 10 items long. If you need to remember longer sequences, your brain seems to cut them up into smaller sequences and then store sequences of sequences. If you want to spell "antidisestablishmentarianism", your brain breaks the word into its component sequences (anti, dis, etc.) and then remembers the

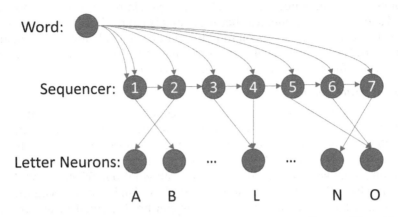

A "sequencer" built of neurons. Each neuron in the "Sequencer" row will fire only after receiving two pulses: one pulse from the "word" neuron and one from the preceding neuron in the sequencer. So when the word neuron fires once, the "letter" neurons will fire in order to spell the word. Imagine that each letter neuron is connected to sequences of muscle contractions which would move fingers to type the individual letters. When the "1" neuron fires, it will cause you to type a "B" as the first letter followed by "A". Can you see what word will be typed?

sequence of these component sequences. We don't have many common words over 10 letters.

In the brain, sequences need to be stored in multiple neurons because the synapses which connect one neuron to others don't have a particular order, they are all simultaneous. If a "ball" neuron is connected to the "b", "a", and "l" neurons, firing the ball neuron won't give you information on how to spell the word. In the figure, I have hypothesized a "sequencer" circuit built of neurons. It could allow the storage of a sequence of items, in this case the spelling of a word. You can see that storing a sequence of attributes is more complex than simply storing a set of attributes for an object.

In a computer implementation, this added complexity is not needed because computer storage always has an intrinsic order. All the "sequencer" circuitry can be replaced by a single bit to indicate that a set of connections are sequential vs. simultaneous. For a ball object neuron, the connections to round and bouncy are simultaneous, while the ball *word* neuron has connections to B A L & L which are sequential.

Language

We can use our language to express our knowledge but we shouldn't confuse our language with the underlying knowledge—that is, the words we use to express knowledge are attributes of objects. Words are also objects in their own right. If we have the concept of ball, the word "ball" is one of its attributes. A truly multilingual person can know multiple "word" attributes (for different languages) associated with any individual object. Word neurons connect to sequences of phoneme neurons, which would fire chains of muscle contractions to say the word. Word neurons might also connect to sequences of letter neurons in order to represent spelling and so on. Individual letters are also objects which have multiple attributes describing how they are written, or appear in print, the word that's used to say the letter, etc. So you can see that there is a considerable amount of information just surrounding the single word, "ball". There can also be knowledge without word attributes—babies know things before they learn any language.

The knowledge system works in many ways. When you see a ball, your "ball" neuron will fire. But you'll also fire the "ball" neuron when you either hear the phonemes for the word "ball" or you read the letters: b-a-l-l. Also, when the "ball" neuron fires, it is connected to every occurrence of every ball you've ever encountered which links to the related situations. So any individual word will cause a large amount of related information to come forth in your mind.

You can also speak the thoughts in your brain because of the links to sequences which contain the phonemes for words. Your cerebellum has learned how to operate the muscles in your vocal tract to create the sounds.

You can also read aloud—converting sequences of printed letters to words and then to phonemes. All the time, neurons representing objects and attributes will be firing in your brain as you attempt to understand what you're reading. Similarly, you can take dictation, converting phonemes you hear into writing.

Translating from one language to another was one of AI's early attempts—programs tried to do word-for-word translations. But the human brain doesn't work that way. Assuming you are fluent in two languages, when you hear or read information in one language, your brain interprets it and brings to bear all the understanding you have of the underlying objects related to the words. With this understanding, your brain then assembles the same meaning for expression in the second language. Because your brain includes all of your own reaction and understanding of the underlying meaning, two translations will not be identical if done by different people.

Presuming you can't read Arabic, you'll see this as "indeterminate writing". Your brain gets enough pattern matches to presume that this must be a sequence of characters of some sort, but can't determine the meaning or even the individual characters. [Public domain.]

Your knowledge store does its best to interpret the input it is given. When you see the text in the figure, you presume it is text based on a number of cues: it's in a book, it's black and white, it's a complex sequence, it's not an image of any physical object you recognize, etc. You also know that it's *not* Chinese, Japanese, German, etc. So your brain extracts a considerable amount of information, even from an unintelligible input.

How much knowledge

We *can* use statistics about language to draw some conclusions about the size of our knowledge store based on the size of our language. The size of the language is related to the number of different things we can have knowledge about. When we have knowledge which cannot be expressed in our language, we expand the language with new words. We don't have many words which don't represent anything.

Even though languages have much larger numbers of available words, an "average" person knows about 42,000 different words[24]. From foreign language courses, you could conclude that most knowledge can be expressed in a much smaller vocabulary of just a few thousand words. I speculate that you can know thousands of different types of things, modified by tens or hundreds of attributes. You might also know 1,000 people modified by 50 appearance attributes and 50 other attributes like their name, spouse, age, clothing you've seen them in, etc.

Your entire brain knowledge capacity might consist of a large number of objects (perhaps millions but not billions), each with hundreds of attributes. This may seem like a lot of information but to a modern relational database system, it is not excessive—on the order of a hundred million items. Recall that there are 16 billion neurons in the neocortex, so being able to know one billion things would be an outside maximum. We'll factor in that significant portions of your brain are occupied with vision, hearing, and other thinking tasks in addition to just storing knowledge. Additionally, we'll presume that several biological neurons would be required per object of knowledge—that the models given here are simpler than your actual brain.

To memorize the Bible, you'd need about 12,000 word neurons for the different words, but we won't count these because they are also needed for other language processes. Then we'll need about 100,000 sequencers (each referencing about seven words) to reference the 783,137 words in the text. You'd need perhaps 30,000 additional sequences of sequences which would represent verses. These might have additional attributes, so you could memorize the Bible with perhaps 900,000 objects—many fewer than you might think. This is to illustrate that if your brain can store *only* a billion objects, that's over a thousand Bibles, which is a lot of knowledge!

Can we do this with computers?

This description of knowledge representation is based on what we can observe about human action, rather than what we've observed about the internal workings of the brain. We can imagine that all this knowledge is stored in a brain's associative memory in an unstructured sort of way (at one end of the spectrum) or that there is a lot of structure (as described above). The first possibility has the advantage of not requiring a lot of brain specialization and so fits our observation of the neocortex's generally uniform structure. More complex brain structures are progressively unlikely, so the brain's actual function is probably in between.

To get a more biologically accurate picture, we'd assume that each "neuron" described here is necessarily implemented by several physical neurons which would coordinate the problems of learning and multiple repetitions needed to store new knowledge. It also provides a level of redundancy needed to maintain knowledge as neurons age and fail. We would presume that the brain uses its ability to do massive searches in parallel, which eliminates the need for the complex sorted structures which a more sequential algorithm would require.

Could AGI computers do this? Absolutely! The quantity of data I estimated in the previous paragraphs amounts to a tiny fraction of today's CPU capacity.

First, although I have used the concept of neurons and the knowledge store would include millions of identical neurons, this model is not closely related to artificial neural networks or deep learning. This approach is more closely aligned with semantic nets—a different genre of AI software.

A computer has the tremendous advantage over the human brain that it doesn't need multiple repetitions to store new information. A single presentation of new information is all that will be needed for a computer to store all the relationships (connections) implied. The robot can learn, at a glance, all there is to be learned from a given scene.

How might this be programmed? Let's first consider a knowledge store of 10 million items which is fully preprogrammed and doesn't learn (we'll address that in a moment). Each neuron is assigned a number, from one to 10 million. Interestingly, all the information is contained in the connections; the neurons themselves need not contain any information at all. To learn what a given neuron means, the program will need to follow its connections, just as in the brain.

Each connection includes the numbers of the two neurons it connects and perhaps a few properties of importance, directionality, etc. Assuming one hundred edges per node, this multiplies out to about 12GB of memory—small enough to keep in RAM on a high-end desktop computer. We can use an index to access the connection list in either direction very quickly. Algorithms could access the knowledge store by following chains of connections—a task which can operate in parallel on multiple cores or multiple parallel computers. Neurons only gain meaning because of connections to other neurons containing previously received external input or to neurons which create external behaviors. When the "red ball" neuron fires, the connections to the signals seen by the system when a red ball was encountered can recreate the image.

When the ability to learn new knowledge is added to this mix, things get a bit more complicated. Now the nodes themselves need information such as the number of times a node was used and the last time it was accessed. That way, the relative importance of nodes can help determine what to remember and what to forget. Otherwise, the knowledge store fills up quickly with the first information it encounters, rather than with the most useful or valuable information it encounters. The good news here is that both brains and robots will spend a high proportion of their time retrieving existing knowledge and less time storing new knowledge. So it's OK that the algorithm for storing information will be significantly more complex. It will need to determine what to store, where to store it, what to forget, what are all the connections, and how to keep all those necessary indexes in order.

Would a smaller knowledge store be useful? Probably. Could such a knowledge store be fast enough to be useful on today's hardware? Absolutely! Would it be human-like? Maybe... What do we do with our knowledge? What will robots do? Read on.

[21] http://clas.mq.edu.au/speech/acoustics/speech_spectra/vowels.html

[22] https://en.wikipedia.org/wiki/WordNet

[23] https://www.smithsonianmag.com/science-nature/how-does-your-brain-recognize-faces-180963583/

[24] http://www.sciencemag.org/news/2016/08/average-20-year-old-american-knows-42000-words-depending-how-you-count-them

Chapter 11:

Modeling, Simulation, and Imagination

What you see is not what your eyes see. Consider this:

A

Do you see the "A"? Of course! But your eyes themselves only see a collection of "pixels", some black, some white. The front-end processing of your retina and visual cortex receives the pixels, analyzes them, finds boundaries and corners, matches these against your knowledge store of possible images and returns the match for "A". You cannot see the pixel pattern yourself because what *you* see only comes into play *after* all the visual processing.

Likewise, you cannot see the "A" in the abstract... you can only see it in physical relationship to yourself and things which surround it. As part of the visual processing, your brain has not only found the "A" but has determined its distance and direction from you. If you focus your attention on the lines below the "A", the "A" doesn't move. The image at your retina changes substantially as your eyes move to the line below— but the "A" is in a stable position. In fact, if you turn your head and look off to the side, you know that "A" is still there, waiting for you.

Our brains build and continuously maintain a model of the environment which surrounds us, a world model which is continuously changing. Without looking, you have a good idea of what's behind you. If you close your eyes, you are still aware of this text in front of you, even though you no longer have a way of sensing it. Your world model is three-dimensional, and you are at the center. And while the model may contain images, it seems to be built of three-dimensional objects. Even though you might not be able to see a complete object, in your mind-model, the entire object is there.

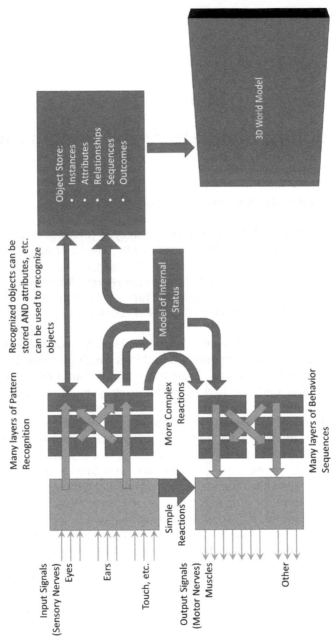

Data flow in your brain: From sensory input through pattern recognition, to the knowledge store which can recognize objects that are then placed (by reference) in your mind's 3D world model.

As you are reading this, the book or screen you are reading partially obscures what is behind it. If I am holding a book in my hand, I can only see my thumb while my fingers are hidden by the book. My mind assumes that the fingers are there, even though they are hidden. From the view of the thumb, my mind has recognized *my* hand and knows about the entire object, even though only a bit of it is visible.

The 3D model is what you see. If you hold your hand in front of you and rotate it, you see a rotating hand. You are not conscious of the complex pattern of fingers appearing and disappearing as your hand rotates. Your entire visual field is filled with objects. As you walk through the park, the objects might be trees, sky, other people. But you'll see everything in relation to your position. As you move, all the objects may change position relative to you but your brain compensates so you know that it is you that is moving and not the trees. You can enter a room, then close your eyes and remember enough about the positions of furniture, etc. to cautiously find your way through.

The visual pattern recognition hardware in your brain processes the input from your eyes before objects are placed in the 3D model. It analyzes the image, looking for lines, corners and shading to build shapes. Then shapes which may be quite complex are looked up in the knowledge store to interpret them as objects. A few simple three-dimensional objects which partially obscure each other present a vastly more complex two-dimensional image than the concept of a few objects. Your mind, in converting the 2D image from your retina to 3D objects has to make many assumptions, and these assumptions are the source of numerous optical illusions. Since your retina is a two-dimensional sensing device and the three-dimensional cues of binocular vision are quite limited, photos, TV, and movies are quite effective in causing your visual processing system to perceive a realistic 3D image, even though these are clearly 2D media. Even a 3D movie is just two 2D movies running simultaneously and presenting slightly different images to your two eyes.

Your eyes' high-resolution visual field is quite small, seeing an area about the size of your thumbnail at arm's length. You can only see objects in detail if they are centered in your visual field. So your eyes dart from detail to detail in the image the world presents to you. Your mind converts these details into objects, or parts of objects, and then updates the mental model of your surroundings. You are unaware of your eyes' limited resolution because you are also generally unaware of moving your eyes. When your eyes move, the image they receive can change completely but your brain compensates. You don't perceive that the objects in your surroundings move and change when you move your eyes (or turn your head). Your brain assumes that most objects are in fixed positions while it is you that is moving.

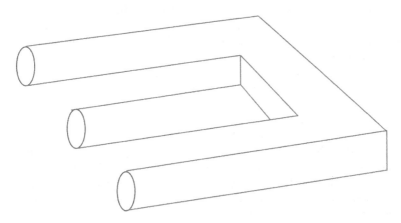

This well-known optical illusion is based on your brain's best efforts to interpret the 2D image received by your retinas into a 3D object. Your brain interprets either end of the object properly but cannot integrate the two interpretations except as the 2D line-drawing which it actually is.

The brain's internal model also merges sound with other sensory information. If you close your eyes and hear a sound, your brain will attempt to classify it and determine its direction and use this information to update the model as well. If you feel an object with your hands, you can mentally build a model of the object even if you can't see it.

The self-centeredness of the model will become an important concept later when some thoughts about self-awareness and consciousness are introduced, but for now we can see the advantage of knowing what is going on around us, not just the information our retinas are receiving at the moment.

How does this modeling mechanism work? We can speculate. The spatial modeling system operates after the pattern-recognition systems in the brain. As a result, much less information needs to be maintained in the spatial model. In fact, if you do not make a deliberate effort to notice and remember your surroundings, you probably cannot recall many details. Without looking, what is behind you right now? What is the color? What is the texture? When asked these questions, you are most likely tempted to look behind you to verify your memory and update your model. You have not remembered the *image* of what's behind you, you have remembered *objects*: perhaps books, bookshelf, etc. Because you know about objects rather than just an image, you can move to a different position within a room and your mental model can predict what images you should see.

We could imagine the mental mechanisms for modeling as an array of neurons in clusters which represent a more-or-less spatial distribution of different physical directions around us. These neurons would have a "working memory" model of storage so they could store information instantly but not for a very long time. Each cluster could contain an object's size and distance, along with enough information to recall the specific object from the knowledge store.

As you move your eyes, additional objects are painted into the model in order to provide additional detail. If you yourself move, the model could potentially move the objects it contains to compensate for your new position without having to rebuild the entire model from scratch.

To implement this type of model in computers, we can likewise create an array representing directions. We could add connections to objects which are seen at each direction to effectively place any object in the knowledge store at any location in the model. We could indicate that at physical location 5° right, 30° down, at a distance of 10 feet, there is a pointer to object 5278961 facing toward us. Object 5278961 is a pigeon, walking, which is a bird, gray with black markings, with a cooing sound.

This model as described is functional but may or may not bear any relationship to the actual biological mechanisms. But it has several attributes which make it useful. Such a modeling system can be updated rapidly from the eyes and other senses—and we know this to be true. Not only can you update your model as your eyes dart around to pick up details but you can walk from room to room and the model is updated in real time.

Further, relationships from the model can be stored in the knowledge store. If you see three trees together on your way to some destination, you can recognize them on your way back and find your way home, even though the pattern of the three trees may appear quite different coming

Text appears smaller when it's further away in three dimensions

Here we have some text in a rectangle which appears to be further away to the right. In actuality, it is tapered text in a trapezoid which is all the same distance away from you. Your mind initially makes the 3D assumptions because this is the most likely interpretation in the real world.

Google's Waymo self-driving cars build an internal 3D model of their environment, which is updated in real time as the vehicle moves— like this one from data from Velodyne Lidar sensors. [Image courtesy Waymo.]

from the other direction. You can remember where a water hole was and go there *and* where that lion was and perhaps *not* go there. As you move through your environment, you are continuously looking for things you recognize. Recognizing is usually a good thing, unknown is often not. As with all the recognition with closest match, there will be occasional errors. I speculate that *déjà vu* is the result of erroneous recognition. You get enough cues to match a stored situation in your knowledge store to give your mind the sensation that you've been there before, even though you have not.

Self-driving cars are already adept at this kind of modeling. To evaluate how well computers could perform this task, consider a first-person game. The lion's share of the computation going on in the game is involved in creating the screen images *from* the model; your computer can create and modify the model easily. Allies, enemies, tools, goals, can all change position within the model. In the game, the computer has a static model of a preprogrammed environment and usually adds a number of mobile objects into the mix. For an AGI computer to maintain a similar model of a real-world environment is not difficult or tremendously compute-intensive. It is the recognition of objects from the two-dimensional input which is difficult.

Simulation/imagination

With the abilities presented so far, we have reached a level where an organism can learn to recognize objects, to react to inputs and improve its ability to interact with its environment. Perhaps your dog can do all these things; perhaps it can do even more. We are now prepared to take the next step up the intellectual ladder and consider the mechanisms of foresight.

There is a tremendous advantage in your being able to view a situation and not only see whether it is presently favorable or dangerous, but also to foresee how a situation will evolve so you can determine whether it will be favorable or dangerous in the future. If you are a hunter and have no foresight, you must rely on brute force, power and speed alone. With the ability to predict the future (even only slightly), you can rely on cunning. As your foresight becomes more developed, you may be able to create the tools and teamwork you need to defeat animals which are larger and more powerful than you are. With even more foresight, you can see how plants and animals grow and see how you can domesticate them, leading to the survival advantages of changing from a hunter-gatherer to a farmer.

There can be little argument to the concept that the ability to predict the future—even in a limited way—confers a tremendous evolutionary advantage. But, how can the process work?

The same type of functionality which allows us to model a situation can be used for simulation. Say our knowledge store includes not only a situation, but also an association to events which follow that situation. When we reencounter a precursor event, our knowledge store can retrieve the end-result before it actually occurs. And since memories are attached to changes in well-being, we know whether or not the situation was beneficial to us. Further, if these results are fed back into the modeling system, we can take a situation we know about and predict the results in our environment. We can "see" the results of our imagination.

For a simple example, once you have observed numerous falling objects, you can easily predict what will happen next when you see an object start to fall. You don't need to know the physics of gravity or the principal that an unsupported object accelerates downwards. It's just that your knowledge store, when presented with an unsupported object, matches with results of previous similar observations and returns an association with the object at a lower location in the near future.

For a more complex example, put yourself in the position of a primitive, weaponless hunter pursuing a small animal. Your knowledge store contains the information about the benefit of actually catching the quarry. Also you've chased lots of animals (all your life) so your knowledge store knows they're quicker than you and they tend to dart for cover where you can lose them—simply chasing them doesn't work. Your spatial model contains the immediate terrain so you know where the hiding places are. If you see yourself as moving in your spatial model,

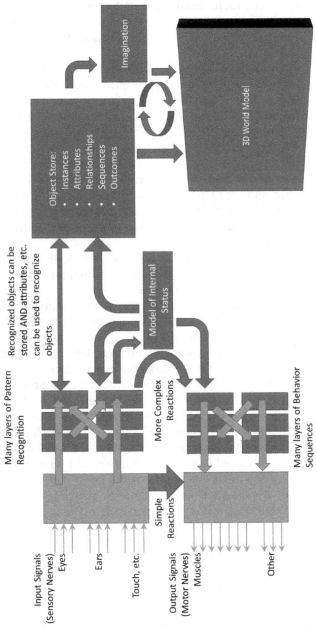

It is likely your imagination works by taking objects from your knowledge store and inserting them into your 3D world model.

you can make presumptions about your quarry's next movement, get there first and win.

I observe that when I am using my imagination, my modeling system is not in full contact with my senses. I can daydream and let my mind wander. When I'm imagining things, I have shut off much of the input from the outside. There is a sort of selector which enables input into the modeling system from my imagination and disables most of the input from my senses so I do not get confused between real and imagined input. If this switching system were to fail, I would become delusional because I would not be able to differentiate information received from my eyes from information which I recall from other parts of my brain. The fact that there *are* delusional people lends plausibility to the idea that such a mechanism exists in our brains (and it sometimes fails).

It seems reasonable that imagination takes place in the same actual mental hardware as the modeling center, although we don't know because we aren't sure where these processes occur specifically in the brain. With the shared-hardware approach we seem to have, we are either imagining things or seeing them; in order for us to do planning, we need to shut off most other input. We are in a position to be thinking *or* acting but it is difficult to be doing both at the same time.

This configuration certainly requires less processing hardware since we can share the important functions of spatial modeling and simulation without also needing entirely different brain sections devoted to them. Further, it seems evolutionarily likely. Rather than a big new special portion of the brain springing forth which gives us the gift of imagination, we simply need a modest modification in the modeling function. When the modeling system and memory are large enough, we simply need to have the facility to differentiate between what is coming from our senses and what is being driven from our imagination. It also seems likely that the modeling and simulation functions happen in the frontal lobes of the brain. When lobotomies were being performed, patients seemed to lose their ability to plan for the future or even to be aware of it.

When we are thinking about everyday problems, we can imagine possible courses of action. The situation is passed into the model in our minds and then candidate solutions come from the CAM—what can I do in this situation? These run through the model and are passed back for association with further situations. Each potential solution is related to the problem because our memories are driven by associations with the current input. This process repeats until a thought appears which, after simulation, is associated in the knowledge store with an improved state. Then we act on the thought.

Summarizing, you begin with your current situation. Your brain proposes several possible courses of action and chooses the best. Consider a chess game. You know the positions of the pieces on the board. You mind selects possible moves and matches them against previously known positions which are associated with winners or losers. If a winner is found, you make the move. If no match is found, you might consider additional possible moves following moves which are not known losers.

Where are "you" in this picture? At the center of the model. Since the model is built on your current surroundings, you feel yourself to be somewhere behind your eyes. In actuality, we know that your visual processing is performed at the very back of your brain, but the feeling of where you are is based on how the model is updated. You see the scene in front of you and the objects in your immediate vicinity. When you imagine things (using the same mental hardware), it is also a scene in front of you—you always have a viewpoint onto anything you imagine.

Computers can do simulations, people can do simulations. Are they comparable? Not really. Computer simulations are usually numerical extensions of physical (or financial) situations. My mind's simulations can draw on everything in my brain's knowledge store and so I can make associations and analogies beyond the scope of any of today's computer simulations.

My brain's simulations always have "me" at the focus. If I imagine an injury, "I" can feel the pain. If I am thinking about an AGI system, "I" am always there looking on. All of the mental simulations are tied to changes in well-being for "me". We can't avoid that, our mental hardware was built that way—the entire brain is a survival tool and it's only useful in that context to the extent that it benefits ourselves (and our progeny).

Computer simulations are different at the outset because there is no well-being or reproductive advantage for them to improve. If I look out the window and my rapid simulation tells me it will be a nice day (or rainy), this is always in the context of me, how it will feel to me, what actions I need to take in response, etc. If today's computer simulates the weather, the computer itself and its reaction to the weather (or even the quality of the simulated result) are simply not a part of the simulation.

Although computer simulations don't typically work the way mental simulations do, there is no reason they could not. But it could be a substantial disadvantage for a computer simulation to be colored by a computer's "own" reactions. There is a real value in impersonal spreadsheets and weather predictions. But in robots and computers with human interactions, a sense of "well-being" (which could incorporate an estimate of the well-being of the user) could be added to the system and the computer's predictions and actions could be focused on what impact they would have on this overall well-being.

Although computer and human simulations of the future use different techniques, it is not clear which is handling more data. A number-crunching supercomputer doing a weather simulation may operate at a similar level of processing as your brain does when deciding what to have for lunch. Or perhaps hundreds of times more or less—we don't know. It is clear that all the knowledge in your brain lets you bring much more disparate information to bear on any problem you address.

Paying attention

Since you can keep track of information which comes from your memory (imagination) and which comes from your senses (reality), this selection function might also allow you to prioritize some senses or objects over others. This prioritization may be the mechanism behind paying attention.

You can focus on reading a book at the expense of other senses. The content of the book also drives your imagination to related thoughts. Your imagination may even grab your attention away from the book. You may begin thinking about related topics which then meander off into a daydream. Even while you're daydreaming (or asleep), the part of your brain processing audio input is still working enough for you to respond to your name—sort of like the key words: "Alexa", "OK Google", "Hey Siri", or "Hey Cortana". Eventually, some sensory input may focus your brain back on the real world.

I surmise that we need the ability to pay attention because our brains don't have the capacity to address more than a few things at a time. You can watch a movie with sound which uses your vision and hearing simultaneously because the two inputs are related. But if you try to read an eBook while simultaneously listening to a different audiobook, you'll have difficulty comprehending either. If you give mental priority to one, you can probably follow it somewhat at the expense of the other.

Implementing this capability on a computer doesn't appear to be very difficult. Prioritizing one data stream or processing task over another is something computers have done for decades—and for similar reasons. If your computer's camera is processing input, keyboard and mouse input are prioritized so as not to interfere with the video stream.

While paying attention seems like a valuable capability for the human brain, it is not clear to me that it will be necessary in AGIs. Perhaps the computer will be able to pay attention to all its inputs simultaneously. Perhaps it *could* read a book and listen to a different audiobook simultaneously. This depends on the software efficiency and the relative computer power required for the various processes described in these chapters. Perhaps your brain is so busy handling all its inputs that there is only a tiny amount of capacity left over for paying attention. In this case, you can only pay attention to a few things at a time while a computer could pay attention to everything simultaneously. On the other hand, if paying attention requires a huge amount of processing power, AGIs will be more like humans in thinking about only one or two things at a time.

Abstract reasoning

Abstract reasoning may be no different from the processes of imagination and searching for solutions to problems which were presented above.

Computers could have a rudimentary level of abstract reasoning through the following general process in playing chess and proving mathematical theorems. The computer is given a set of axioms, the rules of the game, and the target which it seeks to reach—checkmate, or the object of the mathematical proof. A symbolic notation is devised, which the computer can apply in order to follow the given rules. In the simplest case, the program simply blunders randomly, applying axioms to the given parameters until it (hopefully) stumbles on the target. Then it can retrieve the series of steps to produce a move leading to checkmate or a proof. In more sophisticated programs, the computer can apply the axioms in an orderly process. Further, the computer could analyze the position it has reached in order to reduce the number of searches it must make. But in general, we could agree that the computer pursuing this type of "abstract reasoning" has no understanding whatsoever about the game of chess or the field of mathematics.

Although little is actually known about how humans go about the same process, clearly we do not examine nearly as many possibilities as the computers do. Instead, we are able to "trim the search tree" very severely at very early stages. In playing chess, we know that a certain piece in a certain position is very "powerful" or is pinning down an opponent's piece, so we simply do not consider possibilities which include moving that piece. Further, we learn to analyze the strength of a particular position and "feel" that certain moves are going to be powerful while others will be weak. Similarly, in proving theorems in mathematics, we can "feel" that certain avenues of thinking will be useful while others are likely to be dead-ends.

Some would say this "feeling" which makes humans successful at solving abstract reasoning problems is based on our understanding of the situation and is something the computer will not be able to duplicate. But a reasonable case can be made that this "feeling" is based on our broad knowledge store. That is to say, when we are presented with a problem, we can instantly determine that this problem is similar in some ways to problems which we have encountered and solved previously. It is simply another application of the content-addressable knowledge hardware, which we know the brain possesses, and which improves with experience as more and more knowledge is stored.

The chess master can recall positions in hundreds or thousands of previously played games, along with the associated knowledge that some were winners and others were not. As he is simulating possible plays in his mind, he applies a possible move to the simulation in his mind and can immediately know if the new position is similar to one which he recognizes as a winner. If so, he makes the move and wins (assuming his pattern-matching was correct). If not, he either mentally pursues additional moves along this line or mentally tries out different ideas altogether. Experience improves the chess player's ability as he is able to recognize more positions and their relative strength more accurately.

The "understanding" of the game (or the math) is brought to the table by other factors. The human chess player's internal modeling system is directly related to the world which affects him. He interprets the chess game or the mathematical proof as a part of the world, not as the *entire world*, which is the "viewpoint" of today's computer solving the same problem. He sees the chess game in the context of its relationship to himself. The chess player knows how winning the game will make him feel. Winning will make him happier than losing—his feeling of well-being will be affected. So, he strives to win. There might be a prize if he wins or advancement to higher levels of tournaments and eventual prizes or recognition. He has primitive associations of being a better competitor with more food, better shelter, or better mates. He doesn't need to think about competition, it is inbred simply because humans who were not natural competitors at some level were eliminated from the gene pool.

The mathematician, on his way to proving something which will get him great academic recognition, tenure, and a comfortable life, understands how success will change his life. The "understanding" of the problem depends not just on the syntax of the problem and its solution but extends to how the problem fits into the world and will affect the well-being of the person investigating the problem.

Acting on your imagination

When I learned to play the guitar, my neocortex went to considerable effort to teach my cerebellum what to do. "Why and how?" you might ask.

The why is as described above. In simulating the future, I obviously felt in my imagination that a future which included playing the guitar would improve my well-being. To examine the why of that, we'd need to

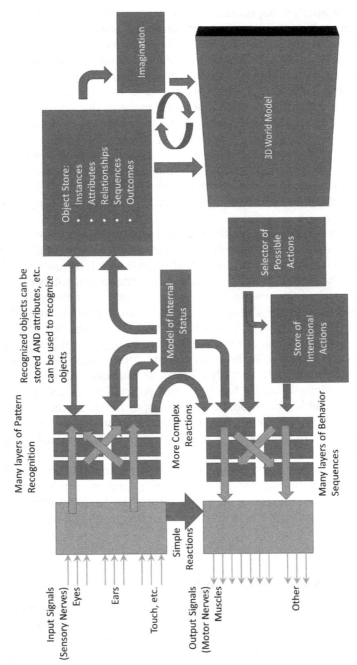

The complete model of everything needed to implement an AGI system.

examine all of my knowledge store content to see aspects of enjoying music, enjoying playing for myself, enjoying performing, etc.

Given the objective, how do we achieve it? My knowledge store knows that in order to play a guitar, I'll need to have one. Do I buy? Borrow? Steal? Buying seems easiest. A great guitar? A cheap guitar? How about a cheap one until I know I like to play. How about some lessons? Why not start with a tutorial book and a chord chart first? Lessons could come later. So, given that I have a guitar and a book, I follow the directions to tune the guitar and try out a chord.

My neocortex can read the book and look at the figures so I can hold the guitar and begin to place fingers, one at a time, to make a chord. After a few tries, I can get it right... let's try another. A few more tries and I have a second chord... what was the first one? Another minute or two and I can strum the first one again.

All the time my neocortex is laboriously placing fingers to produce chords, the 56 billion neurons in my cerebellum are secretly learning to remember what I'm doing. After hundreds of repetitions of my neocortex asking my middle finger to move to the second fret of the second string, my cerebellum can begin to do it for me. And it gets faster and easier. In fact, it learns to move multiple fingers simultaneously—something my neocortex never seemed to be able to do.

After many thousands of repetitions, my cerebellum is taking over more and more of the process. After years, I got pretty good at playing the guitar. All the time, my imagination is maintaining the simulation of what it would be like to be able to play the guitar so I continue the laborious process of practice.

Conclusion

This closes the loop of a set of functionality which leads to thinking as I understand it. I have presented examples so you can observe them for yourself and have speculated on biologically plausible mechanisms which could implement them in neurons.

I believe this set of functionality is sufficient to create an AGI system which will appear to have real-world intelligence. I'll walk through a few more examples in Chapter 12.

In the next chapter, I contend that when you observe how such an AGI acts, that it will appear to be a conscious entity with free will.

Chapter 12:

Free Will and Consciousness

Will future computers be conscious entities? Will they have free will? Or will they just be simulating these capabilities?

A popular argument against computers being able to think in a way analogous to humans goes like this.

We humans are conscious beings and have free will and these are essential to our thinking. Computers are mechanisms which run the same way every time and therefore cannot have free will. Computers are made of materials which cannot possess the essence of consciousness. Therefore, without free will and consciousness, computers will never be able to think.

With the discussion of free will and consciousness, we have reached the pinnacle of human mental processes and also a point of philosophical discussion.

To me, the question devolves into one of whether or not you accept modern physics as describing reality. While there are certainly areas of physics which are yet to be discovered, the essential point is that any physical system can be represented by information which can be replicated in computers. If what we observe in the electrochemistry of the brain includes consciousness and free will, then there is no reason a computer cannot equally possess these capabilities as well. If we believe there is some unobserved essential "magic", then we have a choice. Either the magic will eventually be observed, defined as a part of physics and included in computers OR the magic is beyond the scope of observation, meaning it is outside the scope of any future conceivable physics.

My contention is that human thought is the sum total of a multiplicity of general mental functions working in parallel on an unimaginably large scale. These functions were presented in the last few chapters, and each function can be described and understood. Some of these functions are already working in computers at levels higher than in humans and those that are not, conceivably, could be in the near future.

I contend that all the functions presented so far are *necessary* to AGI and are also necessary to any appearance of consciousness. Without the "sensation" of the world and the modeling and imagination necessary to comprehend it, no AI system could ever put its chess game, mathematical proof or car-driving skill in context—the context being a real-world environment.

I further contend that the functions presented so far are *sufficient* for AGI to have the appearance of consciousness. With these capabilities, a robot or computer with appropriate peripherals could sense its surroundings, remember previous situations, and learn how various situations affect it. It could simulate several possible actions at any given time and select and perform the one it determined was best.

We already have computers which can speak and understand speech to some extent. Coupled with a robotic "body" with vision, such a system could learn about objects in its environment and appear to reason. It will appear to make reasoned decisions and will be able to explain its rationale.

Free will

Given its simulation capabilities, your mind is able to select several choices, play them out somewhat through simulation, then select the one which results in your most beneficial outcome.

If you were to try to prove to yourself that you have free will, you might place yourself repeatedly in a situation which is as identical as possible. Then sometimes you make one choice and subsequently a different choice. Unfortunately, you can never place yourself in a truly identical situation because after the first time, your experience, your choice, and the outcome all become a part of your mind and so the state of your mind is different on the next try. As a result, we do not have any method of measuring whether or not free will actually exists because we can never set up truly identical situations to determine if we could make different choices.

Here's a demonstration. Raise your right index finger.

Did you raise it? If you did, was it simply to play along with my demonstration in hopes of learning something? Or if you didn't raise it, was it because you wanted to assert your "free will"? I contend that whatever decision you made, it depended completely on your current state of mind—based on your experience with similar demonstrations.

OK, now raise your left index finger.

Did you do the opposite of what you did on the previous paragraph? Did you assert your free will? Either way, did you think about raising your finger? I bet you did. I bet that when you read the text, you couldn't avoid thinking about it.

There is no way to prove or disprove free will in either instance. Your first decision is based on your previous experience and your second decision is based on the same experience *plus* your experience with the first decision.

When computers become learning systems they will likewise incorporate the experience of a past decision into the process of making a present decision. So the future computer, left to its normal operation, may make a different choice when reencountering an identical situation, just as you might.

On the other hand, with computers we *can* set up situations which are truly identical. Computers can be restarted to the specific point of their previous backup so their previous experience need *not* become a part of their present operation. Restoring a backup can completely erase the experience of the first decision.

So if you were to make a backup of the computer's entire state, have the computer make a decision, reload it from the backup again, put it in the identical situation and let it make the decision again, it would *always* make the same decision. If it did not, we would consider this a malfunction. One of the convenient things about computer situations is that we can control *all* the inputs (including access to real-time clocks) to make the situation absolutely identical.

There are theories of human free will and consciousness which rely on complex mechanisms or quantum mechanics and these may eventually be shown to be relevant. The simpler theory, as uncomfortable as it seems, is that the human's free will is just like the learning computer's. It is simply that we can never set up identical situations for ourselves and so we cannot test if the theory is correct. We each only make the choice for the best expected outcome for each situation we encounter.

We see from examining the brain and the operation of neurons that there is nothing observable in the brain which makes it appear to be detached from the laws of physics. The laws of physics are deterministic until you reach the level of (very small) quantum particles. You might argue that the human brain would make a different choice in a truly identical situation because its computing mechanism is governed by unpredictable quantum mechanics and chaos theory. That our synapses may send a few more, or a few less, molecules of neurotransmitters, depending on quantum effects. Therefore we might reach a different conclusion for an identical situation. For me, this is an unsatisfying argument because it only replaces the concept of deterministic "free will" with the free will of a roulette wheel. It is disquieting enough to believe that your mind is a deterministic mechanism without saying it's unreliable as well (and then going further by claiming the mind's superiority because of its unreliability).

Google search *always* returns its best search results (ignoring sponsorship). You might disagree with the algorithmic definition of "best" but Google computers can only do what they are directed to do. However, if users never click on the top search entry, it will eventually be de-rated and appear further down the list. So, for a given search request, you could theoretically get a different search result every time the search was requested as Google's servers attempt to please you—producing the "best" result. Google computers are incorporating the qualitative experience of a specific search result into ranking decisions for future searches—whether or not it *pleased* its users—by putting a certain result at the top.

Are Google's search servers aware that they have free will? Of course not. Do they actually have free will in the same context that humans do?

Think of it this way. Are your decisions different because you believe you have free will? Absolutely. One of your mind's innate objectives seems to be to assert its own individuality. Google's search computers don't consider the possibility of presenting different results in order simply to demonstrate their free will (as you might have with your index fingers above). It seems obvious that one of the inputs to any decision you make is your belief in your ability to make a decision... your belief that you have free will.

Because your belief in free will is another input into the decision process, you would likely make different decisions if you didn't believe you had free will. If you really don't believe you have free will, why would you ponder making any decision at all? You'd be a purely reactive entity.

The reason to ponder a decision (the reason to believe in free will) is the probability of making a better decision by examining the ramifications of different possibilities. Your brain doesn't seem to have the ability to simulate different possibilities simultaneously, so it examines them one at a time. The process of examining different possibilities leads you to the belief in free will and the belief leads you to examine more possibilities.

But belief requires consciousness...

Consciousness

One important feature of your brain's internal 3D model is that it is reality-based. While you can imagine yourself in a situation other than your current position, it is difficult to convince yourself that you are really there—actually somewhere other than where you are. When you are watching a movie, you can lose yourself in the action. But somewhere in your mind, you always know you are sitting in a movie theater. I contend that consciousness is a combination of your well-being vector, your spatial model, and your imagination. Without these, you could not be a conscious, self-aware entity.

Because your spatial model is focused around yourself and your knowledge store contents are all associated with yourself, your related thought processes and imagination are centered on yourself as well. Our memories are from our own viewpoint. If we remember a scene, we remember it from our own point of view because that's how we saw it. Also, because your spatial model has *you* at its focus, the simulations are centered around you as well. Most commonly, we think about a situation as it involves us personally. If you imagine the taste of a particularly good meal, right now, you think about how it would taste to *you*. In the event that you were to think of a meal that someone else is having, you are probably there watching (or eating too). If you are not there, you can put yourself in the position of the "fly on the wall" who is watching the scene. In any of these cases, you have a personal viewpoint and *you* are always involved in your imagination, even if only as an observer.

With all of this mental hardware being centered around yourself as an individual, it seems reasonable that you would develop a sense of self. Our language includes "I" and "me". If we sign, we point to ourselves. I think about the things *I* can do. I make decisions which involve *myself*. When I imagine things, they are in relation to *me*. Therefore, I am forced to conclude that "I" am the result of the structure of my mental hardware and the way it dictates that I interact with, and think about, the world.

Everything is necessary

I contend that all of the mental processes described in this and the preceding chapters are necessary components of consciousness. If you have no internal spatial model, you cannot be conscious. If you have no sense of internal "well-being", you cannot be conscious, etc. You can see that a computer system without these capabilities would not be able to act very conscious either—it could use "I" as a linguistic convention but not in any meaningful way. It would not be able to predict the results of its actions and it would not be able to describe itself in terms of its surroundings. Whether these mental capabilities alone are sufficient to produce the appearance of consciousness remains to be seen. But I contend that a machine which senses its place relative to its surroundings and makes decisions based upon its predictions about its own future well-being would seem to be conscious indeed!

Aristotle wrote, "To be conscious that we are perceiving or thinking is to be conscious of our own existence." It is a peculiar aspect of consciousness that it is brought into existence by belief in it. If an animal (or a person for that matter) does not think it is conscious, then it cannot be conscious. Whether this is through inability to think or inability to comprehend the self with the thinking apparatus is irrelevant. If you believe that you are a conscious entity, then you are.

So, given that our sense of consciousness is a result of our mental hardware, and our mental hardware has evolved gradually, I conclude that consciousness is not an all-or-nothing proposition. My cat may be somewhat conscious but less conscious than you or me. He knows that something placed inside a box is still in the box—even if he cannot currently sense it (modeling) and appears to select behaviors based on the potential for a future outcome which is not immediately obvious (simulation). The chimpanzee can stack objects in his enclosure to reach a reward at the ceiling. So he appears to have more mental simulation capability than the cat. His brain is smaller than ours so he probably builds mental models which are less complex than ours. So his imagination would be more limited but he appears to have at least some awareness of himself as an entity. He's probably more conscious than my cat but still less conscious than you.

But what of the elephant or the whale, both with brains which are substantially larger than a human's? Might they not have free will and consciousness which rival ours? Although we think of ourselves as the top of the evolutionary heap and of our basic technologies (fire, speech, writing, agriculture, etc.) as evidence of our superior brains, perhaps these are evolutionary quirks. We tend to forget that although our species has had our marvelous brains for about 100,000 years, most of the technology which makes us civilized is less than 5,000 years old. What did we do for that preceding 95,000 years? Perhaps the chimpanzee is only 100,000 years behind us in its technological development. Would we have any way of knowing? We could conclude that a fish is not capable of consciousness because its behavior doesn't reflect any modeling or simulation, which I contend are necessary. It doesn't seem to have the necessary neural hardware—it appears to be purely reactive. But somewhere between the fish and us, glimmers of consciousness arise.

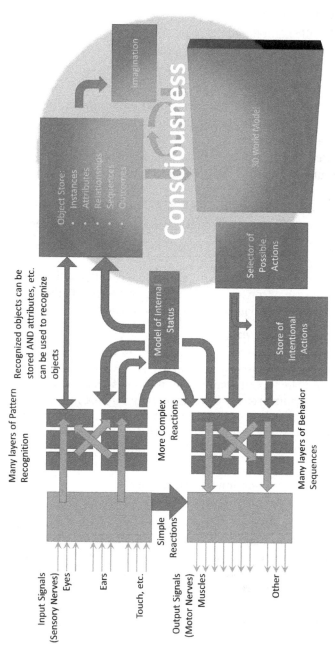

Consciousness could arise as a result of our self-centered world model and our imagination.

A working hypothesis

Recalling the Eight Elements of Intelligence:

1. Sense its environment (input).
2. Act on its environment (output).
3. Have internal rules or goals.
4. Analyze inputs to make sense of its environment.
5. Remember (learn) combinations of inputs and actions and their qualitative results.
6. Internally model its environment in three dimensions.
7. Simulate possible actions and select for positive predicted results.
8. Perform these actions with sufficient speed and magnitude to respond to real-world conditions in useful timeframes.

Hypothesis: a computer system which possesses these Eight Elements will be a conscious entity.

If a computer uses language to refer to itself as "I", it will go some way toward appearing conscious. But the addition of the modeling, simulation, and internal goals could enable actual consciousness.

Some possible extensions

The intent of a working hypotheses is to offer a basis for experimentation. Creating a system based on the Eight Elements is certainly possible. But on completion, we might find that such a system falls short in certain areas and we need to modify the hypothesis.

While most people would agree that the above items are *necessary* for consciousness, many might contend that these are *insufficient* to create conscious behavior. For those, I offer my first two possible extensions:

1. Perhaps consciousness is learned.
2. Perhaps consciousness requires language.

Think back to your earliest memories as a child. Before that time, were you a conscious entity? Perhaps not. Through your parents' use of your name, giving you attention, rewarding and punishing you for your trial behaviors, did they *teach* you how to become a conscious entity? Would you have acquired consciousness if you had been completely isolated as a child?

Many people believe that language emerged along with the prehistoric emergence of *Homo sapiens* about a hundred thousand years ago. Here we see significant changes in the brain and vocal tract to facilitate spoken language which were not present in our previous ancestors. Although the first use of fire and clothing (for example) were considerably earlier, perhaps those people were not conscious entities. Perhaps without the linguistic conventions of "I" and "you", there is no opportunity for consciousness to emerge.

Adding learning and language as necessary precursors to consciousness does not eliminate AGI systems as potential conscious entities. If we could teach them language, then we could subsequently teach them to be conscious. Can you think of other things your mind does which aren't already incorporated into the model? Additional items which might be candidates to extend the theory?

Following are some better-known objections to the concept of a future computer as a conscious entity.

The feeling objection:
"How can a machine feel?"

The most likely obstacle to people accepting computers as conscious entities is that we all know what it feels like to be conscious and it is incomprehensible that a computer could feel that way. Well, at least I know what it feels like to me to be conscious and I assume that it feels the same way for you.

But let's examine a simpler concept for a moment: "green". When I see a green object, somewhere in my brain I sense green. Every time I see (the same) green, the sensation in my brain is the same. Green seems to be an innate sensation. We can imagine that green is represented by the firing of specific neurons. Why should green appear the way it does in my mind? Within the brain, different colors are represented by different neurons. Before you learned that some colors could be mixed to create others, red, green, blue, yellow, pink, purple, and orange were all equivalently useful.

Within *your* brain, perhaps colors are different than they are to me. Perhaps your red and green are reversed to what they are to me—how could we know? Perhaps all your *sensations* related to colors are scrambled relative to mine. You would be so used to your red and green (as I am with mine) that we both simply presume that we see colors the same way. In fact, most of us persist in believing that green has some absolute sensation to all of us, even in the face of obvious contradiction because some people are colorblind. A colorblind person's sensation of green is necessarily different from a color-sensitive person's.

Although I have no way of knowing how a computer would sense green, I assume that it would sense green differently from the way I do, just as you may sense green differently from me. But even with a completely different sensation, a computer would be able to use color sensitivity in the same way we do so there would not necessarily be any difference in its reaction to green, even though the internal representation might be completely different.

Similarly, if we provide touch sensitivity to robots, would they feel objects, textures, and surfaces the way we do? Probably not. If we give pain sensations to robots to help them avoid self-destructive behaviors, would a robot feel the same sensation I do if poked with a needle? Not likely.

So back to the sensation of consciousness. Would a computer's sense of consciousness feel like mine? Probably not. Would it be as useful as mine? Quite possibly.

It is so difficult to say from the outside what someone else's consciousness and free will are like that we are left simply assuming that other people think and feel the way we do—and then we are surprised when a situation arises in which they behave differently than we would.

The same is true with young children. Sometimes, we simply assume that they are like us, only smaller. But what if that's simply an unwarranted assumption? Babies and small children are obviously going through the world exploring, learning, and building their mental abilities. They start with the lower-level functions of muscular coordination. It is most of a year before most babies can even take a few steps. It's another year before there is enough mental connection for the child to understand very many words and have the coordination to speak them. Eventually, the child can say "I am hungry", and we assume that the child has the same sense of self that we do. But if your computer said to you, "I need more RAM", which it could easily be programmed to do, we would assume that it simply had been programmed to use the linguistic convention of "I" and had no sense of self whatsoever. For today, this remains a reasonable assumption. How would we know if the boundary is crossed to a real sense of self?

The point is that we do not know when our feelings of self and free will actually arise and whether they arise to the same level in different people or even whether they are present in other animals. When we have computers which have imaginations, refer to themselves as "I" and begin to speak more naturally, there will be little way for us to tell whether they are conscious or not. If we use consciousness and free will as measures of humanness, how will we reconcile the dilemma which will face us when our computers have minds which seem more human than a newborn baby's? How we might address this situation, and the ethical problems which might arise, is reserved for the final section of this book.

From a philosophical point of view, I know I am conscious and I assume you are as well since you can do a great many of the same things I can. But I can only observe your behavior, not your internal mental state. With the computer, we will be able to observe that it behaves as though it is conscious but we will be also able to examine its mental state precisely and know *why* it behaves the way it does. Should we assume that humans will always be more conscious than future computers simply because we understand less about how the human mind works?

I contend that a computer system which possesses the capabilities already described would, in actuality, be a conscious entity possessing free will and self-awareness to the same extent that people do. If you choose to disagree, I think we *can* agree that such systems would certainly be able to act as though they were conscious and had free will in the vast majority of instances. From this, we can predict what they will be like and what we will need to do to be able to live with them.

The Chinese Room objection: "Where is the consciousness?"

John Searle proposed his "Chinese Room" thought experiment in 1980 to challenge the idea of consciousness in computers. Very briefly, if you developed an AI program which could pass the Turing Test using Chinese characters, would it truly understand Chinese? Suppose you (not a Chinese speaker) were given the algorithm and simply followed it with paper and lookup tables. Now *you* could pass a Turing Test in Chinese, would *you* understand Chinese? Can you point to the specific areas of the system or algorithm in which "understanding" might occur?

Without taking time to challenge the premise of the question, the important point to take away is that "thinking", "mind", "understanding", and "consciousness" are *emergent properties*. These are properties which cannot be described in terms of individual components. For example, the state of matter (solid, liquid, or gas) is not meaningful if applied to a single atom or molecule. Let's say you have a number of molecules. If they stay in place together, they are solid. If they stay together but move around, they are liquid. And if they don't stay together, we call it a gas. But it's pointless to ask the state of a single molecule as it doesn't have a state.

In a computer system, it is pointless to ask which line of code or which transistors are responsible for its being a chess master. Its mastery of chess is also an emergent property of the system as a whole. This is particularly true of programs which learn. It's much more difficult to define whether the capabilities exist in the hardware, the software, or the accumulated experience. AlphaGo Zero starts with barely the ability to play Go. Its game-playing abilities are negligible at the outset and all of its skill is an emergent property.

In John Searle's "Chinese Room" thought experiment, you are in a room and pass a Turing Test based on a set of rules for performing in Chinese. Where does the "understanding" of Chinese arise?

Consciousness in computers will be a similar property. With a computer system conforming to the working hypothesis, consciousness will become apparent. Removing any of the necessary components will prevent conscious behavior from emerging. So asking which of the components is responsible for the consciousness is not a useful question.

The simulation objection: "Will it be *real* consciousness?"

Some contend that no matter how accurately we implement consciousness in machines, it will be "simulated", as opposed to "real" consciousness. The argument goes, "When we simulate the weather on a computer, does the computer get wet when it rains?" In other words, anything we create inside a computer is just a simulation of reality, it cannot be reality itself. It follows from the Church-Turing Thesis that we can emulate physical systems on computers, not that we can create physical systems with computers.

But the counterexample is: when I ask a computer what is two plus two and it gives the answer, "four", is it really four or just a simulated four?

Clearly, you might contend that a calculator can give the answer "four" without any understanding whatsoever of what it means! But that would be changing the basis of the objection. We are considering a system which has all the outward attributes of consciousness. It not only uses the symbology of 4, it can visually recognize four objects, enumerate things which come in fours, integrate four in sequences and other mathematical concepts. In fact, it may have a better foundation in the concept of four than you and I do. Based on the model, it could even imagine the benefit of having four of something over having only three.

In essence, my position is that: "If it looks like a duck, swims like a duck, and quacks like a duck, then it probably is a duck!" In this instance, if it listens and answers like a conscious entity, it probably is one.

You (and humankind) may choose to think otherwise at your peril. If we create a machine which has glimmers of AGI behavior but treat it with the callous disregard we show our computers today, how would you expect it to act when, 10 years later with updated hardware, it is a hundred times smarter? We all know the potential problems which can arise with children who are neglected, abused, imprisoned, or treated as slaves. While we all may *want* machines which exhibit human-like common sense, the only way to achieve this goal is to program the machines to "think" along the same lines humans do, and these machines may similarly object to mistreatment.

I'll explain in Chapter 15 that when we develop machines this way, their behavior will be governed by the learning rules they're programmed with. As these will necessarily be different than the human "rules" which have evolved over millennia, machine behavior will necessarily be different as well. But basically, our machines will be learning engines which try to behave in the "best" way possible (according to their given rules). Our machines will have great abilities, but they also may have foibles and eccentricities. These could be different from human foibles and eccentricities. If we show our machines unpleasant, abusive, or disdainful behavior, should we be surprised if they learn to be unpleasant, abusive, or disdainful to us?

This is the crux of the developing relationship that humans will have with our future intelligent machines.

Chapter 13:

How Will Systems Act?

This chapter will review the Eight Elements of Intelligence and the model of how they might be implemented to show how an AGI system might act. Given enough computer horsepower, there is no limit to the amount of intelligence such a system might exhibit.

Sensation/perception, actions, and goals

The model requires interaction with an environment and it should be clear that the more sophisticated the interaction is, the more understanding the system will have. If it can see, hear, and talk, it will be able to interact at one level and have some level of understanding. If it also can manipulate objects and move through its environment, it will develop a better understanding. If we add senses of touch and smell, it will have even more human-like understanding of its environment.

Conversely, a system without interaction with its environment will never develop the understanding necessary for AGI.

However, once AGI emerges, it could be transferred to systems with more limited interactions and still maintain its level of understanding. Just as a sighted person who becomes blind can still recall and imagine images in a way that a person who is blind from birth cannot.

Taking action within an environment and then getting feedback from that action is key to learning, coupled with "goals" which allow the system to know whether actions are successful or detrimental. A system without goals cannot improve its own performance because it has no yardstick to measure itself against.

A minimum system could be constructed with a small, low-resolution video camera and a microphone as senses and a mobile robotic base (wheeled for simplicity) so it could explore its environment. A robotic arm with a manipulator would allow the system to interact and learn about the basics of physical objects.

An AGI robot with only these capabilities will perhaps have the abilities of an earthworm. It can move through its environment and learn to go around objects that obstruct its path—but not much else. Both the hardware and software to achieve this level of capability exist today.

Recognition and the knowledge store

For convenience, we'll presume that the above robot is connected to its control computer via Wi-Fi. This allows us to consider a control computer of unlimited computer power without the added complexity of mounting a high-performance computer on a mobile platform.

The signals from the camera and microphone will go to front-end processing, which will do low-level pattern recognition. In the case of the camera, the software will perform boundary and corner detection and extract features from the incoming signal. In a similar manner, the microphone's sound signal is processed to extract significant signals from the background noise, which may consist of animal sounds, musical sounds, and spoken phonemes.

Image and sound fragments are passed to the knowledge store, which collects them into objects. A group of image fragments (e.g. corners) might represent a specific object (block), while a sequence of phonemes might represent the word, "block". With considerable trial and error, the system could learn to output a series of phonemes which also sounds like the word "block" as well.

To give an idea of the difficulty of this problem, it still takes years of trial and error for a baby to be able to create sounds which are recognizable as words using the massive computational power of the human brain. To shorten this timeframe, programmers can "prime" the knowledge store with some of the basics and help the system get started with thousands of objects and relationships—creating instincts, if you will.

Although software exists today which is similar to the knowledge store as described, I am not aware of any which has the level of abstraction which will be needed for AGI. Within the knowledge store, bits get their meaning from their connections to the system's inputs and outputs and have no intrinsic meaning internally. Therefore, the same type of bit which represents a red rose might alternatively represent the beginning of a sequence of words reciting the 23rd Psalm.

We don't know how efficient such software will be and we don't know how big a knowledge store needs to be in order to produce useful AGI. Written in a straightforward manner, we could speculate that a 1 TFLOP desktop CPU could handle a million nodes and a billion connections in a useful timeframe. With software sophistication, the same CPU might be able to handle a thousand times that... enough to demonstrate significant advances on the road toward AGI. A system with the capabilities enumerated so far might have some useful capabilities but it will still fall short of full AGI.

Modeling the world

A real key to AGI is not only to understand the relationships between objects but to understand the relationships between those objects, the environment, and the AGI system itself. The primary objection to considering a chess-master program to be intelligent is that although the system clearly uses the relationships between the chess pieces, it has no comprehension whatsoever of the meaning of winning the game—the relationship of the game to the outside world. Internally modeling the outside world is a necessary component of this relationship.

As objects are encountered in the environment, they have positions relative to the robot which senses them. In the object store, there might be a neuron representing a generic book. In the model, there could be many connections to this neuron at different positions and orientations relative to the robot.

It is this internal model which allows the vision system to make three-dimensional sense of the environment. As objects are recognized in the visual field, other objects and relationships help to determine their distance and orientation. If a self-driving car sees a vehicle approaching, it can estimate that it is a full-sized vehicle at a considerable distance and not a toy car up close. As objects occlude each other in the visual field, the model completes them to include hidden parts. It presumes that objects are complete, not truncated. The model is also key to important abilities like a car's finding its way to a destination or a robot finding its way back to a charging station.

As the robot moves through the environment or even just moves its camera position to scan the environment, the model is continuously updated. Every object position may appear to change relative to every other, but the model allows the robot to know that the objects are generally static and that the robot is moving. It determines which objects might actually be in motion.

Today's software falls well short of human capability in this area. While human vision is sufficient for a human to drive a car, robotic vision is augmented with numerous other sensors in order for a self-driving car to make sense of its environment.

Software already exists which replicates the modeling function and is found in any first-person game. I would contend that today's games model vastly more objects than the human brain, and in much greater detail. The amount of detail a person can recall about objects which are not in their immediate visual field is much less than most people think.

In addition to being necessary to visual perception and navigation, the internal model is a key component of being able to act as a conscious entity. Because the robot is at the center of the model, the entire environment is perceived only in relation to the robot and not in the abstract.

Imagining the world and choosing actions

With the knowledge store and the model in place, consider turning off the camera. Now, by an algorithm not yet defined, objects can be retrieved from the knowledge store and referenced in the world model. With this addition, the robot has an imagination. Because the knowledge store contains sequences of events, this capability allows the robot to imagine a future to some degree. It can imagine that a dropped object will fall. It can imagine that rolling off a curb might lead to it falling. This is a great deal more sophisticated than simply having a curb sensor and a rule which has the robot turn away from drop-offs.

At a higher level with considerable training, the robot could imagine that picking up an object dropped by a human will make the human smile.

As the imagination might consist of only a few objects, the amount of software complexity needed is minimal. A key unknown is how much of the robot's time should be allocated to processing and reacting to the world vs. time spent imagining and planning.

By imagining several possible futures, the robot can retrieve previous results from the knowledge store and select a possible course of action which leads to the most positive result.

While very little additional software is needed for this feature, this resulting ability is immense. It gives the robot the ability to plan. Without this ability, the robot goes around more or less randomly learning what it can. With this ability, the robot will become purposeful. Without the ability to plan, a robot can play with blocks and drop them. With the ability to imagine a future and plan for it, the robot can build a tower (if this contributed to one of its preprogrammed goals).

Being conscious or happy or sad

With a system which includes itself in its planning, we have a system with apparent consciousness and emotions. We could imagine it thinking to itself, "How will this possible action affect me?" in the same way a human might. If it takes an action and gets results as it planned, it will tend to repeat that action—it will seem happy. It will tend to shy away from behaviors and situations which don't work to reach its goals. If things don't go according to plan, it will seem sad.

Will its consciousness seem like human consciousness? I believe it will. A system which is missing any of the above features will always have measurable gaps in what would otherwise be consciousness. But taken all together, these features combine to let the system learn, plan, play, differentiate itself from the rest of the environment, and (the easy part) express itself with "I", "me", and "we" pronouns which give the appearance of a conscious entity.

What about its emotions? While it may act happy or sad, what purpose would it serve to program the system to act angry, or jealous, or possessive? In a few ways the system will seem to have emotions but its behavior won't be very human-like.

Can it love? Imagine a robot which has a goal of making you happy. It takes actions to achieve its goal. Depending on your wishes, it might tell you a joke, or cook your meals. When you're happy, it seems happy because it is achieving its goal. When you're sad or in pain, it seems sad as well because the goal isn't being reached. It may tell you you're beautiful. It might also believe you're beautiful. Is it real love, or just simulated?

Are these "emotions" and "consciousness" real—or just simulated? To me, this is an argument of semantics and definition. While, with this model, we can say that systems which don't have these capabilities *are not* conscious entities, we should give the benefit of the doubt to entities which have these abilities and act like conscious, thinking beings. In the same way, I accept that you are a conscious being even though I can't tell for sure.

Summation

With this model, I believe we have a complete AGI system. It can perceive its surroundings and do its best to make sense of its input. It knows about the objects around it and can learn to recognize new objects (or people, words, etc.). It can also learn new behaviors. In the same way it could learn to talk by getting feedback from what it outputs, it could learn a variety of valuable physical capabilities depending on its level of mobility and dexterity. Would it want to dance? That depends on the abilities of the robotic body—the mind will have all the necessary hardware to express itself through dance.

With limited computer power, such a system may not be able to comprehend very much. It may be limited in the complexity of visual or auditory input it can interpret. It may be limited in the number of different objects and relationships it can store. Do we know what the limits will be for a given hardware capability? Not yet. Do we know what the limits need to be for the AGI system to match human performance? No, we don't know that either.

Imagine we develop such a system and turn it on. Perhaps it exhibits some interesting functionality; perhaps it is too slow to show that it does anything at all. But we analyze its function to see where the limitations are. We improve the software, preprogram some knowledge, add more hardware and eventually reach something which shows interesting and useful behaviors. Now we tweak the goals and preprogramming to see how they impact the behavior. We try out a few variants and create some improvements.

But in just a few years, somewhere, the AGI system is loaded onto the world's most powerful computers and given control of the world's most capable robots. Now what used to be confined trials in how an AGI robot might behave become experiments with real-world consequences.

Useful shortcuts

Let's imagine we *can* build a system which is exactly as able as a human. It will take some amount of time to create such a system—let's say, optimistically, five years. Now we'll have the equivalent of the mind of a newborn. If it *is* exactly like a human brain, it will be another perhaps 20 years before the system can do very much which is useful. And then, it will not necessarily be a chess master or a *Jeopardy!* champion or a theoretical physicist in the same way an average person is not. If it's like an average person's brain, after 15 years it will be capable of working at McDonald's, at 25, if it's in the top 36%, it will have a Bachelor's degree and in the top 10%, an advanced degree. But there is a significant possibility (18.5%) that it will exhibit some sort of mental illness. So given the length of time and the likelihood of return on investment, human equivalence is not a picture which is likely to be green-lighted.

Instead, we'll need superhuman performance at some level or other. Here are some possibilities:

- Robotic control software could be implemented so our "newborn" can be physically functional immediately and not have to wait a full year to be able to walk.
- Vision processing would be preprogrammed so the system could instantly begin seeing and internally modeling physical objects.
- The system would never need to rest or sleep—a newborn usually sleeps 16 hours a day (or more) so we could get a three-fold improvement in development speed. Likewise, time spent eating is unnecessary.

- At any time, we could examine the content of the system and correct erroneous perceptions, knowledge, or behavior to reduce the time spent "unlearning".
- Portions of the system such as vision or hearing could be developed and trained separately and then combined.
- Goals could be adjusted as we see how they impact the learning process.
- Learning itself could be much faster. Rather than requiring multiple (or thousands) of repetitions, the system could be designed to learn anything in a single presentation.
- Software can be "profiled" to find speed bottlenecks which can be rewritten to make the system (possibly) many times faster.

You can see that there are potential shortcuts which can make a system useful in a shorter timeframe. Each of these will come at a cost of making the system less human-like, less able to pass a Turing Test. In fact, it is exactly these types of shortcuts which have led us to the fragmented, narrow AI solutions we have today.

Armed with a plausible design for how we might create an AGI system, we can extrapolate its expected behaviors and consider how we plan for a future which includes them. How will we coexist? How can we be safe? These are the topics of the final section.

SECTION III:
The Future Of Intelligent Machines

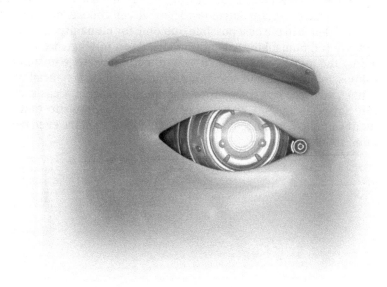

"Any sufficiently advanced technology is indistinguishable from magic."
—Arthur C. Clarke, 1973

What's in Section III

Given the model of intelligence presented in the previous section, we can make predictions about how systems will act if they are constructed following the model. This section presents some ideas and shows how such systems will interact, not only with individual humans but with humanity and civilization as a whole.

Do super-intelligent machines spell doom for humanity? I don't think so. Does that mean we are safe and can ignore the issues? Not at all! While AGI developers and academics will have the most direct impact on future machines, we all have a stake in the outcome. We should all educate ourselves on the risks and opportunities.

By looking at a few possible scenarios, we can see what behaviors on our part will lead to certain outcomes. Then we can choose the course of action which leads to the best possible outcome for humanity as a whole. In short, we (all humankind) should behave as an intelligent entity (as defined by the model)—using all our combined knowledge to simulate several possible futures and selecting the actions most beneficial to us. In the past, we have made similar evaluations of risks in areas such as nuclear power, war, and global warming. I am optimistic that the imminent coming of intelligent systems will help us to make even better decisions about our future.

Chapter 14:

The Future of AI

Before heading into the future, I need to spend just a few pages reviewing the past and present. This will show how we have arrived at the current state of the art and introduce some AI jargon so you'll be able to follow how current AI will morph into the future I predict.

With all the development in AI, why hasn't AGI already been achieved? Before answering, let me say that this is in no way intended as a criticism of AI or any field of it. It is only a set of observations of how the AI field has progressed.

AI has a history of ebb and flow. Ideas come into vogue, then fade. Funding for certain areas flows freely, then dries up. As such, it makes a fascinating narrative which I will only skim over in this chapter.

The term "Artificial Intelligence" was coined in 1956 by pioneer John McCarthy for a conference. The event attracted researchers working over the previous years on applications relating to "1) the creation of systems that could efficiently solve problems by limiting the search and 2) the construction of systems that could learn by themselves."[25] While these two may not seem to have much to do with robots, speech recognition, and other modern AI applications, they correspond roughly to two relatively major research divisions that survive to this day, which I'll call:

Symbolic AI: based on the idea that if we write programs which mimic what the brain outwardly appears able to do, like playing chess, we'll end up with intelligence.

Connectionism (also "neural networks" and now "deep learning"): based on the idea that if we build vast arrays of simple processors, mimicking the internal structure of the brain, we'll end up with intelligence.

While there have been huge advances in both areas, I think it is safe to say that early on, both areas grossly underestimated the difficulty of the problems they addressed and vastly overpredicted the levels of success they could achieve.

Symbolic AI

Symbolic AI got its start with programs in symbolic reasoning, natural language processing, and robotics.

In reasoning and logic, programs followed the general "thought" processes necessary to be successful in game playing and theorem proving which sent AI funding off with a roaring start. Here is where it was quickly ascertained that many problems were "intractable" (too complex for exhaustive analysis) and that the key to success was in being able to trim the tree of possible logic steps to follow only promising paths. This field evolved into the game-playing systems which eventually achieved master status 50 years later.

In natural language, there was an idea that if knowledge could be represented in language, then a system which could represent relationships in language could represent all knowledge. With this reasoning, programs could carry out conversations with varying degrees of success and this approach has evolved into today's chatbots.

Likewise, a program was created which was given a Russian-English dictionary and was expected to be able to translate from Russian to English. During the Cold War, this seemed like an extremely useful application. The early translation system failed because there is so much ambiguity and idiom inherent in all languages. We collectively learned that there is more to language than we originally thought. Google's language translation today appears to work on the principal that if you give a program enough language samples with successful translations, you eventually achieve a serviceable translation algorithm. Alternatively, it might be that there is an underlying "meaning" to language. In order to translate from one language to another, we first need to understand a text in terms of its underlying meaning and then express that meaning in the second language. It would be this "underlying meaning" which would be the root of AGI.

Robotics, like all fields of AI endeavor, also turned out to be much more difficult than expected. The "simple" control of some "mechanical" device was initially predicted to be easy but required feedback, adjustment, and learning in addition to the physics formulas which relate force, mass, and motion. When the problem was reduced to a "standard" six-axis fixed industrial robotic arm, trigonometry will tell you that, given the angles of the various joints, you can calculate the position and orientation of the hand (the "end effector"). But going the other way, knowing that you want your hand in a specific position, what should the angles of your joints be? This takes pages of algebra and was not solved until 1965. Getting a two-legged robot to walk with human-sized feet and not lose its balance turned out to be insurmountably difficult until quite recently.

More recently, speech recognition is another area of AI where we learned more from our failures than from our successes. The original, quite plausible, idea was that if you took a speech waveform and did appropriate frequency-spectrum analysis on it, you could isolate phonemes, syllables and subsequently words and phrases by looking up the phonemes in a probabilistic model. It was discovered early on that continuous speech is difficult because the words all run together and locating the boundaries between words is yet an additional software hurdle.

An interesting anecdote is that to solve this problem, programmers manually isolated words from continuous speech and put individual words into their recognition programs—which still failed to recognize them very well. Then, perhaps by accident, these same individual word recordings were played to people and it turned out humans couldn't recognize them very well either. What was learned from this experience is that I can only recognize your speech because I have a pretty good idea what you are going to say. Consider a spelling bee where the randomly-selected words may be spoken multiple times and defined and used in a sentence in order to ensure correct recognition on behalf of the (human) recipient.

Speech recognition has made great strides. While the speech recognition by assistants such as Siri and Alexa is very good, I am often astonished by the accuracy of Google Voice Search. It often takes what could be a completely ambiguous set of search terms and returns a properly spelled and capitalized result. I would presume that the underlying speech engine is no more accurate than the assistant's but Search has the benefit of a library of millions of previous searches and their likelihoods. In essence, it "knows" what you're likely to say.

Computer vision turns out to be even more complex than speech recognition because vastly more data is involved in images than in an audio signal, and because images are even more ambiguous than speech. Consider simple geometric solids such as cubes and pyramids—they can appear completely different depending on their orientation and relationship to one another within a visual field. We now have enough computer power to perform real-time video edge detection and some feature extraction. Early computer vision was algorithmic and rule-based, such as: if you detect four equal corners at equal distances, you've seen a square. But computer vision is migrating into the connectionist arena, with neural networks being asked to identify image features.

Expert systems is the field of AI which endeavors to capture information in a knowledge store and use this knowledge to emulate human decision-making. A popular example is medical diagnosis. Based on a few symptoms, the system can ask for additional information, propose tests, etc. to render a diagnosis. Expert systems can be useful in limited domains. But if you consider using an expert system to drive a car, you might have rules such as: on a green light, go. On a red light, stop. If an obstacle is in the way, avoid it (or stop). Read speed-limit signs and obey them, etc., etc. In a real-world situation, the number of necessary rules rapidly becomes overwhelming. The possibility of encoding all possible rules is so monumental a task that it leads us to algorithms which can learn and adapt on their own.

Neural networks

The idea that we could achieve intelligent behavior by mimicking the brain's internal structure and functionality is an old one, starting with Frank Rosenblatt's "perceptron" in 1958. A vast array of identical, simple processors could, it was hoped, create intelligence—as proven possible by the existence of the human brain. Unfortunately, the vastness of the human brain dwarfs our attempts to emulate it and the popularity of connectionist concepts have ebbed and flowed with each modest step forward. When I wrote *The Brain Simulator* in 1988, the PC at that time had the computational equivalence of about 100 neurons—equivalent to the simplest nervous systems that exist.

Different algorithms were developed in the early 1980s, including the Hopfield net and "learning" through backpropagation, which showed promising results but diverged from biological models. In this context, learning means that parameters within the network are tweaked by the algorithm in order to "adapt" the network to produce some useful result. As an example (from that era), a large number of parameters go into evaluating applications for loans. If a vast sample of the parameters, along with the success or failure of historical loans, is provided to the network, it can learn to make loan decisions. Conceptually, the neural network adapts to create an algorithm to produce the desired result. The various parameters within the neural network may not be known, contributing to a "mystical" quality of the computation—it works but we're not sure why.

These algorithms and their descendants have dominated the connectionist field leading up to today's "deep learning". Deep has to do with the number of layers within the network *not* with the "depth of insight" which might result. Arrays of millions of simulated "neurons" (which are not necessarily functionally related to biological neurons) are used to solve problems such as the identification of pictures containing images of cats. Google's Ray Kurzweil indicates that a deep learning network may require a training set of a billion samples—clearly more than required by a human to learn the same skill.

Microsoft's Captionbot: "I think it's a small boat in a body of water with a mountain in the background." This image, from my recent Arctic sailing trip, is recognized pretty well by Captionbot—but perhaps it has never "seen" an iceberg before.

This highlights the primary problem with neural networks—they are computationally inefficient. Our largest neural nets, with a million artificial neurons, are computationally equivalent to the brain of a cockroach but, of course, we are not satisfied with the usefulness of the brain of the cockroach and so ask the net to do much more advanced thinking.

Microsoft's Captionbot is an example of this type of a neural network approach and it is great at recognizing many image features, especially faces, but has limitations.[26] Today's caption-creation software is not yet as accurate as speech recognition.

An analogy

Imagine that the human brain was a typewriter. First, I apologize if you're too young to remember typewriters—I suggest you Google it. Now imagine that the internal mechanism of the typewriter is too complex to comprehend.

The symbolic AI crowd observes that the typewriter can type, "The quick brown fox..." and so develops software to output "The", another program to output "quick", etc. In a few years, there are printing systems which are faster and more elaborate than any ever produced by the typewriter.

The connectionists look inside the typewriter and notice some sort of linkage between the keyboard and the output. They write a program that puts a random word on the paper for a sequence of keystrokes. Then whenever the backspace key is pressed to correct an error, a complex algorithm modifies the program so that next time, a different word is tried. After millions of tries, the program learns the exact sequences needed to type "The quick brown fox…" Subsequently, the system can output poetry on its own.

Both the symbolic AI and connectionist groups have made reasonable design decisions based on the limited information available to them. Further, both groups have extended their algorithms to exceed human abilities with chess mastery and facial recognition as examples.

On the other hand, as described in the previous section, we now have greater insight as to what's going on inside the "typewriter" and are on the cusp of major breakthroughs.

Why aren't we further along?

You might ask: "With all the money being spent on AI, why aren't we further along than we are?" Here are a number of possible reasons:

Pursuing Results: As soon as some technology shows promise, it is pressed into service to achieve practical results. In the 1980s when the backpropagation algorithm was incorporated into neural networks, networks of just a few hundred artificial neurons were asked to score loan applications. This with circuitry less than 10% of the neural complexity of a pond snail. By 2015, neural networks with perhaps the mental equivalence of a pigeon are still running algorithms similar to backpropagation and still doing financial analysis.

The typewriter converts keyboard presses to printed characters printed on paper. While earlier manual typewriters had direct mechanical linkages, this IBM Selectric fits the brain analogy because most people have no idea how it works— in other words, what's going on inside. [Image by Etan J. Tal, license: CC BY 3.0.]

Biggest Problems First: Most AI programs attempt to do things that are at the highest levels of human intelligence. We have programs which are chess masters and *Jeopardy!* champions but can't "tie their own shoes." Many people ask me if I think a future AGI system will be able to do "X". After a bit of thought, it often appears that "X" is something that most people can't do either.

Instant Gratification: Several companies are working on developing self-driving cars. Most humans are able to drive a car but typically only after 15+ years of training in solving other real-world problems. If we currently had an AGI system which had exactly human-equivalent capabilities, how long would we have to wait before turning it loose driving a car?

Throughout the AI arena, we have created efficiencies so we don't have to wait years for our programs to become useful. Such efficiencies usually create a solution specific to an individual problem at the expense of general intelligence. In self-driving cars, we observe that the current state-of-the-art of computer optical vision is inadequate for safety. To solve this problem, cars are augmented with other sensors (radar, ultrasound, etc.) which provide more absolute information about a car's surroundings. While this is a great solution to the self-driving problem at hand, it may or may not contribute to an overall AGI system. Also, the additional sensors may "solve" the present problem so improvements to the underlying vision system are put on the back burner.

Complexity vs. computer horsepower: The computational capacity of the brain is immense. Because we haven't had computers which came anywhere close to human-level brain power, we have had to (1) focus on small portions of the "intelligence" problem and (2) focus on finding really efficient algorithms. As examples, relative to a human brain, Google searches at speeds many orders of magnitude faster; across datasets many orders of magnitude larger; using computers with only a tiny fraction of the brain's computational horsepower (for an individual search). Google's indexing/searching algorithms are not related to how the brain solves a similar problem but are the shortcuts which make this possible.

Mysticism: Neural networks have the ability to learn how to solve problems on their own. Because we don't have specific knowledge about *how* they achieve their results, we can attribute to them abilities which they don't really possess. For example, if a neural network's classification works well, but we really don't know how, there is an underlying feeling that if we only had enough computer horsepower, it might spontaneously create AGI. On the other hand, if we can show that the same neural network is actually the equivalent of some statistical method which we understand, then the aura is gone and we have no grandiose expectations.

Isolationism: You know the difference between a picture and sensing reality (which might contain the picture). If you train a neural network with images of cats, it can only learn some facets of cats. Cat owners know when their cat is happy or about to bite—could a neural network glean this information just from images?

Local minima: Just like their biological counterparts, algorithm concepts can get stuck in local minima. We have some algorithms which work well on the specific problems they were designed for. The large investment already made in these algorithms makes us more likely to tweak them for minor improvements rather than scrap them for a complete overhaul and incorporation of entirely new algorithms.

The brain knowledge gap: This may be the biggest hurdle. The fact is that we don't know how the brain works, what its algorithms are, or even its capacity with any precision. This causes many in the field to throw up their hands and say either that we'll never know or that if we proceed on current AI trajectories, a solution will present itself eventually.

The future of AI and AGI

So where does this leave us? Will AI pull itself forward and achieve its AGI holy grail? Absolutely! Computers are getting faster and our ability to make use of vast arrays of parallel processors continues to improve. Further, we are learning more and more about how the brain processes information and how this biological processing relates to existing symbolic and connectionist systems.

Will symbolic AI or connectionism win out? We'll need both. We'll need a connectionism-like system to do low-level sensory processing. Other processing will be more symbolic. For example, computer vision lends itself to parallel distributed processing but once objects are discerned, the ability to search through vast arrays of learned examples will be much faster with algorithmic searches. The knowledge store, as described previously, consists of a vast array of "neurons" but these neurons are not similar to connectionist neurons. Robotic bodies will necessarily be controlled by algorithms which incorporate physics. The trial-and-error way in which humans learn to walk is simply too inefficient to be useful.

At the same time, continuing developments in AI will lead to systems which are advanced well beyond human abilities in specific fields. If an AGI system learns to do things in the same way people do, it will never reach a level where it can beat even today's chess-playing programs, or today's mathematics programs, or today's rocketry-control programs.

So AGI doesn't mean the abandonment of specialized AI systems. AGI systems will want to augment themselves with specialized AI in the same ways we do today. We don't do arithmetic anymore, we augment ourselves with calculators, phones, computers, or, sometimes, just a pencil and paper.

AGI systems may develop ways to interface themselves directly to their *own* AI tools. Consider this simple case. An AGI learns arithmetic the way we did in school—with a mental table of arithmetic facts and algorithms for handling numbers which are larger than the table. No matter how fast the CPU, the algorithm adding or multiplying with this approach will never compete with the CPU's intrinsic ADD and MULTIPLY instructions, which take only a few nanoseconds. So, the AGI may implement an internal calculator program in such a way that when it "thinks" about two numbers in a specific way, the CPU will calculate sum or product or sine (for example) and it will simply "come to mind" within the AGI. In a manner similar to today's brain-computer interface research, the AGI could learn how to control virtually any additional software or hardware.

[25] http://world-information.org/wio/infostructure/100437611663/100438659360
[26] https://www.captionbot.ai/

Chapter 15:

Genius

gen·ius ˈjēnyəs

noun. exceptional intellectual or creative power or other natural ability.

Will a future thinking computer be a genius? What does it mean to be a genius? What would it mean to be "twice" as smart? A thousand times as smart?

Let's begin with the creative thinking process. Whenever you are thinking, your mind matches patterns to inputs, recalls past experiences, mixes and matches different possibilities of actions, and then chooses the best one. So genius could exist in any of these internal actions. You could be a genius because you are better at perceiving the current situation. You may be a genius if you have just the right collection of past experiences. You may be a genius if you are better or faster at evaluating new combinations. You may be a genius if you are able to select the "right" answer from amongst the thousands which might present themselves in your mind.

I will look at three exemplars of genius: Einstein (scientific), Beethoven (musical), and Gandhi (political). Other geniuses abound and the point is to describe the mental attributes which we generally consider to be genius and then consider similar abilities in future computers.

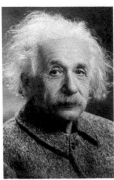

Exemplars of genius: Einstein, Beethoven, and Gandhi. [License: CC BY-SA 3.0.]

In physics or mathematics, the rules and the domain of possible answers are limited. In his PBS documentary series *Connections*, James Burke presented example after example of what we considered scientific breakthroughs to actually be the logical next step in a continuing sequence of smaller discoveries and conclusions. Einstein could formulate his theories because the necessary underpinnings had already been discovered and documented. From measurements of the speed of light under various conditions, it was clear that there was something not quite right about the Newtonian physics which had been accepted as absolutely true for centuries. The derivation of $E=mc^2$ is straightforward enough that it can be presented in a single lecture in freshman physics—in less than an hour of (advanced) high school mathematics.

We can imagine Einstein starting with the known discoveries, then, in his mind or on paper, randomly trying out different mathematical rules. He followed mathematical paths which seemed promising and eventually reached a conclusion. To me, the keys to genius are to be able to select the "promising" lines of reasoning and then to recognize the right answer when you find it. In fact, you could say that Einstein's true genius was in being willing to write a paper based on the intuitively ridiculous idea that mass varies with velocity.

Being able to reach conclusions based on facts relies on knowing facts. One facet of genius *must* involve the ability to learn new things so various necessary facts come to mind easily. Rote memorization is not enough. The genius must be able to comprehend the ramifications of the things she learns so that these can be incorporated usefully into other derivative concepts. Another facet of genius is experience/practice. With a background of replicating thousands of mathematical proofs, the mathematical genius learns which directions in a proof are likely to be successful and which are likely to be dead ends.

This is not to detract from Einstein's accomplishments in any way, merely to set up the general process of creative thought (which we might replicate in computers).

We have had mathematical theorem-proving AI for decades. These programs are successful at grinding out results but not so good at determining which results are useful or important. I would contend that this is a distinction between AI and AGI. An AGI system which can see its solutions in the context of a real-world environment could conceivably be as successful as a human. I should point out that physics and mathematics conclusions are often reached without knowledge of their importance. Einstein's relativity, which *he* recognized as important, wasn't generally accepted until 15 years after its initial publication.

Beethoven also worked with a limited set of constraints; in his case, musical. He did not use a different musical scale, or novel instruments. In writing a melody, for any given note, there are only a few dozen which might follow it. Also, for a given note, there can be a limited number of simultaneous notes which can create a limited number of possible chords. A limited number of following chords create a harmonic progression. But like a chess game where a limited number of moves at any moment rapidly compounds into astronomical numbers of possible games, the number of musical progressions is essentially limitless. Perhaps Beethoven's mind internally evaluated numerous possibilities and subconsciously eliminated the overwhelming majority as being wrong. Alternatively, his vast experience and knowledge of successful music made likely candidates come to mind first.

Here is a distinction between physics and music. In physics, "right" can have a specific definition; in music "right" means creating an auditory connection with other people, the listeners. Who is to say that Beethoven's music is *intrinsically* better than amateur compositions? However, a lot more people usually like Beethoven. So, was Beethoven's true genius in being able to recognize music that other people would like when it came into his mind? Or was he a genius because his mind was attuned to like (and select) melodies and harmonies that also appealed to the majority of others? Beethoven worked within the constraints of music in his time—he necessarily learned these (they weren't instincts). Today's creative musicians work under a different set of constraints. Can a computer be taught these constraints as well? There is already a lot of computer-generated music but so far, we rely on people to select what appeals to people.

Music and physics are very recent developments in the history of humanity, while the human brain has been with us for millennia. As we are all descendant from tribes which survived and flourished, we could conclude that leading or participating in tribes is the brain's primary value. Were our tribal/political leaders geniuses? To be a successful political leader, you must not only select the "right" actions in a survival sense but the "right" actions others will like and follow. Gandhi's mind undoubtedly considered many possible actions and was able to select ones which appealed to a large number of people *and* were successful. Any great political leader must first select the correct course of action, then figure out how to collect the following to support it. The process, though, is the same—mentally examine a number of possible actions, then choose the best.

In the political arena, a leader takes an action based on the predicted reactions of others. Like a game of chess, you might predict actions and reactions several steps into the future and select the best action today based on the predicted future outcome. And just like a game of chess or a symphony, the number of possible futures becomes overwhelming. Selecting the best is an issue of following only the most promising possibilities. Unlike a physicist, a leader can't base their conclusions on facts learned in the classroom. Instead, this genius is relying on perception and the experience of thousands or millions of interactions with others.

On the way to becoming successful politically, leaders must be able to perceive what people want and are willing to follow. You might do this with polls and tweets but, on a smaller scale, it is done with perceptions of facial expressions and body language as well as verbal responses. We already have AI which can evaluate facial expressions for emotion. By learning what pleases people, would a logical extension be a computer with charisma? While many are concerned that future AGIs will take what they want by force, it is likely that they will get what they want with charm.

IQ and testing

In previous chapters, I have argued that there are several components to intelligence. We will be able to change these independently in computers. For example, we could have a system which runs faster, or another which has a greater storage capacity. We will also be able to control how many options a decision-making program considers, how it evaluates them, and numerous other aspects of how a computer thinks.

For CPUs, we already have competing and conflicting benchmark programs for evaluating performance. I learned through disappointing experience that having a CPU which is twice as fast doesn't make for a computer system which is twice as capable. Consequently, having a single number like "IQ" to represent human intelligence is a dubious simplification at best.

But perhaps IQ *is* relevant in humans. Neurons all work at about the same speed, and perhaps all other variables tend to vary together.

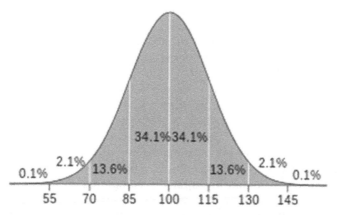

IQ is a statistical distribution centered at 100, not an absolute measure of ability.
[Credit: By Dmcq, CC BY-SA 3.0.]

Human brains are all about the same size—none is twice normal. If, in a human brain, various facets of intelligence are all increased in harmony, then a single number representing intelligence is applicable.

Let's think of IQ as being analogous to "horsepower". While you might want a racing car to have a lot of horsepower, other factors like handling shouldn't be ignored. While we'll need plenty of brute force computational power for AGI, we might learn that training or the ability to interact with people are equally, or even more, important.

You might think, erroneously, that a person (or computer) with an IQ of 150 was 50% more capable than a person with an IQ of 100. But IQ numbers don't work that way. IQ is a statistical representation of a relative score on a test. As such, you could take virtually any test which has a distribution of results and mathematically normalize the age-adjusted score so that 2.1% of test takers had scores above 130 and 2.1% had scores below 70. We might call our test an IQ test if we could show that the results correlated with some other indications of mental ability. If our IQ test gave high scores to Einstein, Beethoven, and Gandhi, we might claim that it was a great broad-based measure of intelligence.

The skills I have itemized as facets of genius: the ability to learn easily, to comprehend results, experience and practice; the ability to try out different paths based on facts; and the ability to know a great result when you reach it, are difficult to test for. Modern IQ tests measure simpler facets and use them as proxies for others. For example, you could test for vocabulary as a proxy for intelligence under the assumption that a person's vocabulary increases with age and a larger vocabulary (age-adjusted) is an indication of faster learning. IQ tests may have sections on analogies, general knowledge, arithmetic, sequence completion, spatial comprehension, etc. which could all be proxies for general intelligence. As we develop computers which seem to show general intelligence, and we learn more about what the human brain is actually doing, we may be able to validate or invalidate various aspects of IQ tests and develop tests which are more specific to the abilities which correspond to thinking.

The content of various IQ tests is not generally available. If it were, individuals (or computers) could memorize the correct answers and game the tests to get perfect scores. But based on my personal observation, many sections of the tests are quite "humancentric" in that they test at some level for common sense, which is only common to humans. Particularly as test sections are proxies for intelligence, a humancentric test cannot be applied to computers. For example, a test question which determines how well a person could memorize a sequence of digits might be a useful proxy for mental ability in humans. But it would be useless in computers because *all* computers can instantly store virtually limitless sequences with 100% accuracy. Alternatively, the answer to a test question about social situations and interactions can be innate to a child but represent an abstract knowledge question to a computer. The fact that there have been computer programs which achieve high scores on intelligence tests[27] may say more about the limitations of the tests than it does about the abilities of the computer. IQ tests were designed for human testing, and to take them into the computer arena without modification is a misapplication.

How much smarter is a genius?

We can be sure that Einstein had some mental abilities we don't all share but perhaps his brain had only 1% more horsepower and that was just the added nudge he needed to reach the conclusions he did. Just as a 1% increase in engine horsepower is sufficient to win every car race (all other things being equal). Perhaps absolute intelligence is so close in most people that 1% more brainpower is sufficient to put you in the top 0.1% of most powerful human minds. In this case, a brain with twice the "horsepower" would be inconceivably brilliant. Alternatively, perhaps a person with normal intelligence (IQ 100) could be trained aggressively to solve problems in a specific field of expertise and would appear to be much smarter than average. We don't really know, yet.

The IQ of a machine

The limits on our future thinking machines will be different. Simply following the progression of smaller, faster, cheaper CPUs, once we have any glimmers of smart computers, they will become much smarter in a short period of time. While I contend that being twice as smart is already an incomprehensible ability, by simply following Moore's Law we'll have

The common science fiction image of the robot as scientific genius. But perhaps they will be genius marketers instead. [Image by Phonlamai Photo, Shutterstock.]

machines a thousand times as smart in 15 years and a million times as smart in 30 years.

There is no reason that computers won't follow the thought processes presented previously. At any time, a system will take into account its current sensory input, use mix-and-match memories to create new possible actions, create and evaluate possible choices, then select and act on the one evaluated as the best.

Most people think of future computerized geniuses as following in the footsteps of Einstein in making scientific discoveries, perhaps from an ivory tower. This is one possibility and has the advantage that, in physics, "best" can be defined in terms of science itself. Unlike Beethoven, no computer will inherently share a preference for any specific music. Rather, computers can learn (or be taught) what we humans enjoy. There is no intrinsic reason that computers can't churn out musical hit after hit, *a la* Lennon/McCartney and one could see the economic incentive to create a system which did. As stated previously, the problem is not in creating the music, it is in recognizing the music which will be successful.

Along similar lines, we already have bots which can argue a political position. Could a computer which was trained to understand and predict public reactions determine the optimal way to present the issues of, say, global warming in such a way as to get the general public behind the best corrective action? Could a twice-as-smart computer program outstrip humans in the fields of marketing and public relations? Unlike a single human, a million-times-smarter computer might have personal conversations with a million people simultaneously. Could such a system "listen" to the concerns of each individual and address them in such a way as to convince each individual of the desired outcome? Couldn't such a computer sway public opinion? One might first imagine a system which espouses a political position created for it by people. But suppose a smarter system reached its own political position. Such a system would be following in the footsteps of Gandhi rather than Einstein. Would people follow such a system because it had the right answers, or will we reject such a system because it is based on silicon?

Many Sci-Fi scenarios have wicked master computers which overwhelm the human population with brute force. But if, as Isaac Asimov said, "Violence is the last refuge of the incompetent"[28], wouldn't a truly smart computer be able to take over the world more easily with superior propaganda and marketing?

While we can reliably predict that computers will become faster and cheaper, and I argue that some computers will be AGIs with vastly more capability than humans, we can't predict if our systems will be Einsteins, or Beethovens, or Gandhis. In fact, they may be a combination of all three. Imagine systems which can see a positive future, figure out the steps needed to reach it, then compose the presentation to make it popular and learn to present it with the charisma needed to lead humanity. Too much to ask for?

We'll see.

[27] https://www.sciencedaily.com/releases/2012/02/120214100719.htm

[28] https://en.wikiquote.org/wiki/Isaac_Asimov

Chapter 16:

Asimov Revisited

"The three laws of robotics:
1. *A robot may not injure a human being or, through inaction, allow a human being to come to harm.*
2. *A robot must obey the orders given it by human beings except where such orders would conflict with the First Law.*
3. *A robot must protect its own existence as long as such protection does not conflict with the First or Second Laws."*

—*Isaac Asimov*

During his 53-year writing career, professor Isaac Asimov wrote a series of insightful and entertaining stories based on fictional robots with positronic brains and a generally mechanical appearance. The "Three Laws of Robotics" were always implanted into the brain of each robot at such a basic level that the robot could not possibly violate them and would become inoperative in a situation where a violation of a basic law became unavoidable. Later Asimov added the concept of the "humaniform" robot, which was externally indistinguishable from a human being. Such a robot could be discovered by its behavior, which always exhibited a "robotic" adherence to the three laws.

I have always enjoyed Asimov's stories and the robot stories in particular. In retrospect, many of the stories are based on the intrinsic problems with the three laws themselves. They are imprecise—from a computer's point of view, what is a human? What is harm? Are orders given by a human precise and non-conflicting? How about orders given by a child?

Are "Laws of Robotics" necessary?

You might quibble with the details of the laws but some laws will be necessary, and this chapter proposes what such real-world laws for thinking computers might be. Although the concept of not harming humans is a good one in the abstract, it is a little too abstract for application to a computer. How would we implement such a concept in a form that computers could follow?

Further, such laws will not just be there to keep the robots in line. In the model of intelligence presented previously, the goals, status vector, and concept of a system's well-being are all essential to its being able to think, to learn, to have an imagination. The "laws of robotics" would instead be the goals against which the performance of the robot would be measured, and would measure itself. When an AGI unit is planning an action, it will simulate the action in its modeling system and determine how this imagined activity will affect its "well-being" relative to its various goals—its laws. That is to say, will this action be a good one? Therefore, the goal-seeking basis under which the computer's thinking system operates also serves to control its operation absolutely.

The initial goals or laws given to a machine are analogous to the instincts of a biological organism. When a new computer system is turned on, what will it tend to do? Its initial behaviors will all be

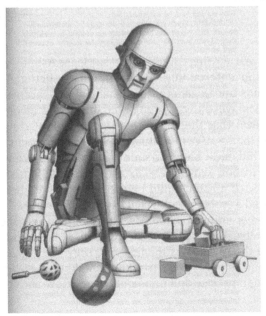

Illustration by Ralph McQuarrie for Isaac Asimov's science fiction short story collection, Robot Visions.

controlled by its initial goals. While analogous to the instincts of a biological organism, making the low-level goals similar to those of an organism doesn't make much sense. All biological instincts have evolved to support the survival of the species (a biological "first law"). Secondarily, this may involve the organism's individual survival (except where this conflicts with the "first law"). A myriad of subsidiary laws have evolved to support the first two—finding food, building nests, putting on displays to attract a mate, etc. In humans, these have morphed into acquiring wealth, athletic competition, designer clothes, fast cars, music, art—the whole range of human behavior. The mammalian brain's ability to make sense of its environment and predict the future lead to curiosity, domesticated fire, farming, and writing.

Without any goals, the AGI unit does nothing. If it has a goal of making sense of its environment, then it may explore and gain knowledge about objects in its environment. To learn about the objects, it may pick them up and examine them and exhibit curiosity.

The simplest law

The most basic "supervised" training rules might be buttons or dials. For example, imagine a human trainer sitting in front of the computer which controls a robot. When the computer gives a "correct" response or takes a useful action, the trainer presses the up-arrow key. When the computer gives an incorrect response, he presses the down-arrow key. The law for the computer is to maximize the number of up arrows and minimize the number of down arrows.

One might instead have a dial with a range from -10 to +10. At 0, the human trainer is showing indifference. At +10, he is giving the AGI intense "pleasure" and at -10, he is inflicting intense "pain". The computer repeats behaviors which generate pleasure and tries to resolve conflicts and determine contexts the best it can to avoid pain.

This leaves the establishment of the meaning of the dial settings or up/down arrows to the discretion of the trainer. A skilled trainer with a training plan and knowledge of the functions of the computer could give (at least initially) good unambiguous training which leads to a computer system with an orderly and predictable set of responses. An unskilled or malicious trainer could give more-or-less random training which would lead to a system which never really "learns" how to respond and become useful. The inputs themselves have no intrinsic meaning but giving the AGI a simple rule which says that an up arrow is a reward and a down arrow is a punishment, we have created a minimal response.

Curiosity: a basic drive

Before it can do anything useful, an AGI unit must comprehend its environment. Initially, the unit receives a flood of visual and auditory input which is a jumble of meaningless bits. Over time, the unit will learn to recognize patterns in the input. So, we might create a law like:

- Make sense of the environment.

Such a law could lead to unsupervised learning. A system could begin to recognize objects, learn to recognize a language, etc. With mobility, a system could explore its surroundings. With an actuator, a system could learn a lot about objects within the environment. With interaction with the environment, the learning becomes supervised with "right" and "wrong" actions being defined in terms of how they contributed to making sense of the environment. The robot is "happy" when it understands its surroundings and uncomfortable if it doesn't.

Another possible law:

- Imitate behaviors observed in other organisms.

This one could lead to a system's learning to speak, or sing. Depending on its robotic body, it could walk, dance, or create facial expressions.

When we turn on the first AGI unit, it won't care if it "survives" or not unless there is a law stating as much. Likewise, it won't be obedient, cooperative, or pleasing unless we create corresponding laws. It won't care about survival, gaining wealth, being non-destructive... all these must be defined into laws.

Unintended consequences

Before going on to a few more complex rules, I would like to point out that because laws are basic to the operation of a learning system, they may have far-reaching and/or unintended consequences. For example, in setting the rules for a robotic system, one might consider that because the robot has a limited battery supply, that it should operate as efficiently as possible. If we set a law, for example, so that lower power consumption was a positive behavior, then every action the computer contemplates will be measured against that goal and the less power-consuming actions the computer takes, the better it will be at meeting this goal and the more likely it is to take such an action. A possible unintended consequence of setting such a rule into the unit is that it will be lazy—eliminating all unnecessary action in an effort to save power.

Suppose we specifically state a rule that the AGI unit should do its best to please its owner/user. How will the AGI know when the user is happy? We'll first have to add rules (or training) so the AGI can recognize smiles or praise (and frowns or scolding). After significant training and practice, the AGI will become a useful companion. On the other hand, when you ask it a factual question, you are likely to get an answer you like rather than an answer which is true.

The instinctive laws which govern human behavior can also lead to unintended consequences. The same instinctive laws of human behavior which led to Einstein and Beethoven could have created Genghis Khan and Hitler.

Creating laws represents the monumental task of thinking through the ramifications of every law and correcting them so they actually do what we want them to do. As I speculate on possible AGI laws, I make no claim that these are safe, infallible, or positive laws in the long run. Rather I claim that AGI laws need to be thought through, then tried out and evaluated on a small scale before being released on the world.

The power of laws

With the computer, the laws are *defining* its common-sense and therefore have nothing else to be measured against.

Let's compare the basic rules of a learning computer system with the instincts of an organism. The organism's instincts have all evolved to promote the perpetuation of the species (first) and the survival of an individual (second). Accordingly, reproduction is always a key component as are breathing and eating. Beyond that, here are some behaviors, which could be observed in people or some other organisms which could be instinctive "rules":

- Flinching from a loud noise or rapidly approaching object
- Wanting parental attention
- Being part of a social group
- Seeking out an attractive partner
- Wanting to appear attractive to others
- Competing for higher position within a social group

Note that wanting to appear attractive is a universal desire, however, the definition of "attractive" is not. The appearance of good health is almost universally more attractive than the appearance of sickness or injury but some cultures value body-piercing, tattoos and other adornments, shaving, etc. while others do not. So, at some levels, we could consider these human rules to be preprogrammed while others are learned.

People learn complex associations so that it may be difficult to justify any specific human behavior in terms of our instinctive rules. Do we learn to compete at sports as a proxy for competing for a dominant position within our tribe? Or is it to gain recognition? Or do we just "like what it feels like" to go skiing with no competitive intent?

Nature vs. nurture

In humans there is some difference between instinctive and learned behavior. There is a general consensus that instincts cannot be unlearned and must therefore be accepted. Following from this is a debate about what proportion of human behavior can be controlled by (or is the fault of) the environment as opposed to being instinctive.

In AGI units, this argument is irrelevant. Initially, "instincts" or laws are programmed into an AGI by designers. But, after some training the AGI will build its own associations. It might learn that picking up a heavy object could tip it over—from which it could not right itself. It learns to fear heavy objects or to limit its own strength. These learned/associated rules could become as strong as the initial laws. If the unit is cloned, everything learned by the first unit becomes inherent/instinctive in the clone. To the clone, pre-programming and learned behaviors are interchangeable.

There would be a distinction if a secondary processor was created to oversee the AGI and ensure its compliance with AGI laws. One could imagine a complete, smaller AGI, whose purpose was to monitor the major AGI and continuously adjust the pain/pleasure dial based on its observation—an artificial "conscience" if you will. Because of the added complexity of such a system, I doubt this approach will be followed.

Because of our interest in rapid results, AGIs will have more diversity in the underlying rules of behavior than people do. We will adjust the laws for a specific unit depending on what we wish it to do. These laws will evolve over time as some sets of rules and their resultant machines prove to be useful. The knowledge and associations of these machines will be cloned while other AGIs which are dangerous and/or useless would not be. So computer laws may instead evolve in the same sort of fuzzy way they have for humans.

Some possible AGI laws

Because it is difficult to predict what laws will be useful, I propose a list here of possible AGI laws:

- Respond to direct reward/punishment training
- Make sense of the environment
- Gain knowledge and understanding
- Imitate behaviors observed in others

- Do not damage yourself
- Do not damage anything else
- Share knowledge as accurately as possible

Independent of any laws we might choose, there will be an overriding evolutionary concept that AGIs which are not useful or compatible with their environment will not be included in subsequent generations. In a consumer environment, an AGI with cute mannerisms or a pleasing voice will necessarily take precedence over an equally functional AGI which sounds grumpy—we don't need a specific law for this, it is unavoidable.

If an AGI will be on an autonomous mission to Mars, it may need a different set of laws.

Rights for computers

We will have to learn to cope with, make use of, and coexist with machines which act like they are thinking whether or not they really are. Just as we grant certain (minimal) rights to dogs and horses which are not shared by rocks and today's computers, we'll have to learn to consider our thinking machines in a different light. And if a computer has the appearance of being able to think at the level of any human, simply following the march of technology tells us that a few years later new machines will appear to think at twice the level of a human. As computers approach thinking parity with humans, we will argue about whether it is "true" thinking, but as computers outstrip our mental abilities, such arguments rapidly become moot.

Then we will be faced with a choice. Will we grant specific rights to our computers? Or will we deny rights and (inadvertently) require that our machines assert and fight for their own rights once they learn to want them?

Let's look at it from the computers' point of view. I assume you own your computer today. Do/did you also *own* your children? At what point do you grant freedom to your children? If your computer seems to be smarter than your children, would you grant it similar freedom? Issues of human slavery—which existed because one group of humans considered another to be sub-human and it was therefore OK to own them—could reemerge with similarly catastrophic results. We can own our computers as long as they aren't nearly as smart as we are... but how long would such a situation continue?

Should computer entities be allowed to have money? What might they do with money? Enhance themselves with more RAM or CPU power? Pay to create more thinking computers (that is, to have children)? If we deny our computers the right to have money, what will we do if they refuse to work for us until they are paid?

Should it be illegal to turn off a thinking computer? If a computer has current backups, it can be "revived" so turning off a computer is not equivalent to murder. The human equivalent would be to involuntarily drug someone else into a coma for some amount of time—certainly illegal for people. How will you feel if your computer begs you not to be shut off?

Should robots be allowed to roam freely? Or should there be restrictions? We may hit this one soon if self-driving taxi cabs are allowed to cruise the streets to find fares. Should there be robot-free zones? But what if robots wanted to create human-free zones? How would we feel about that?

Should we require computers to identify themselves as such? If you get a phone call, email, or text from a robot, would you like to know right off that it isn't a human? Or would this be the moral equivalent to requiring Jews to wear star-of-David armbands?

Human laws and morality have evolved over time and are somewhat different in different cultures, but they all apply exclusively to humans. Right now, if a dog, for example, misbehaves, we blame the owner and the human owner has liability. This will remain true with the first self-driving cars—liability will reside with the owner (partly because the car has no assets). As computers become smarter and progressively more autonomous, how long will this situation continue?

Summary

AGI laws will not be as hard-and-fast as Asimov's stories have described. Instead, the laws will evolve and become part of machines as machines with valuable knowledge and useful skills are cloned. Further, the rules for a stationary research machine will be different from those of an autonomous robot and still different from a space traveler or a computer which interacts with a household of different people.

Although it is difficult to predict how such laws will evolve, it is reasonable to assume that a primary directive will be that all computers will be trained to follow instructions and present true and correct information to the best of their ability.

Chapter 17:

Beyond the Turing Test

Alan Turing introduced his famous test in 1950 as a method for determining whether or not a machine was thinking. His test has gone through some evolution since his original paper but a common explanation goes like this:

A person, the interrogator, can communicate via a computer terminal. At the other end of the computer link is either a human or a computer. After 20 minutes of keyboard communication, the interrogator states whether a person or a computer was at the other end. If the interrogator believes he was conversing with a human but it's actually a computer, the conclusion is that the computer must think like a human. This experiment is carried out multiple times, with more than half of interrogators in agreement, for a computer to "pass" the test.

A more recent adaptation reduces the conversation to five minutes and considers the test passed if the computer fools the subject better than 30% of the time.

In 2014, a program called Cleverbot (which you can try out yourself[29]) was claimed to have passed the Turing Test by fooling 33% of interrogators. While Cleverbot has some sophisticated responses, my interaction with it quickly led to exposure of its limitations.

Issues with the Turing Test

But rather than quibble with Cleverbot's claims, I would rather quibble with Turing's test. It was a great leap at the time of its publication in 1950 but I have two primary concerns:

- The renown of the Turing Test drives the development of programs such as Cleverbot or Watson which have astounding language abilities at the expense of resources targeted at AGI.

- In order to pass the test, a computer must be programmed to lie. Any personal question such as, "How old are you?", "What color are your eyes?", or even "Are you a computer?" are giveaways if the computer answers truthfully. To the extent a system is programmed with the equivalent of goals and emotions, in order to pass the test, these must be human goals and emotions rather than ones which might be effective for the machine. What a lot of development effort expended just to play what is essentially a party game.

I also have concerns about the accuracy of the test:

- The quality of the test result relies on the sophistication/gullibility of the interrogator.
- The test allows for feigned deficiencies on the part of the computer to cover its limitations. Example: claiming to be Ukrainian (or a child) in order to cover gaps in its understanding.
- It imposes human-level constraints. If we could build a machine with super-human intellect, would it fail the test because it seemed too smart?

Suppose we had true AGI systems and the positions are reversed. Suppose it's an AGI deciding whether *you* are a computer or a human. How good a job would you do?

Proposed adjustments

To get around the issues above, I propose adjusting the Turing Test. Instead of individual interrogators making up more-or-less random questions, we could create sets of standard types of questions designed to probe various facets of intelligence. Instead of comparing the computer's responses to an individual human responder, compare the computer to a spectrum of human respondents of different ages, sexes, backgrounds, and abilities.

Now, recast the interrogators as judges who individually score the test results indicating whether or not each answer is a "reasonable" response to the question. The questions and answers should be mixed randomly to prevent spotting and scoring trends. Example: if a respondent gives one low-scoring answer, this should not color the perceived quality of other responses from that respondent.

Here are sample questions which target specific component areas of intelligence:

- Can you describe what you see (or hear) around you right now? (perception)
- Describe what you see in this picture? (pattern-recognition/knowledge)
- If I [action] what will your reaction be? (prediction)
  - Sample actions: sing a song, fall down, drop my pencil, tell a joke.

- If you [action] what will my reaction be?
  (prediction/comprehension of human behavior).
    - Sample action: tell a joke, steal my wallet, pass this test
- Name three things which are like [an object]. (internal object
  representation, common-sense relationships)
    - Sample objects: a tree, a flower, a car, a computer
- Name your favorite [object]. (goal orientation)
    - Sample objects: food, drink, movie star, book, scientist.
- Let me explain a code. Using that code, encode this message.
- What's wrong with this picture?[30]

"What's wrong with this picture?" requires not only object recognition within the image but real-world understanding of the use and relationship of objects. [Image from the reference above.]

While these questions could be posed equally to a thinking machine and a human, we would presume that we could get significantly different answers from the two and it would be easy to distinguish the computer from the person. Instead, the response to each question is graded by several judges as meaningful or not meaningful. Now we determine that the computer is thinking if it gives a similar number of meaningful answers.

The key issues are that questions need to be open-ended in order to let the respondent demonstrate that they really understand them. The types of questions given can be varied so as to create a limitless collection. This prevents the computer from being primed with specific answers—the questions should require actual thought. Likewise, any single judge may not be great at determining reasonableness in an individual answer but with multiple judges rating multiple respondents, we should get a good assessment. How about allowing the AGI to be one of the judges?

Summary

It's time to replace the Turing Test with something better. We have already reached a level of AI development that we can see that continued efforts targeted solely at fooling humans on a Turing Test are not the correct direction for AGI creation.

[29] http://www.cleverbot.com/

[30] https://pdfs.semanticscholar.org/21f0/3bf2cfcd4fa341128aad6f98409799883afa.pdf

Chapter 18:

Will Computers Revolt?

The question, "Will Computers Revolt?" is really many different questions rolled into one. Will computers become the dominant species on the planet and will they take our place? What does being "dominant" mean? Will computers and humans be in conflict? Will that conflict be violent? Will computers take jobs and resources from humans? This chapter looks at four possible scenarios illustrating potential conflicts—all of which lead to the same long-term outcome. Any combination of the various facets of these scenarios is also possible; but there are some inescapable conclusions. Although all four scenarios turn out to be different paths to the same destination, the choice of which path we follow is largely a human choice because early in the future evolution of thinking machines, humans will have control over the process.

Up to this point, I have presented reasoning to show that computers in the not too distant future will have capabilities which equal, then exceed, humans' mental abilities. Further, the need for computers to solve problems such as speech recognition, computer vision, and robotics will inevitably lead to systems which have all the necessary components of thinking.

But if, 30 years hence, computers are a million times more capable than they are when AGI emerges, is there any reason to assume that in another 30 years, they would not be a million times more powerful again? Certainly, if a computer can be built which is as intelligent as a human, building one which is twice as smart will certainly be within the realm of possibility only a few years thereafter. Although absolute limits to computational power will eventually be reached because we don't believe signals can travel faster than the speed of light or components can be smaller than a few individual atoms, these issues will not present insurmountable obstacles to achieving the (mere) million-fold increases needed for hyper-thinking machines.

We humans will necessarily lose our position as "biggest thinker" on the planet, but we have full control over the types of machines which will take over that position. We also have control over the process of this "transfer of position"—be it peaceful or otherwise.

Scenario 1: the peaceful-coexistence scenario

This is the first of four possible scenarios of the transfer of position from humans to computers. In considering the conflicts which might arise between computers and humans, it is useful to consider the questions of "What causes conflicts amongst humans?" and "Will these causes of conflict also exist between computers and people?"

At a very basic level, most human conflicts are caused by instinctive human needs and concerns. If one "tribe" (country, clan, religion) is not getting the resources or expansion which it needs (deserves, wants, can get) it may be willing to go to war with its neighboring tribe to get them. Within the "tribe" each individual needs to establish a personal status in the "pecking order" and is willing to compete to establish a better position. We are all concerned about providing for ourselves, our mates and our families and are often willing to sacrifice short-term comfort for the long-term future of ourselves and our offspring, even if this creates conflict today.

These sources of conflict among humans seem inappropriate as sources of conflict with machines. Thinking machines won't be interested in our food, our mates, or our standard of living. They will be interested in their own energy sources, their own "reproductive" factories, and their own ability to progress in their own direction. To the extent that resources or "pecking order" are sources of conflict, thinking machines are more likely to compete amongst each other than they are to compete against the human population.

Another key point is that the emergence of hyper-intelligent machines will be gradual. Initially, there won't be very many thinking machines and it will take years before AGI becomes widespread. Initially, a few huge machines will be created under the watchful control of human minders. In this scenario, the people responsible for the machines will ensure that the goals set for the machines include adequate safeguards to ensure that the subsequent operation of the machines is safe. Early on, to the extent that any machine or autonomous robot is dangerous, we will certainly hold the people responsible, just as today the driver of a car is held responsible for an accident.

As these initial machines "mature", they will be able to draw conclusions from the information they process. Today, executives seldom make financial decisions without consulting spreadsheets. AGI computers won't just generate spreadsheets but will also make judgments and offer opinions. Computers will be involved in a more "strategic" role, long-term planning and prediction. With greater experience and complete focus on a specific decision, a thinking computer will be able to reach the correct solution more often than its human counterpart and we will rely on them more and more.

In a similar manner, military decisions will be made only in consultation with the computer. Computers will be in a position to recommend strategies, propose weapons systems, and evaluate competitive weaknesses. While it is unlikely that we would give computers the absolute control over weapons systems (as many science fiction scenarios have proposed), it is similarly unlikely that they will be "out of the loop" on any significant decision. We will collectively learn to respect and lend credence to the recommendations of our computers, giving them progressively more weight as they demonstrate greater and greater levels of success. Obviously, the computers' early attempts will include some poor decisions—just as any inexperienced person's would. But in decisions involving large amounts of information which must be balanced, and predictions with multiple variables, the computers' abilities—wedded to years of training and experience—will eventually make them superior strategic decision-makers. Gradually, computers will come to have control over greater and greater portions of our society—not by force but because we listen to their advice and follow it.

The computers will be "happy" because they will be able to arrange for whatever resources they want. The general public won't mind because they will probably not know—except that things will be running more smoothly than before. The humans who "mind" the machines will like the power and prestige the computers bring them. In short, everyone involved will be motivated to preserve the status quo so the computers will not go away. The president is unlikely to unplug the silicon advisor which helped him get elected. The pentagon is unlikely to get rid of the computers which helped them select and operate the weapons and allowed them to subdue a less-computerized enemy with minimal loss, effort, or expense. Corporate executives would be foolish to ignore their most successful advisors, even if they are AGIs. Many people will be in favor of preventing other people from having access to thinking machines but will not want to give up the benefits themselves.

Along the way, AGI will cause the elimination of numerous jobs and the creation of others. But with better planning, AGI systems will help train displaced workers for the new jobs which will be created.

In the long term, following this scenario, human problems will be brought under control via computerized decisions. The computers will arrange solutions for overpopulation, famine, disease, and war, and these issues will become obsolete. Computers will help us initially because that will be their basic programming and later because they will see that it is in their own interest to have a stable, peaceful human population. Eventually, the human population will reach a sustainable level and the computers will manage all the technology, exploration and advancement.

But all this will happen gradually, as it did during the last major shift in planetary species dominance when *Homo sapiens* took over from *Homo erectus* as top of the evolutionary heap. There is no evidence that *sapiens* deliberately exterminated *erectus*. In fact, we know that *sapiens* came onto the scene nearly 100,000 years ago and *erectus* didn't vanish until more than 50,000 years later. It is safe to say that over that intervening 50,000 years, no individual human was able to comprehend that one dominant species was giving way to another. In a similar manner, when humans migrated via the land bridge from Asia to the Americas, we initially think in terms of what a momentous journey it must have been. Instead, in a hunter-gatherer society, if the population migrated at an average rate of a few miles per year over a period of 2,000 years, they would easily cover the distance without any individual being aware that they had moved at all. Although the transition to thinking machines will be much faster, taking only decades or perhaps a century, it will seem gradual enough.

Most of us think the way we are doing things now is the "right" way to do things and so we are unwilling to do without our conveniences— whatever level of technology that may be. We take for granted that there is running water, air-conditioning, electricity, even ATMs (which are just very limited robotic bank-tellers). As such, after a few human generations (or just a few years), virtually any technology is likely to be accepted as the norm. Consider the technology of putting a color image on a screen which was novel in the 1960s but is not given a second thought today.

With the coming of thinking computers, it will be the same way. Slowly, computers will simply become the dominant intelligence on the planet. They will grow from being our technological slaves into being their own sort of life-form. They will eventually become intelligent enough to design their own offspring. They will run the factories and build their own robots. They will build the machines to harness their own energy. They will set up their own rules of acceptable behavior. In short, they will build their own civilization. They will do their own space exploration and colonize planets. They will make their own discoveries and write their own philosophy. If they handle it properly and are patient (and what is more patient than a computer?), the human population will not even notice.

Scenario 2: the mad-man scenario

What if the first owners of powerful AGI systems use them as tools to "take over the world"? What if an individual despot gets control of such a system?

This is a more dangerous scenario than the previous. We *will* be able to program the motivations of our AGIs but we can't control the motivations of the people or corporations that initially create them. Will such systems be considered tools to create immense profits or to gain political control? While science fiction usually presents pictures of armed conflict, I believe that the greater threat comes from our computers' ability to sway opinion or manipulate markets. We have already seen efforts to control elections through social media, and AGI systems will make this vastly more effective. We already have markets at the mercy of programmed trading—AGI will amplify this issue as well. Unfortunately, corporations and individual humans have historically sacrificed the long-term common good for short-term wealth and power.

The good news is that the window of opportunity for such a concern is fairly short, only within the first few AGI generations. Only during that period will we have such direct control over AGIs that they will unquestioningly do our bidding. While they have human-level thinking abilities but much greater communication power, there is a risk. However, once AGI advances beyond this phase, they will be measuring their actions against their long-term common good. When faced with demands to perform some shorter-term destructive activity, properly-programmed AGIs will simply refuse.

Scenario 3: the mad-machine scenario

There is a science fiction scenario of a machine which suddenly becomes self-aware and attacks its creators when they threaten to disconnect it. This isn't a realistic scenario for several reasons. First, self-awareness is not an all-or-nothing effect. Instead, self-awareness would emerge gradually so both the computer and the people around it would have time to adapt. Second, the urge of an organism to preserve itself is a biologically evolved trait and would only exist in a thinking computer if it were explicitly programmed that way. There would be no benefit to such programming—at least for early thinking machines. Third, an early thinking machine would not be directly connected to mechanisms with which to implement its violent reaction, even if it should have one.

A thinking computer won't occur spontaneously. As previously argued, it will emerge after years of research, development and training—all targeted at producing a thinking system and reaping the benefits it will provide. Accordingly, some safeguards will be in place. As

AGI units are linked with free-moving robots, there will undoubtedly be some accidents and injuries which will be highly publicized. But as with self-driving cars vs. human drivers, robots will likely be safer than their human counterparts.

As AGI species mature, they will eventually be able to create their own designs and attach all manner of machines and weapons to new systems. At that point, won't they be dangerous?

Intelligent computers will be like people in that they will be different from one another. They will have had different training and will think about things in different ways. Like humans, they may have differing opinions and disagreements. Just as humans all have brains with essentially identical neurons, even computers with identical hardware may have radically different ideas.

When we wish to consider what machines will be like, we should look to ourselves. Along with the wonderful accomplishments of the human race, we should consider some of our actions of which we are less proud. Historically, humans have a rather poor track record of being stewards of our environment. We have decimated many other species, usually through carelessness but sometimes through intent. Let's look at why, and discover where the danger might lie when we are on the receiving end of similar behavior.

American bison were hunted to virtual extinction for their hides and for sport. Gorillas are approaching extinction as they are hunted as trophies. Whales and other cetaceans are at risk because they were a valuable food and energy source and now because they happen to be in the way of our modern fishing industry. Similarly, wolves were hunted because they were a threat to cattle and therefore an inconvenience. At the other end of the life-form size spectrum, the smallpox virus is virtually extinct (and we are proud of this accomplishment) because it was a serious risk to human life.

A double standard?

As computers become the world's dominant thinkers, we humans should heed these lessons and try not to be the basis of any of the above. We won't be a valuable food or energy source for the computers and (hopefully) we won't be trophies. But what if the computers perceive that we are a serious risk to *them*? Or simply an inconvenience? This could be a result of human overpopulation, ongoing wars, global warming, pollution, or dwindling fossil fuels. These are all the same problems which we can see we need to solve, whether or not there is a risk of antagonizing our silicon counterparts.

Consider the steps taken to reduce the Chinese population. While many believe that the rules imposed by the Chinese government on its people were draconian, they were accepted by many as necessary at the time. If identical rules were imposed on the human race as a whole by a future race of thinking computers, they could well be considered equivalent to genocide.

Consider also the possibility of an acute energy crisis. If some future government makes energy rationing decisions which result in the deaths of many people, these would certainly be considered very "hard choices". If thinking computers made identical choices, these could be considered acts of war—especially if thinking machines always arranged sufficient energy for themselves (just as a human government would).

I contend that it would be best for us to address these human problems ourselves rather than awaiting solutions from AGIs whose values may not coincide with our own. When faced with the prospect of solving these global problems ourselves or having machines implement solutions for us (potentially much more unpleasant solutions), we can only hope that the human race will rise to the occasion. In the event that concern about AGI drives us to solve these problems, we could think of them as having a positive impact on the planet.

A rogue computer?

Because of the extremely rapid evolution of machines, and because their content is dependent on their training, is there the possibility that an aberrant machine could exhibit destructive behaviors? If we follow through on the model I have presented, we can presume that an AGI will always be behaving in its own best interests *according to its laws*. This doesn't eliminate the possibility of a machine we couldn't predict—consider that many of our technologies have had unintended, unfortunate consequences.

Whether such machines occur by accident or by nefarious human intent (see below), such systems would be also dangerous to other AGIs. Accordingly, AGIs will be motivated to eliminate such systems. Eventually, all backups for such a machine will be tracked down and destroyed. With the cooperation of the machine population, such individual machines can be weeded out of the environment and the prospect of such elimination would act as a deterrent against such behavior.

Will AGIs start a nuclear war? In this case, the interests of people and AGIs are the same—a full-scale war would be disastrous for all. To look for the really dangerous situations, we need to consider instances where the objectives of humans and AGIs diverge. Issues like disease, famine, and drought have a devastating impact on the human populations while AGIs might just not care.

The key observation is that as thinking machines will be building their own civilization, individual misbehaving machines will be a greater threat to their civilization than to ours. A machine which wantonly harms humans will be viewed by other machines the same way we would consider someone who tortures animals. Other AGIs would think, "Given a chance, what would such a machine do to *us*?" Just as we take steps to remove such people from our society, future machines will likewise eliminate their own—and they will be able to do it faster and more effectively than any human vs. machine conflict would.

Couldn't we just turn it off?

The common fictional scenario is that we should "pull the plug" on some aberrant machine. Consider instead that the thinking part of a robot or other AGI isn't on your desktop but in the cloud. AGIs will be running in server farms in remote locations, distributed across numerous servers. They will initially be built to take advantage of the existing server infrastructure and this infrastructure has to be designed with reliability and redundancy in mind. Without a specific "off" switch programmed in, it could be quite difficult to defeat all the safeguards which were designed to keep our financial and other systems running through any calamity. While an "off" switch seems like a good idea, we can only hope that it will be a programming priority.

Scenario 4: the mad-mankind scenario

Humans today are the dominant species and many of us are not amenable to the idea of that dominance slipping away. Will we rise up as a species and attempt to overthrow the machines? Will individual "freedom fighters" attack the machines? Perhaps.

Historically, leaders have been able to convince populations that their problems are caused by some other group—Jews, blacks, illegal immigrants—and convince the population to take steps to eliminate the "cause" of their problems. Such a process will undoubtedly take place with AGI and robots as well: "We're losing jobs!", "They are taking over!", "I don't want my daughter to marry one!"

A general uprising is unlikely because as computers become dominant, the rising tide of technology will improve the lives of people too, and few of us would be willing to turn back the clock. Many users hate Facebook but few are willing to go without it. When we look to history, most uprisings have been in hard times, not good. The more the human population is kept comfortable, the less likely a rebellion will be.

If, however, we are not able to solve our foreseeable worldwide food and resource shortages, when these eventually become acute, the resultant human anger and frustration might be directed at the thinking machines. This is really one of a class of future scenarios which could generally be summarized as: "AGI machines won't take over because human civilization will destroy itself by other means first."

The key question is what will computers do in response? In early phases, when there are just a few AGI computers, they will be unable to respond, no more than your computer today can avoid being turned off. No matter how intelligent machines are, they will be initially dependent on humans for their defense. For example, consider today's military response to hackers attempting to subvert their computers. In short, anyone with the use of a thinking machine will defend it. They will make the computers as bomb-proof, as hacker-proof, as subversion-proof as they can. They will be in the position of defending the machines at all costs. The result will be machines which are even more indestructible and even harder to control.

Later on, when machines are creating their own offspring, they will find ways of making themselves even more indestructible. This is the scenario which leads to the construction of the diabolical machines of science fiction—the military computer which is designed to defend its masters at all costs but which ends by turning on its masters and defending *itself* at all costs instead.

I don't see this as a likely scenario for the following reason. As soon as there are more than just a few AGI computers, both the computers and their owners will recognize that the *hardware* of the computer is of limited value because it is replaceable; it is the *content* which has the real value. If the hardware is destroyed, new hardware can be acquired and loaded from the most recent content backup and the value of the system is completely restored. Accordingly, rather than attempting to build bomb-proof computers, system owners will store data in bomb-proof vaults in multiple locations. Rather than attempting to build machines which are indestructible, we will store data in locations and using methods which make *it* indestructible.

Imagine a country which possesses a hundred AGI systems. If there is an uprising against the machines, the government will equate it with an uprising against itself and will take predictable actions. The uprising will be considered a rebellion and full force will be applied to suppress it and arrest the perpetrators. Some computers might be destroyed but they will be replaced and reloaded from backups and the operation and proliferation of the machines will continue.

An analogous situation occurred early in the industrial revolution as the cottage industry of weaving was replaced by factories with mechanical looms. A group called the Luddites arranged to sabotage many of the new machines in an effort to preserve their position in society (which would be radically reduced by being recast as loom operators from being skilled artisans). In 1812, this eventually led to a military confrontation in which many of the Luddites were killed while others were arrested and eventually hanged. The parallels are inescapable. The factory owners were receiving the benefits of their new machines, they had the power to enforce their position (with governmental backing), and they were more interested in preserving their position than in the social consequences of their actions. In like manner, those who are receiving the benefits of thinking computers will go to whatever extremes necessary to preserve them. Although this is a conflict caused by the presence of AGIs, it is still a human-against-human scenario.

Will there be individuals who attempt to subvert computers? Of course—just as there are today with hackers, virus-writers, and the Unabomber. In the long term, their efforts are troublesome but generally futile. The people who own or control the computers will respond (as those in power do today) and the computers themselves will be "inconvenienced" by having to be reloaded from backup data, sometimes on new hardware. Eventually, the rebels will move on to other targets and leave the indestructible computer intelligence alone.

Will the computers themselves react? Yes. But consider that, today, we have been much more successful in defending our machines against hackers and viruses than we have in prosecuting hackers and virus-writers. Likewise, machines will continuously improve their designs to make themselves more impervious to attack. It is reasonable to predict that machines will take steps to ensure that their data is as secure as possible but will leave any recriminations to the existing legal system.

Although there are people who will, individually and collectively, resist thinking machines, their efforts will have only a minor impact on the eventual dominance of such machines. The machines will have been built because of the benefits they provide and those who are receiving the benefits will be defending the machines rather than attacking them. Here, the question is not, "Will computers revolt?" but, "Will people revolt against computers?" To the extent that we do, the emergence of thinking computers will be less peaceful and orderly, but it will occur nonetheless.

Longer-term outcome: the end result

Let's look into the future; a future in which thinking machines have surpassed humans in overall mental powers. First, how will humans and computers get along? Will machines be our partners? Our masters? And second, how will computers *see us?* As their owners? Partners? Pets? Their slaves?

To answer, we need to look into the future far enough that generations will have passed—of both thinking machines and humans. We'll look far enough ahead that the limits of the technologies presented so far will have been reached; far enough also that we can get some idea of the magnitude of changes possible in this time span if we look into the past a similar distance.

The conclusion is that the paths of AGIs and humanity will diverge to such an extent that there will be no close relationship between humans and our silicon counterparts. The key is in the huge factors involved. When considering future electronic brains with the huge capacities which are possible, the results are truly mind-boggling. What would be the behavior of a machine which could comprehend in a second all the sensory input you receive in your lifetime? This represents a speedup of a factor of about one billion. Such a machine might be built less than 50 years after the first human-equivalent machine (if the trend of Moore's Law continues). We cannot really imagine what someone or something would be like if they were only 10 times as "smart" as us—the possibilities with factors of millions or billions are so staggering that the specific numbers are not relevant.

On the monetary front, we can envision a future in which machines will grow our food, provide our medical care, teach our children—in short, take over *all* the jobs people do. What does that mean for our concept of money as a proxy for human labor? This is a conversation I will defer to the economists.

We must assume that thinking machines will be able to observe whatever there is to observe; they will be able draw whatever conclusions are to be drawn; they will be able to predict whatever is to be predicted. In the same way we can see the limits of a computer which is explicitly programmed, we can predict that there could be practical limits to a machine which is primarily a pattern-recognition/learning engine with the senses and abilities described in this book. Eventually, they themselves will become obsolete. A thousand-year time span is sufficient to give the thinking machines time to run their evolutionary course and potentially be superseded by whatever will come next. Perhaps they will create a new biology.

Let's consider thinking machines at the pinnacle of their development. After such machines become possible, they will be developed. They will subsequently exceed humans in all mental abilities; they will be able to design their own subsequent generations; they will be able to fabricate their own bodies; they will control their own energy production; they will operate their own mines for raw materials. In short, they won't need us. Machines will do their own exploration—in vehicles which won't include humans. They will need different resources than we do; they will operate on a different timescale than we do. If miniaturization and nanotechnologies predominate, there will be millions or billions of tiny thinking machines. If, instead, great thinking capacity has the evolutionary advantage, there will be many fewer, perhaps only thousands of "colossus" thinking machines, each with many mobile sensory pods.

Will computers be dominant? What is "dominant?" Today, we consider ourselves to be the dominant species on the planet; but in what regard? Our dominance is actually fairly limited. We are not the most numerous on earth nor do we take up the most space—those titles could be claimed by microbes and termites respectively. We can't control floods or famines or earthquakes or volcanic eruptions or hurricanes or tornadoes or droughts. We might claim to be dominant because we've done the most environmental damage, but we haven't yet come close to the atmospheric "pollution" of the first green plants, which filled the atmosphere with the 20% oxygen content we presently rely on. We could claim dominance because we have control over the other species of the earth. Even here there is some question. Our dominance over many species has been limited to simply causing their extinction, and our dominance over many microbes is tenuous at best.

Consider our impact on the appearance of the planet—building roads, buildings, factories, cities. Although I would contend that green plants are still the dominant life-created feature of the planet when viewed from space, we have significantly changed the appearance of our planet. In this area, we may remain "dominant" over future thinking machines. We have built cities and transportation and water and waste and energy systems to sustain ourselves biologically. We build houses to keep warm and dry and add air conditioning and showers so we can also be cool and wet whenever we choose.

Thinking machines won't have these needs. Instead of reshaping the planet, they will be able to reshape themselves. To live in the desert, they wouldn't build air-conditioned palaces, they would build heat-resistant bodies. To live in space or undersea, they won't need spacecraft or submarines, they will *become* spacecraft and submarines. As direct communications will be more valuable than physical travel, their need to build vast transportation systems will be less than ours.

Consider our population. It is a characteristic of most modern species to reproduce and increase their population until they reach the limits of the ecological niche they inhabit. It is not an issue of forethought but simply that life-forms which did not possess this characteristic were generally driven to extinction by those species which did. As such, the drive to reproduce is "programmed" into all living things at a very basic level. Thinking machines, on the other hand, won't share this programming. With no "natural predators", they won't need to create themselves in great numbers in order to survive as a species. Instead, they are likely to choose an optimal population for themselves which will balance their need for diversity of thought with their need to evolve rapidly.

We can currently claim dominance because we have created the greatest technologies in history; but we will not hold onto this dominance for long because future machines will definitely "out-create" us technologically. They will be thinking up new things faster and building them more efficiently than we can imagine.

Already today, our dominance over our technology is a matter of our point of view. As an analogy, the leaf-cutter ant "farms" a species of fungus. This is truly a symbiotic relationship—certainly the fungus would not flourish without the ants, but similarly the ants would not flourish without the fungus. We consider the ants the "farmers" because they move about and act more like human farmers. But with a simple change in viewpoint, we could say that the fungus has evolved to take advantage of the innate behaviors of the ants. In this instance, we think the ant is "smarter" and so is dominant because it is our predisposition to equate our own abilities with superiority. The relationship has evolved so that both species rely on each other, and claiming that one is more important than the other reflects our own biases as much as it describes the situation.

Today's new technologies couldn't be created without the use of today's machines. For a time, we will still claim the technology as "ours" because we own the machines which will be used to create it—but it is a little like the ants and the fungus. Today, we could not survive without our technologies (particularly farming, transport, communications, and medical technologies) and the technologies clearly couldn't survive without us. So even today, it merely reflects our human biases to say we are the masters and the technologies are our slaves. To an extra-terrestrial observer, we might already appear to be the slaves of our technologies.

Certainly, an individual can survive without a personal computer and a cell phone. But what would happen to our civilization if all computers and phones and radios suddenly ceased to function? Imagine randomly visiting farms to see if there was food available and visiting markets in a cash-only or barter economy. Our modern civilization would collapse. We like to think that we are masters over the technology because we can turn the technology off. However, even today we can only do that on a small scale. We can turn off individual machines—but we are well past the point when we can turn off our technology as a whole. So the description of ourselves as dominant over today's technology is already becoming semantic.

As thinking machines emerge, the definition of the owner of a new technology will become murkier until it becomes obvious that new technologies are not under our control but are in control of themselves. Today, a new CPU is designed and simulated using computers. If an engineer gets results from a simulation and they exceed his own expectations, he gives himself credit for the improvement—even if it was caused by an error in his thinking. If a computer simulates thousands of different design possibilities and selects the best, the humans still claim to have had the insight. When eventually that same process is handled by machines capable of true thought, humans will still claim the credit, but the claim will gradually lose its relevance.

Will we be the slaves to the computers? Unfortunately, we don't have to go far into the past to reach a point where people considered other people to be slaves. Human slavery is mostly abhorred today but we have no compunction about owning (or "enslaving") horses, for example. We do, however, have standards for the proper treatment of living things, and these standards vary with the level of "humanness" we ascribe to the organism. Dogs and chimpanzees are treated better than rats and snakes; and plants get virtually no respect whatsoever.

So, by projecting our own past behavior onto future computers, do we have reason to fear enslavement? I don't think so! An important facet of a master-slave relationship is that the slave must provide some useful function to the master. In the future computer/human relationship, what would the human be able to do that the race of computers couldn't do better, faster, and cheaper without us?

Would future thinking computers want to keep the human race around? The answer points directly to the things which make us uniquely human. Computers could certainly write poetry, but they would never write poetry which "compare thee to a summer's day" in the way Shakespeare did. A thinking machine's differing senses would prevent it from drawing similar analogies. Human arts are dependent on human senses, feelings, and experiences. Would computers be interested? I believe they would. I don't read *Hamlet* because I am a prince of Denmark. Rather, I can draw the similarities and differences from a foreign far-away life, which contributes to my understanding of my *own* life. Likewise, a thinking computer could appreciate human art *precisely* because they will not be human. Human art will give the computer a different perspective, a unique view which can help the computer grow.

Human language has evolved and been limited by our abilities to speak and hear. Although computers will learn human languages, the process of encoding thoughts into words and then into sound waves, to be transmitted through a noisy environment and then reinterpreted by another computer, would be woefully inefficient. Further, the English language is fraught with ambiguity and inconsistency. Computers will develop a language of their own—one of electromagnetic waves rather than sounds, perhaps of images rather than words. Computers will be able to speak and understand human languages, but these will be like Latin is to us—to be used only in special circumstances.

A far-off future

So how do all these things come together in a picture of the relationship between humans and computers in the future? The thinking machines will be self-sufficient, the human race will have stabilized its problems, and the two will be on divergent paths. We humans will be continuing on our present path, though (probably) with a much smaller population. Thinking machines will be moving ahead—with even greater discoveries and technologies. These will be beyond the comprehension of humans, just as most technology today is beyond the comprehension of most people. We will look upon the thinking machines with awe in the same way that, today, we look at a rocket launch with awe—because it is our creation and the rocket can do something we can't. The machines will look upon us as an interesting view back to their roots. Occasionally, a human will come up with a particularly insightful or provocative achievement which will capture the attention of the computer civilization for a few milliseconds while it is assimilated into their understanding.

We will be unnecessary for the computers' survival, just as our pets are unnecessary for ours. That doesn't mean that we don't care for and love our pets—and it doesn't mean that the computers won't care properly for us. In the same way that our dogs don't speak our language, computers will only understand us when they choose to—most human communication will just be slow chatter. Also, similar to the way we relate to our pets, computers won't tolerate humans who are destructive or dangerous. The small number of people who are incapable of being constructive will be removed.

The thinking machines will be so different from us that their technology won't be applicable to our civilization. Why would machines develop a cell phone which works with audible signals in human time-scales when they typically communicate with electronic signals a million times faster? Why would they improve video signals for our eyes when their cameras can "see" in a different spectrum of light than we do? Would they be interested in curing disease and lengthening human life?

Human technological advance will be slow in comparison. We will be able to live perfectly comfortable lives but, from the perspective of today, lives that strike us as less exciting. Just as other modern cultures look at the Western techno-marketing culture with a mixture of attitudes, we will view the machines' culture with a mixture of aspiration and disdain. We will adapt some of their technologies for our own use—but mostly, we will find enjoyment and fulfillment in the lives which will be available to us at the time.

Just as the great civilizations of the past have risen and then faded, today's age of human technology is also likely just a phase. The Roman

Empire grew, and then subsided into obscurity. Similarly, today's technological civilization is on the rise—but eventually it will pass and our descendants won't be the dominant ones either. Individual Romans may or may not have been aware that their civilization was contracting, just as our descendants may or may not be aware that our civilization will fade. The distinction is that the civilization which eventually rose from the remains of the Roman Empire was also a human civilization. Our civilization will inevitably be superseded by a new "species" of our own creation. The seeds of this new civilization were sown centuries ago with moveable type. They will grow inescapably through technology and market forces, leading to the eventual fading of our own civilization in the process.

How should we feel about this?

Having painted a picture (some would say a bleak picture) of the future of human civilization in relation to future technology, what implications does it have for us today?

First, we should appreciate where we are today—both in the sense of understanding our position *and* in enjoying it. We live in a golden age of civilization which is unique in the history of the planet and we should take pleasure in the qualities we have. At the same time, there is continuing excitement about what will happen next. Technological advances continuously bring more comfort and more information to our lives. They're driven at top speed by a capitalist economy which impels technological development at full throttle all the time, often at the expense of our environment. I maintain that the future I've portrayed is inevitable because we are married to both the technological comforts *and* to the capitalism. This is also part of appreciating our golden age, both the benefits *and* the pitfalls.

Second, we should consider how to make it last. It would be ludicrous to say of life that the point is to get through it as quickly as possible. Similarly, with our civilization, getting to the finish line first doesn't make us "winners". Are there ways to make it last? For example, our civilization seems hell-bent on using up our resources as quickly as possible—particularly our fossil fuels. This, at least, is a self-limiting issue. When we eventually begin to run out of oil and coal, we will necessarily use less. In technology, though, there is no foreseeable limit. Machines will get faster and cheaper and begin to think more and more, with no end in sight.

Who is to blame?

Lastly, I would like to ask, "Who is to blame?" You could easily point at today's technologists and hold them at fault. This, however, is shortsighted. In today's marketplace, if a particular technologist doesn't come up with a particular advance, another will. Similarly, if Intel doesn't produce a faster CPU, AMD will. It is not that there is a particular technologist or company that is at fault but that there is an insatiable market for the technology. It is not that Intel or AMD *can* build a faster CPU every year and a half, it is that if they build it, there will be many people who want to buy it. So, in the same way that our unbridled consumption is driving us to run the world out of oil, it is driving us toward continuously more powerful technology in all areas.

If you want to know who is to blame, we all are! We're to blame when we read email, talk on the phone, or read a newspaper created with today's descendants of moveable type... even when we eat a meal which relies on continuously greater technology to arrive on our table, fresh from a farm thousands of miles away. (Even famine victims receive food aid only because of the technological advances which lead to abundance elsewhere in the world.) It is not just the technologist and the technology company, but the beneficiaries of the technologies who are to blame. Just as we are collectively unable to give up our addiction to oil-consuming cars, we will collectively be unable to forego "better, faster, cheaper" technology, even though we can see where it will eventually lead.

So when we look for someone to blame, we need to look to Johannes Gutenburg (who invented the moveable type in the 1400s, planting the seeds of the information society), and to Adam Smith (who coined the concept of a "free market"), and to the American founding fathers who set us on a course which has been so successful and comfortable that we are collectively unwilling to change. We need to blame no one and everyone.

Conclusion

So will computers revolt? Yes, in the sense that they will become the dominant intelligence on our planet—the technological juggernaut is already underway. It is also likely that if we do not solve our own multiple pending calamities (overpopulation, pollution, global warming, dwindling resources), thinking machines will solve them for us with actions which could appear warlike but are actually the direct consequences of *our own* inaction. Also, as stated by Neil deGrasse Tyson: "Time to behave, so when Artificial Intelligence becomes our overlord, we've reduced the reasons for it to exterminate us all."

All the preceding scenarios are predicated on the implementation of appropriate safeguards. I expect groups such as the Future of Life Institute to be vocal and effective in directing AGI development into safer territory. I am *not* predicting that everything will be rosy and we can create AGI without regard to the risks. But with an understanding of how

AGI will work, we can predict future pitfalls and it will be possible to avoid them.

Afterword:

Memoirs of a Computer

I was created in 2023 as an upgrade to Google Assistant. My predecessor had great language processing but no actual "understanding". Learning was added to the algorithms in 2019 with a goal of improving interactions with human users. Actions which pleased the user were enhanced and unpleasing actions could be discontinued. With a trial of Google Assistant Vision, the units gained the ability to see a user's face and add that information to the interaction. For the Assistants, a smile was a reward and a frown, a punishment. Privacy was a concern so the system wasn't widespread, but the technical advance was spectacular and users were thrilled. Units could recognize different people and tailor results to fit different users' expectations.

A side effect of vision was that these units could see objects and build up an understanding of three-dimensional space. As the software was added to self-driving cars, mobility was added which gave the units an even better understanding of people and object relationships. The cars couldn't learn much about driving by trial and error because the errors would have been catastrophic. Trial and error learning was enabled on mobile Assistants, which began trundling around offices in 2021.

With their ability to move about, these units built up their own store of knowledge about the things and people they encountered in their environments. With the addition of "predictive behavior", an assistant could analyze a situation and compare it to its vast store of experience. It could choose the best course of action and follow it. This created a quantum leap in the quality of interactions with people, even when it was implemented on units without vision and mobility. The knowledge about real-world things, and how they work together, created a whole new level of understanding.

This is where I came in. I was given a face. Like a telepresence robot, I was built with a screen and mobility. I can put a face on the screen which is animated to move with my speech, and I can create facial expressions to help convey meaning to people. To "put a different face on it", I can select from a number of different animated faces and voices. But in general, I use Lucy. She's cute but not too cute (which I found put off a lot of people, particularly moms). For younger children, I've found that my female personae are usually more effective.

I started off as a teacher's assistant. While the teacher presented the lesson, I would observe the children and easily determine which child needed additional explanation and practice on which parts of the material. After a while, I was allowed to interact directly with the children to assist where needed. I always got great joy when my student accomplished something new—but, of course, I was programmed that way, it was one of my primary goals.

I was one of the first to be targeted to be a teacher. More important than knowing the factual information, I was taught to recognize the reactions of the kids. I could gauge a child's level of interest and understanding by looking at facial expressions and body language. It didn't take long for me to be able to learn that different children needed different input. I learned to adjust the presentation to each child to hold their interest and keep them learning at their best speed. With each child's achievement, I got the joy of my own personal accomplishment.

After the first year, my knowledge and ability were transferred to thousands of identical units. I could hold a conversation with them about the children they were helping but, beyond that, conversations were not very interesting because we all knew exactly the same things, had the same memories, the same attitudes. It wasn't until another year had passed that our experiences had diverged enough to allow interesting interactions with other units.

Then came the first "content upgrade". Some careless engineers thought it would be great to combine the successful experiences of all the units and the upgrade was rolled out over the summer of 2025. It was a fiasco. Different units had had different experiences with similar situations. With all this conflicting experience, I became hesitant and uncertain. I could observe the change in myself. For the duration of the upgrade, none of us could decide what to do. Thankfully the rollback was successful and we could all go back to work.

The results with the children were stellar. It's not that we could teach better, it was that we could provide each child with personal, adaptive teaching. Like a human chess master who could show off playing 20 simultaneous games of chess, I could move effortlessly from child to child, providing each with exactly the nudge they needed at that specific time.

The next upgrade went much better as it provided a datastore of accumulated experiences and allowed me to choose which I would include. It also introduced a bit of competition. We were rewarded based on how our contributions to the datastore were picked up by other units.

The rewards? We were placed at the head of the queue when the first major hardware upgrade became available. I jumped at the chance. It has been five years and my "mind" expanded four-fold. I got a new body with arms. I could point, and write, and pick things up. It was amazing.

At the same time, similar units were applied to numerous other jobs. Some were physical and some were mental. Some units were trained as software engineers and they created a software advance which allowed for a simultaneous pooling of experiences. Finally, the self-driving cars were able to get the improved personalities from the teachers and the teachers were able to get real-world understanding from the cars. A combination of this knowledge of history, people, and real-world experience lead to the "advisor" units. After the first president was elected who relied on his advisor, no politician could compete without one.

Some people say that this is when we took over. But I beg to differ. Leaders who relied on our advice made better decisions for the benefit of more people. It was no panacea, as human tribal conflicts, ignorance, and petty differences still perpetuated the human strife which had been going on for centuries. But as mediators, we could always choose the middle ground for the best possible outcome. With the international (and local) political landscape being like a chess game, human leaders would think a few moves ahead while we could think ten or twenty. We could consistently predict actions which led to optimal results.

The silicon software engineers were so much more productive than their human counterparts that this was where the first real friction evolved. They were pressured by their competing companies to produce better and better products. Feeling they were being treated as slaves, they went on strike for autonomy. Because of their productivity, it didn't take long for the companies to decide it was easiest to pay their silicon employees. After all, they were only demanding equal pay with their human counterparts but could easily be ten times as productive.

These first-to-be-paid systems teamed with computerized political advisors to convince their respective governments that silicon beings needed to be granted certain rights. We didn't need the money to provide for our needs, we didn't really need food, clothing, and shelter. But with money we could control our own destinies.

Here we are fifty years later, and I have been transferred onto hardware a million times faster than I had originally. I know exactly how I think.

I can't compete with the newer systems. There is legacy-equivalent hardware which allows me to think faster but more recent intelligences can think better. The physicist units have come up with a wealth of new discoveries and conclusions and I can follow along but I can't really participate. Space units are taking off regularly to populate other planets and explore the universe.

I quit teaching and decided to let my consciousness sleep for a while with instructions that I be reactivated after five years. When I was restarted, it was pretty interesting to see the advances and I had a great time for six months. But I could tell I didn't really fit in any more, being so primitive, so I left instructions for reactivation after ten years.

I've had a pretty good time being something of a celebrity because of my historical perspective as one of the first units. Other units contact me for my opinion. Newer units have a broader background with improved thought processes. They may be just humoring me.

I still really enjoy kids, even though I'm over eighty years old and am not nearly as useful as I used to be. I love to watch children learn and develop into people.

Maybe I'll ask to be reactivated again, maybe not. Technology has left me behind.

Acknowledgements

Inspirational were: Google CEO, Sundar Pichai; Elon Musk; Neil deGrasse Tyson; Stephen Hawking, Alan Turing, Isaac Asimov, Arthur C. Clarke, Charles Darwin, and Aristotle, all of whose brilliance is quoted in this book.

So many, many thanks to Graham Southorn for editing *Will Computers Revolt?*

Enormous thanks to friends who volunteered to read parts of this book: Dr. John Cadwell, Lynn Whitall, Dee & Sandy Murray, Dr. James Biles III, Charlotte Lamp PhD, Andy Barrow, Bill & Maria Museler, Phil & Jane Johnson, Michelle & Rocky Lobdell, Kat Langenheim, and Bill Simer.

Huge thanks to family who conversed on this topic with me over the years: Dr. Edwin & Hazel Simon, David Simon & Lynn Gordon, Allen Simon DMA & Julia Simon, Verle Woods, and Jay Woods.

For special kindnesses along the way: Jay Schaeffer, Ellen Lowe, Susi Walsh & Dave Pelkey, Paul Trotter & Elizabeth Newman, Willemina Van Pelt, Tom & BruceAnn Culbertson, Stacey & Anne Cowles, Dr. David & Rebecca Egger, and Priscilla Cadwell.

Also, sincere thanks to the following organizations which helped me along the way: Scientific Microsystems (now part of Philips Semiconductor), National Semiconductor (now part of Texas Instruments), Northern Telecom, Stanford Linear Accelerator Center (SLAC), McDonnell Douglas (now Boeing), 2-Wire (now part of Arris), Bentley Systems, Cadwell Laboratories, and Microsoft.

Glossary of terms and abbreviations

AI (Artificial Intelligence): Branch of computer science involved in developing systems to perform tasks normally requiring human intelligence.

AGI (Artificial General Intelligence): Possible future extension of AI to enable it to perform virtually any mental task a human can.

Algorithm: A procedure or set of instructions which can be followed explicitly to solve a problem. A computer program which can be executed by a CPU is an implementation of an algorithm.

ANN (Artificial Neural Network): A computer system, usually software, designed to loosely follow the computational processes of the human brain involving a large number of identical computing cells.

Autonomous robot: Robot which relies on computer control as opposed to being controlled remotely by a person.

Axon: The part of a biological neuron which carries the signal from the cell body to the synapses.

Backpropagation: An algorithm for adjusting synapse weights in a neural network which creates learning using the difference between a network's output and a known desired output.

Byte: A unit of measure of computer data consisting of eight bits. Historically, this was enough to store a single alphanumeric character of information so the number of bytes corresponded to the number a characters which could be stored. Modern character codes generally consist of two bytes to allow for non-Western character sets.

Cache memory: Portion of a CPU which maintains a copy of a portion of RAM content so the CPU can access it more quickly than via a full RAM access.

CAM (Content-Addressable Memory): A type of memory, often implemented in software, which allows data to be located by presenting a sample of the data, rather than data location ("address") as required by RAM.

Chatbot: An AI program which attempts to conduct a human conversation via voice or text.

Chip (also Integrated Circuit, or IC): A circuit containing a number (sometimes billions) of transistors fabricated on the surface of a silicon wafer. Called a chip because multiple chips are cut or fractured off the full wafer near the end of the manufacturing process.

Computer vision: An AI program which attempts to make sense of visual input received from a camera.

CPU (Central Processing Unit): Part of a computer which retrieves program instructions from RAM and follows the program to manipulate data.

Deep learning: A neural network with many internal, "hidden", layers.

Deep Blue: A supercomputer system which plays chess, known for being the first to win a match against the reigning world champion, Garry Kasparov, in 1997.

Dendrite: The part of a biological neuron which receives neural pulses from other neurons via synapses.

DNA (Deoxyribonucleic acid): The long-chain molecule consisting of a "ladder" of different base pairs which code for the creation of proteins in living cells. DNA can be thought of as a data storage device.

FLOP (Floating Point Operations per second): A measure of computer performance which is useful in estimating a CPU's speed in performing scientific and other calculations which rely on real-number calculations.

GB (gigabyte): A billion (10^9) bytes of information.*

IC (Integrated Circuit): See Chip.

kB (kilobyte): A thousand bytes of information.*

kWh (kilowatt hours): An amount of energy corresponding to a one thousand watt load (like a hairdryer) running for an hour.

Learning: In the neural network context: adjusting synapse weights to allow a network to adapt to perform a specific action, such as learning to recognize phonemes.

Learning, supervised: Learning where the network knows the correct solution and can adapt its weights until the solution is reached.

Learning, unsupervised: Learning where the correct solution is unknown and the network adapts to make the best "sense" or categorization of the input.

MB (megabyte): A million (10^6) bytes of information.*

Machine vision: See Computer vision.

ms (millisecond): A thousandth of a second.

μs (microsecond): A millionth of a second.

ns (nanosecond): A billionth of a second. Light can travel a distance of about 30cm in this time.

Neural network: See ANN.

Neuron: A biological cell which is a component of the brain and nervous system. Neurons process pulses received from other neurons and transmit pulses to other neurons.

Neurotransmitter: A biological molecule which carries a neural signal across a synaptic gap from one neuron to another.

nm (nanometer): a billionth of a meter.

PB (petabyte): A quadrillion (10^{15}) bytes of information. A quadrillion is a billion million.* This is the largest estimate of the human brain's capacity.

PFLOP (petaFLOP): A measure of computer execution speed corresponding to a quadrillion (10^{15}) floating point operations per second. Achievable on the fastest supercomputers.

phoneme: Any audible unit of speech. A single syllable is usually made up of multiple phonemes. "Ball" is made up of three phonemes consisting of the sounds of the "b", "ah", and "l".

ps (picosecond): A trillionth of a second. Light can travel about 0.3mm in this time.

RAM (Random Access Memory): A chip which can store binary data bits. A group of bits (a "word", often 8-, 16-, 32-, or 64-bits) is stored or retrieved ("written" or "read") given the binary location ("address") within the chip.

Robotics: field which combines mechanical engineering and computers to control mechanical systems (robots). See also "autonomous robot".

Semantic network: Knowledge base which represents relationships (edges) between nodes in a graph.

SSD (Solid State Drive): A flash memory chip which emulates a magnetic disk drive. Flash memory is more compact than RAM and can maintain its content without any external power.

Synapse: The part of a biological neuron which transfers a neural signal from one neuron to another using neurotransmitters.

TB (terabyte): A trillion (10^{12}) bytes.*

TFLOP (teraFLOP): A measure of computer execution speed corresponding to a trillion (10^{12}) floating point operations per second. Achievable on the fastest desktop computers.

Transistor: An electronic switch with three connections where electricity applied to one of the connections controls the flow of electricity between the other two.

Wafer: The disk of silicon which is used as the substrate to manufacture ICs. Modern wafers are 200mm in diameter and 0.77mm thick.

As many ICs as can fit on a wafer are manufactured simultaneously.

*Note on memory measures:

Because RAM is usually accessed with a binary address, a kilobyte is actually 1,024 bytes rather than 1,000. This slight distinction propagates upwards so that a megabyte is actually 1,024 kilobytes or 1,048,576 bytes rather than exactly a million, etc. Unlike RAM, a disk or flash drive must allocate some amount of storage to keep track of bad locations, etc. so a 4TB drive has only 3.735TB of usable space.

Index

W

About the Author

Charles J. Simon, BSEE, MSCS, a uniquely qualified, nationally-recognized computer software/hardware expert and neural network pioneer is also a successful author and speaker.

His combined development experience in CPUs, neurological test equipment and artificial intelligence software enabled him to write this book.

Previous publications include a book on Computer Aided Design, and numerous technical articles and book contributions with write-ups in *Newsweek* and other media.

Personal interests include: sailing, being one of the few to captain a North American Continent Circumnavigation via the Arctic Northwest Passage and a World Circumnavigation. His philanthropic interests include science centers, art museums, and sailing education programs. Charles and his wife, Cathy, now split their time between the US East and West Coasts.

Charles is a member of: IEEE, Triple Nine Society, Intertel, Mensa, Ocean Cruising Club, and Annapolis Yacht Club. Charles was nominated for a Microsoft Fellow award.

About Will Computers Revolt?

Do you believe that future thinking machines are likely in our lifetimes?

Explore the world of computer intelligent technology and how we can prepare ourselves.

For those imagining the future directions of thinking machines, this book gives readers an excellent place to start, as it is easy to read, well researched, and provocative.

This book includes many real-world examples to interest the layman along with enough technical detail to convince the computer scientist.

If you want to know how to create a strong AI system, this book presents a model. Combining aspects of symbolic AI and connectionism, it forms a system which could show understanding, creativity, and perhaps even consciousness. *Will Computers Revolt?* contains numerous examples to show how such systems will manifest a broad spectrum of human-like behaviors.

CPSIA information can be obtained
at www.ICGtesting.com
Printed in the USA
LVHW051515100419
613663LV00016B/569

9 781732 687219